Parish

Matt Brown

RESOURCE *Publications* · Eugene, Oregon

PARISH

Wipf and Stock
An Imprint of Wipf and Stock Publishers
199 W. 8th Ave., Suite 3
Eugene, OR 97401

www.wipfandstock.com

ISBN 13: 978-1-4982-0485-9

Manufactured in the U.S.A.   10/08/2014

With gratitude to God for the grace I have known through
Donna, Noah, and Seth

"Perfect love casts out fear"

—1 JOHN 4:18

Contents

Acknowledgments

INCOMPREHENSIVELY MORE THAN MY deserving, I have been the recipient of graces mediated through family, friends, and congregations. Without a doubt the best sentence I ever managed to speak, or at least nervously mumble, was in the form of a question to my best friend—Will you marry me? That Donna took leave of her senses long enough to say yes is testament to God's inscrutable ways. It has been a grand journey these twenty-five years and the joy of watching our sons, Noah and Seth, grow toward maturity has been a treasure without measure. The promise of holding your hand into the future buoys my days and headlines my prayers of gratitude.

I am thankful for the parents who brought me here and for the sons who will someday carry me toward home. For nearly fifteen years, I have been supported and enriched by the fellowship of a group of pastors made up of Jody Welker, Richard Boyce, John Debevoise, and Bob Bardin. To me, they reflect not only the epitome of servant leadership, but also the grace, humility, and character of Christ. I learn from these friends each time I am blessed to be in their presence.

I am abundantly grateful for the congregation of South Mecklenburg Presbyterian Church in Charlotte, NC. I continue to be humbled by their loving support and the opportunity to partner in ministry with them. In particular, I want to thank Nancy Metzler and Terry Gaines for their eyes and insights in reading the manuscript. I also am grateful to the people of Resource Publications and Wipf and Stock for their willingness to take a chance on an unpublished "novelist."

Soli Deo Gloria.

1

The Tree

IN THE MOMENT BEFORE he was hanged at Flossenburg for his involvement in a plot against Hitler, Dietrich Bonhoeffer uttered these last words: "This is the end—for me the beginning of life." Wish I'd have said that. However, I have to admit that as the car careened down the embankment, the only words that escaped my lips in those last seconds of life were, "Oh shit!!" An indelicate closing statement to a life, but miraculous in its own way because I had not spoken a meaningful, cognizant thought in its correct context in so long.

Metal collapsing. Flesh tearing. Shatterproof glass shattering. Body flying. Black.

Tragic? Yes, particularly for my older brother who was driving when the teen queen heading toward us managed to slide the cassette into the player but failed to notice she was drifting to the wrong side, which also happened to be our side, of the road. Instinctively, my brother jerked the steering wheel, only there was no shoulder and the embankment was steep. My brother somehow survived with only bruises, but would live with the irrational guilt of feeling he had failed to protect me. How ironic, because my brother always protected me. He was fettered. I was free. My name is Zachary Parish.

"This is the end—for me the beginning of life." Bonhoeffer said it before he was killed. I would know it after I was killed. You see, I'm a Presbyterian, part of that tortured, contentious, theologically misunderstood, feud-too-much-about-sex, mainline Protestant denomination with the gloomy statistical reports. My brother, who would become a Presbyterian pastor, had a friend who suggested that the Presbyterian Church create an ad campaign with the tag line, "Come worship with us. You can have the whole pew to yourself!" Well, Presbyterians are heirs of the confessional heritage of the Protestant Reformation, and so it is common for us to stand in worship to recite an ancient document called the Apostles' Creed. Considering the head-whipping speed of change in this world, it is mind-blowing to consider that every Sunday without fail, Christians in the far flung corners of this earth have stood to recite this creed for nearly 1800 years. 1800 years! And within that creed you can find this assertion: "I believe in . . . the communion of saints."

The communion of saints. This phrase, that is regularly uttered by rote and without much thought, is a profound affirmation of the idea that we stand on the shoulders of the faithful who have come before us. Their witness informs us and their spirit encourages us in ways beyond our understanding.

Following the wreck, I became a part of that fellowship of saints. I have joined that church triumphant, what some folks call heaven, what others call the Sweet Bye and Bye or the Great Reward or the Kingdom of God. No, I'm not sitting alone on a cloud, flapping my wings, and wishing they had buried me with my *Xbox*. Rather, it is a mystery I can't quite explain, but I've finally come to comprehend those crazy words the congregation used to regularly sing—*Ineffably sublime.* Yes, it is.

On the cross, Jesus turned to the penitent felon who would score no stay of execution, and he said, "Today, you will be with me in paradise." I was never the theologian of the clan. That was and is my brother, but I do know this. It is waaay cool here!

Bonhoeffer was right. "This is the end—for me the beginning of life." You see, my days on earth were constrained by fence posts unlike the usual life inhibitors. I seldom ran a fever and had an impressive record of years without vomiting. I could read the smallest print and see the hyperactive squirrel dancing on the telephone line some eighty yards up the road. I had ten fingers and ten toes, the answer to every expectant parent's prayer. But somewhere in the mixture of flesh, muscle, and bone there was an issue with the wiring.

I could tell you the complete results of every PGA tournament from 1990 when our father joined the Charlotte Country Club and began the twice weekly ritual of taking my little seven year old legs out to the golf course, allowing me to walk along as he taught himself the physics and skills of the game, until April 3, 1997, the day of the accident, ten days before Tiger Woods would win his first Green Jacket at the Masters. I could recite every detail from seven years of tournaments. My dad would clip the results from the sports page each Monday morning for me, and by the time my Lucky Charms were swallowed, I had them memorized. On April 3, 1990, Paul Azinger tied for fourth at the Greater Greensboro Open earning $51,666 in spite of two rounds of 73. I went through a score of spiral notebooks writing all the results, statistics, averages, and earnings of each tournament from memory. I even had a section recording the *Stimpmeter* averages of every course played during a calendar year.

And yet, if asked, I could not tell you whether I was happy or sad. I could not define, offer, or receive forgiveness. I could not grasp the value of a hug or the purpose of a handshake. I was not equipped for conversation, compassion, empathy, or responsibility. The test results offered up words like autism and savant, which meant nothing to me. My mother cried. My father lost his smile for weeks. My brother promised he would protect me. My sister made me a get-well card with construction paper and crayons. I was clueless about the meaning of those words and could not capture the emotions swirling around our house. I could see but not perceive. I could witness but not interpret. I could remember all the details but not understand their meaning.

To live without the capacity for wonder is like a kid going to Disney World and being told he's too short to ride Space Mountain. Not cool. The closest I ever came to a sense of peace was walking with my father on the golf course in the hours before dusk when the fairways were empty and it was just me, my dad, the cardinals and crickets, lob wedges, and Titleists. I now know how important those moments were to my dad, an erudite attorney with a big heart, a small ego, and a Costco-sized reservoir of common sense. That place, that routine, and though I would never swing a club, that game, formed the closest thing to a relationship that I would know. I was obsessed with routine and on a summer Monday or Thursday evening, if dad hadn't appeared in the driveway before 5:30 pm, I would become exceedingly anxious, pacing the floor, reciting the champions of over a hundred years worth of majors, and starting again if he had not yet arrived. Willie Park, Old Tom Morris, Andrew Strath, Young Tom Morris, Tom Kidd, Mungo Park . . .

"This is the end—for me, the beginning of life." As paradoxical as it may seem, death is the final form of healing. The Psalmist sings, "Weeping may endure for a night, but joy cometh in the morning." Affirming this promise, Revelation's author speaks of that place where God "will wipe away every tear from their eyes, and death shall be no more, neither shall there be mourning nor crying nor pain any more, for the former things have passed away."

While my death has weighed heavily on my brother, I am freed from the tangled wiring that so restrained my ability to experience the joy, sadness, hope, and terror that mark life in God's good, but also broken, creation.

And so it is that I've been given a front row seat on the balcony of my brother's life, which could be called a sitcom with substance. I watch with bemused hope, untroubled by the wounds and traumas that may befall him, because I know the story ends well.

Elijah Lovejoy Parish is my brother's name, the name on which our mother insisted at the time of his birth. It is a curiosity to most and only a few historians along with a select number of Presbyterians have a clue about its origin. Elijah Parish Lovejoy was a 19th century journalist, Presbyterian minister and abolitionist who was a terrible insurance risk when it came to printing presses. Seldom has a piece of ink-filled machinery been the object of such wrath.

Born in Maine in 1802 and educated at Colby College and Princeton Theological Seminary, Lovejoy settled in St. Louis, Missouri, started a Presbyterian church, and worked as the editor of the St. Louis Observer where he encountered growing hostility for his anti-slavery themed editorials. Pro-slavery activists destroyed his printing press three times, persuading Lovejoy to relocate across the river in Alton, Illinois. A fresh start? Not really. When Lovejoy attempted to defend his fourth printing press in the face of a pro-slavery mob, he was shot and killed, earning him the epitaph of martyr.

Well, our mom earned her history degree from the University of North Carolina in 1970. She marched with Martin Luther King, Jr. in 1967 after writing a term paper on the brief but courageous civil rights crusade of Elijah Parish Lovejoy. In 1968 she burned the bra that had never been necessary anyway, and 1969 took her to Woodstock where she took a hit from a joint, drank her first beer, ate a loaded brownie, and proceeded to throw up all night. Dehydrated, she passed out and was transported to the hospital by none other than Joan Baez who was on her way out of the festival. The last song of the iconic folksinger's set was *We Shall Overcome*, but mom wasn't so sure because her father, a Presbyterian minister of the South, would be the one driving all day and night to pick her up.

She knew he'd be plenty pissed, but it wasn't like he was the stern Calvinist clergyman seeking to repress everything but his own self-righteousness. Kindness seemed to be his strongest conviction. This would mark only the second time she heard his voice rise to a level that betrayed anger. And it wasn't even that loud. It's just that her hungover head was still pounding and every word ricocheted around her skull like a pinball. "Disappointment." Bing!! "Responsibility." Bing!! "Scared your mother to death." Bing!! Bing!! Bing!! Bing!! And then there was some proverb. What was it? "It is like sport to a fool to do wrong, but wise conduct is pleasure to a man of understanding." To be honest, though, my grandfather always envied her spunk and passion. As far back as her memory would allow, her father never failed to greet her with the words, "How's my little Turbo Tess?"

The Right Reverend Jordan McPheeters, my grandfather, was a good man serving the church in the tempest of the 60's. He had journeyed the route of so many Presbyterian pastors in the South, matriculating at Davidson College and then Union Theological Seminary in Virginia where he met my grandmother, Miss Adele Thompson who was a student across the street at the Presbyterian School of Christian Education.

Following Jordan's middler year of seminary, Jordan and Adele were married in Union's chapel, after which they celebrated a two-day honeymoon in Virginia Beach, before driving to Mocksville, NC for an internship. Jordan would preach while the pastor of First Presbyterian Church was away on vacation and study leave, and Adele would organize and lead Vacation Bible School.

They survived that hot summer, sweltering in an unairconditioned one-room apartment wedged into the attic space of a grand Georgian manor that maintained a certain regal presence in the town in spite of increasing signs of entropy. Here and there, the slats of the shutters were drooping and chipping; and the bougainvillea had swallowed the left side of the porch. The gutter above the kitchen was sagging and the whole place could have used a power washing. Jordan said the house reminded him of his great uncle Nate who always seemed to have some remnant of his last meal forming an ink-blot stain on his white cotton oxford just below his neck as if he was offering a daily Rorshach test to his regular visitors. The elbows of his Brooks Brothers blazer were worn and frayed. He needed a shave, a haircut, and a comb. Yet, he still managed to give off a vibe of refined elegance.

Lord only knows how much money it would take to restore the estate to its former glory, but Jordan and Adele were grateful to have a rent-free roof over their heads, even if it did leak in a couple of spots. As the sweat rolled down their backs and their breathing grew labored during the nightly climb up three flights of stairs, Jordan would smile at Adele and try to put a positive spin on the long hot summer in Mocksville. "At least it's not Bolton," the grim little hamlet you had to drive through to get to Wrightsville Beach that never got the news the Depression was over. The speed limit there on Highway 74 slowed you down to 25 mph so that you wouldn't miss any of the decay. Bolton was like a drive-thru Smithsonian exhibit on Southern poverty.

Mocksville wasn't Paris, or even Greensboro for that matter, but it was an amiable small county seat kind of a town that offered a Rockwellian way of life. For Jordan and Adele, the primary problem was not the town, the summer heat, or even the amount of time spent climbing steps. Rather, what made the summer seem so long, what led these newlyweds to always refer to that summer as The Mocksville Marathon, was the placement of their apartment. Oh, they could handle the stairs and the mildew and the tiny bathroom, but what was continually infuriating was the fact that the antique wrought-iron bed frame sat on a creaky wood plank floor directly over the widow Forney's bedroom. The wealthy widow, a paragon of probity, was legally blind but had the hearing of an owl. In addition, she was a perpetual homebody and had a habit of staying up late into the night, reading large print editions of Jane Austen novels with the help of an architect's lamp and a magnifying glass. Soooo . . . twenty-four years of pent up sexual energy would have to be restrained like the waters behind the lake forming dams of the Catawba during that long hot summer. Poor Jordan. Even though activity down in the missile silo was regularly at DEFCON 2, there would be scant opportunity for any rocket's red glare.

One desperate night the newlyweds tried to pretend they were Russian spies under surveillance in a bugged room where anything but silence would risk capture and execution, but even after Adele sprayed 3-in-One on the bed springs, they quickly found stealth sex to be an oxymoron. A quick effort at afternoon delight wasn't in the cards, either, because whenever Adele wasn't meeting with the young mothers planning for VBS, Jordan was busy visiting the hospital or leading a Bible study for one of the women's circles. You can bet he stayed as far away from the Song of Solomon as possible.

However, the intimacy interruptus did permit the newlyweds to pinpoint the night my mother Tess was conceived. The widow Forney was spending the night at her sister's in Winston-Salem in order to arrive early for her bunionectomy the next morning. It just happened to be July 4th, and growing up, Tess could never figure out why her parents would always be giggling in the middle of the annual fireworks display at the fairgrounds.

Tess McPheeters would grow up knowing only Mocksville as home. When her father completed seminary, Jordan and Adele managed to pack all their worldly goods into the Nash Rambler, even leaving a corner in the back seat for Adele and toddler Tess. That the car was packed tight was probably a good thing; less room for the little duchess of disaster to maneuver.

Ironically, the Rambler died on arrival in Mocksville, where Jordan and Adele would spend the rest of their days, having been called to serve First Presbyterian upon the dismissal of Rev. Turner. Turns out that during the sabbatical for which Jordan had served as a temporary substitute, Rev. Turner had found enlightenment, not in the hallowed Presbyterian environs of Montreat's Anderson Auditorium where Harry Emerson Fosdick was preaching, but in the wanton arms of Bernice Crabtree, a married mother of three who was serving as a Christian educator in Swannanoa. A thicket off Lookout Trail brought forth rapturous, yet contextually and theologically errant shouts to the Lord. But that kind of enlightenment has a price. The subsequent outbreak of poison ivy on the good reverend's hooha was a treat compared to the trouble he would find back in Mocksville the following year when rumors of the affair went viral.

Wise old pastors will witness to the grace of beginning a pastorate after a disaster, as long as the disaster was precipitated by the previous preacher. Even your mistakes will be viewed as endearing in comparison to the bitterness reserved for your predecessor. However, if the disaster was the result of congregational dysfunction, an asbestos pulpit robe will not protect you from the fire and heartburn of conflict. There are a lot of insurance agents and history teachers who were once idealistic young pastors until they innocently walked into the mouths of fire-breathing dragons disguised as charming churches. My grandfather would one day pull my brother Elijah aside on the night of his ordination to say, "Son, be careful out there. Just because the stained glass is lovely on the outside doesn't mean the people are friendly on the inside." I believe it was Mark Twain who said, "The church is always trying to get other people to reform; it might not be a bad idea to reform itself a little, by way of example."[1] (*A Tramp Abroad*)

On the other hand, if church struggles were the result of the previous preacher's negligence, misbehavior, or incompetence, the way may be clear for a sweet ride for the new parson in town. That was certainly the case for Jordan and Adele in Mocksville. Having served an internship there, they were beloved before they even began; and in the light of Reverend Turner's salacious summer sabbatical, the McPheeters were received as a healing balm for wounded souls. When one church member tried to sound merciful, saying, "Rev. Turner just didn't have a stiff enough backbone to withstand temptation," she was interrupted by the widow Forney, "It wasn't a stiff *backbone* that got him into trouble!" Jordan laughed heartily until it crossed his mind that the mischievous sparkle in the widow's eyes might have something to do with what she overheard above her as she read *Sense and Sensibility* late into the nights of the previous summer. The more Jordan's face flushed with embarrassment, the more she grinned. Maybe widow Forney wasn't such a paragon of probity after all.

Relieved that the Turner affair was behind them, the congregation of First Presbyterian opened their arms to the McPheeters and would not let them go. They would serve that church and community for forty-two years. As a toddler, Tess would escape from the playpens in the nursery, twice making it down the aisle of the sanctuary in the middle of worship before the nursery volunteers would catch up to her. Once, the Lord's Prayer would

1. Twain, *A Tramp Abroad*, 1880.

be interrupted as Tess ran down the aisle, pointing to the pulpit, and squealing with delight, "That's my daddy praying!"

Tess would familiarize herself with every corner, crevasse, cobweb,
closet, and classroom of that church property by the time she left for college
in Chapel Hill. She went to preschool there; she broke her arm falling off
the monkey bars in the playground there; she sang in the children's choir
there; she learned her first cussword (and my last word—"shit") from An-
nabelle Strom there; she memorized the kings of Israel there; she fell off the
pew while sleeping during worship there; she was confirmed and received
her first communion there; she got in trouble for calling the youth Sunday
school teacher an imbecile there; she felt the depth of Christ's love during a
Good Friday Tenebrae service there; she made out with Billy Ray Barkley in
the cemetery there; she became passionate about ministry to the poor and
justice for the disenfranchised there; she cheered out loud when the first
woman was ordained as an elder there; she again walked down the aisle of
the sanctuary there, this time wearing a wedding dress; with my father, she
would present Elijah, me, and my younger sister Dina for baptism there; she
will one day attend both of her parents' funerals there; and she would weep
at my burial in the cemetery there. Tess was so woven into the fabric of that
church that you could not discern where it ended and she began.

I don't know if Hillary Clinton actually coined the phrase *It Takes a
Village*, but our family would counter that it takes a congregation to raise a
child. When an infant is baptized in the Presbyterian Church, it is an act of
the whole church community. The parents covenant with the congregation
to nurture a child in an environment where she will know she has been
claimed by God, redeemed by Christ, and loved by God's people. It is not an
exaggeration to say that those Mocksville Presbyterians believed that Tess
was no less their daughter than she was Jordan and Adele's daughter. When
Tess entered the fellowship hall as a child, inevitably someone would pick
her up and swing her around as she squealed with delight. When my grandfather was hospitalized following a heart attack, she stayed with one church
member and rode to school with another church member. Tess gained five
pounds in the weeks following Jordan's release from the hospital because the
refrigerator, freezer, and countertops were overflowing with chafing dishes
holding baked spaghetti, chicken pot pie, broccoli cheese casserole, lemon
bundt cake, double fudge brownies, and chess pie; not to mention plates of
home-baked cookies, ham biscuits, sourdough bread, and gallons of tea so
sweet it made your teeth hurt.

On the Sunday before her graduation from high school when Tess offered the traditional senior sermon, even that old curmudgeonly, leather
handed, John Deere drivin' soybean farmer, Cyrus Jacobs, was seen dabbing

his eyes with a well worn red bandana that he always kept tucked in his back pocket. It takes a tough man to be a farmer with hay fever, and so while it was common to see Cyrus blowing his colossal hawk-billed nose into that tattered rag, this was the first time anyone had seen him pull it out for purposes of emotion. But this was his little girl just like it was Judge Martin's little girl, Dr. Lizzie's little girl, and Sunday school superintendent Mr. Mike's little girl. That church was Tess' home. That congregation was her family. So, when it came time to stuff that VW Microbus with clothes, blankets, pillows, and a typewriter and travel to Chapel Hill for college, it was a traumatic experience for the whole church community.

Tess was what you would call a piece of work. She was equal parts covered dish luncheon on the church grounds and Jack Kerouac reading, rebel always with a cause. I remember my brother often saying that there was never a cause that mom didn't like. So, when Tess McPheeters collided with UNC Chapel Hill, a dynamic, barrier crushing, protest instigating, cause championing relationship was formed that would influence communities and generations to come. Little Turbo Tess was to become a force to be reckoned with. Many a man of the old Southern establishment would be both charmed by her petite beauty and mowed down by her indomitable crusading spirit. Years later, a city councilman would be heard advising a newly elected colleague entering the council chambers, "Remember three things: Always count to ten before responding to any question; always remember that everything that goes on in there is filmed; and for God's sake, don't ever mess with Tess. She'll slaughter you."

Though she would hold no political office, in the circles of local government, my mom's ability to emasculate those who dared to tolerate injustice was so feared, that she was known by a singular name like the superstars of European soccer—Messi, Ronaldo, Chicharito . . . Tess. While some would utter the name with the taste of vinegar on their lips, most came to speak the name with great respect for her indefatigable compassion. The embittered voices were the grudge-holding, defeated opponents who had been twisted into pretzels by Tess' intellect and tenacity. She was never one to raise her voice. She was ever effervescent and abundantly kind.

Tess could not have accomplished so much if arrogance was a necessary trait. In a Southern city like Charlotte there would be many who would disagree with her politics but no one would question the authenticity of her humility. Yet, she killed many an ego with her kindness. Drawn in by her charm, Tess' opponents would find their views shredded like Lexington barbeque by her cleaver sharp questions. At a public forum on school integration in the mid-seventies, Tess carved up a Charlotte-Mecklenburg

School Board member so deftly that by the end you could almost catch the scent of hickory smoke in the air.

"Mr. Catherton, could you . . ."

"Aw Tess, you can call me Prescott."

"That's nice of you, Mr. Catherton. My husband and I certainly enjoyed the Heart for Charlotte Gala hosted by you and Tipper last week. It was a sumptuous affair. It was good to see Miss Effie."

"Yes, she was glad to see you, too."

"How many years has Miss Effie been in your employ?"

"Twenty-two years. She started doing some cleaning and cooking for us when she was nigh but eighteen years old. When our children were born she came on full-time. Why, she practically raised our kids. Effie's like a member of the family. Why, she is family."

"Yes, I'm sure the children love her dearly. Miss Effie has children of her own, doesn't she?"

"As a matter of fact, her three children are the same ages as ours. Very polite. Very respectful."

"Yes, I know them well. Could you remind me how long you have served on the school board?"

"Well you know that. It'll be nine years next week. I was just reelected last year."

"Yes, I guess that's right. Now, where is it your children are enrolled in school?"

"Charlotte Day School."

"Three children. That must be expensive."

"Well, only the best for your children."

"Where is it that they used to go to school?"

"Alexander Graham Junior High School."

"Isn't that where Miss Effie's children attend?"

"Well . . . uh . . . yes."

"Mr. Catherton, if Miss Effie is family, I take it that her children are family, too."

"Uh . . . well, I guess."

"So, why would you find it so objectionable for your children to be in the same classroom with members of your own family, and to pay more than the tuition at Chapel Hill for each child to ensure it?"

"Well, now Tess, it's not like that . . ."

"It is true, Prescott, isn't it, that during your tenure on the school board, you have a perfect voting record against any measure that would support the mandated effort to integrate our public schools?"

"Now, listen Tess! I have been vocal in my support of equal opportunities."

"Mr. Catherton, if they are separate, they cannot be equal. The Supreme Court of the United States, on which your grandfather served, understood that twenty years ago. Don't you think it's time to get up to date? Remember, I've seen your new kitchen and I know the Cathertons loathe the idea of not being up to date."

"Now Tess, I . . . uh . . . I . . . O Tess, you're twisting my brain into a pretzel. I hate it when you do that. You know I'm a good man. I just think it's safer and healthier for children to go to school with their own."

"A good man as opposed to what? Oh Prescott, you know I'm a Presbyterian and we Presbyterians don't cater to the idea of distinguishing good people and bad people. In God's eyes, we're all a mixed bag. Why, I believe I even heard your preacher at First Baptist say not too long ago that the ground is level before the cross."

"Tess . . ."

"I'm sorry. Just thinkin' out loud. But, did I hear you right that you think it would be safer and healthier for your children to go to school with their own?

"Yes."

"Well, Prescott, if Effie is family, as you said, I'm guessing her children are family. So, it just seems a tad odd, or as the psychologists might say, dysfunctional, for a man not to want members of his own family to go to school with one another. Anyway, please send our love to Tipper and tell her I'd love to get her recipe for those delicious cheese biscuits."

"I will, Tess."

Angry? Yes. Humiliated? Yes. And yet, he couldn't help but smile at her as she sat down. "That's just Tess, I guess," he would later say to Tipper. "If she just weren't so damn charming."

"It's not just her charm that gets to you, Prescott. I assume she was wearing the little black dress?"

"Uh . . . Yes. How'd you know?"

Three years later Tess would have Prescott Catherton IV serving on the Community Relations Board working to build bridges between the black and white communities.

It was at Chapel Hill that Tess had learned and perfected the art of subtlety in pushing a cause forward. Turbulent is the word used to describe the atmosphere on colleges across the land in the latter half of the 1960s and the University of North Carolina was not immune to that description. During that period a state appointed commission was studying the feasibility of establishing a state zoo and a bug-eyed future senator named Jesse Helms, a don in the Fox News mafia and godfather to voices like Rush Limbaugh and Glen Beck, notoriously suggested that if North Carolina needed a zoo, all they had to do was put up a fence around Chapel Hill. And to think he started out as a Democrat!

At UNC, if you wanted to propose to your favorite Tri-Delt, you went to the Old Well. If you wanted to worship at the shrine of Tobacco Road basketball, you went to Carmichael Gym. However, if you wanted to shout at sinners to repent, burn your bra, rail against Vietnam, sign up for the rugby club or check out the new pledges of Kappa Kappa Gamma on their way to class, you went to *the Pit*. It is literally a three-foot-deep brick lined pit in the center of campus with two giant pin oaks standing sentry, providing momentary shade in an otherwise sun-drenched brick plaza. If you even thought about starting, joining, or protesting against a movement on campus, the Pit was ground zero. A lot of protesters busted a throat muscle shouting slogans and shrieking epithets against *the Man* in that rectangle of social rage. And Tess? She didn't get it. Oh, she shared their passion for justice and social change, she just didn't see how howling and hollering would be effective in advancing a cause. Her academic results opened the door to teas, receptions, and dinners with chancellors, deans, and significant alumni, and she realized that the art of thoughtful conversation and relationship did so much more to move the fence posts of social reform. A coy smile and a sundress didn't hurt, either.

During her first semester, Tess tried out the whole embroidered parachute skirt—tie dye kurta—hemp sandal bit, but within a month she threw away the sandals because they scratched her feet; she gave away the skirt because when the wind blew she could feel the parachute inflating and she had no interest in doing a Marilyn Monroe as she walked across the Pit; but more than that, Tess came to realize that all those claiming to be nonconformists were actually no less conformist than anybody else. Their dress, their idiomatic lexicon, their hygiene habits, their preferred hangouts, and even their diet conformed to a code every bit as strict as the rituals and habits of the boys of Beta Theta Pi. Many of the self-titled activists were more attentive to maintaining their image than to making a difference.

She figured there had to be a better way to fight for an issue than shouting obscenities from megaphones; and besides, the pervasive body odor that went with the lifestyle grossed her out. So, Tess boxed up a bit of the rebellion, put on some Audrey Hepburnesque drainpipe capris along with her Pendleton plaid jacket and began to pursue other paths to advocate for the forgotten and disenfranchised victims of injustice along with the cause of peace.

Her one capitulation to the Bohemian stereotype was a perfectly maintained 1965 two-toned VW Microbus that she would drive for the next twenty-two years. She even completed an engine repair class at Davidson County Community College the summer before her matriculation at Chapel Hill. She loved that bus and it was that bus that would years later carry us to the grocery store on Tuesday, Elijah's football games on Friday nights, and Sunday school on the Sabbath. It tore her heart when the car coroner pronounced it dead after the tie rod broke, the master cylinder failed, and second gear disappeared. She cried for an hour when the tow truck carried it away.

She thought it was going to the salvage yard but my father had a friend put it in his warehouse, and instead of silver or diamonds, when their 25th anniversary rolled around, dad rolled up the driveway in a completely rebuilt Microbus with Carolina blue metallic paint and white leather interior. The boys from *Pimp My Ride* would have been blown away. And Tess? The most beatific smile anyone had seen since her wedding day. But I get ahead of myself.

Back at the Pit, Tess was staffing a booth, recruiting volunteers for a local free legal clinic. With the influx of migrant farm workers who toiled away in the fields of cotton, tobacco, and strawberries in eastern North Carolina, there was always a shortage of Spanish speaking interpreters to assist the migrant workers when their lives intersected with the North Carolina legal system. Far too many immigrants were sitting in jail cells or being deported because they didn't understand the language, the legal system, or their rights. A busted taillight could thrust a migrant worker into a legal purgatory, and because they didn't read English, they couldn't identify the exit signs.

So, Tess was busy targeting the inner guilt of friends and strangers walking by her table while across the way, some dude with a tinny guitar, a cheap P.A. system, and a bird's nest beard, who looked like Jerry Garcia and sang like Conway Twitty warbled:

> I ain't gonna fight for Uncle Sam;
> Suckin' on napalm o'er in Viet Nam.
> If you wanna know where I'm gonna go;
> I'll be sneakin' 'cross the border to Toronto.

At that moment, Tess looked up and saw a young man wearing a Westminster College hoodie, khakis, and white Chuck Taylors slowly sauntering by her table. He was a decent looking fella of medium height, slim build, and tousled brown hair who wore the easygoing, contemplative bearing of a guy driven more by ideas than success. Tess noticed a grin on his face as if he, too, understood the irony of the troubadour singing protest songs in a ploy to get chicks while mere boys languished in terror deep in a Southeast Asian jungle.

"Westminster College. Presbyterian School. Winston Churchill's Iron Curtain speech. You're a long way from Fulton, Missouri."

Startled, he wheeled around. "I didn't think anyone, outside of a couple of history majors, had ever heard of Westminster out here! That's impressive."

"Not so much. My dad's a Presbyterian minister and his brother went to Westminster. The Rev was there the day Churchill spoke. Drove all night to be there and watch it with his brother. He talks about it all the time. So, what brings you all the way out to Chapel Hill?"

"I'm in my final year of Law School over at Duke."

"Well, that's even more bizarre! Why is a Duke dude settin' foot on campus here in Chapel Hill in March with the ACC tournament coming up next week? You have a death wish or are you one of those test tubes of testosterone who likes flaunting his way into a fight?"

"Now look at my build. What do you think? Yeah sure, I'm looking for a fight. Where does the chess club meet?"

"So, why are you here?"

"I'm doing a little clerking at a law office over on Franklin Street to pay the rent. Just came on campus to buy a cheap bagel for lunch."

"Well, call me crazy since the stereotype rulebook says lawyers are more mercenary than merciful, have you ever thought of volunteering at the free legal clinic? I'll be glad to guilt you into it. Remember, my father's a Calvinist."

"You can give the good reverend my regards, but I've been volunteering at the clinic for two and a half years."

"You saw our poster; why didn't you say anything?"

"You didn't ask."

"You are a lawyer, aren't you? Duke Law School . . . Tricky Dick's alma mater."

"So the Dean keeps reminding us. Not my particular flavor, but it is what it is."

"It is what it is, indeed. So, where's home?"

"Laddonia, Missouri."

"Beautiful spot. I considered vacationing there last summer."

"Sarcasm becomes you. Tess, there are more people standing around the Pit right now than there are residents in my hometown."

"How'd you know my name?"

"Nametag."

"Riiight. That puts me at a disadvantage, I guess."

"I guess it does. My name is Taylor Parish."

"Sounds a bit preppy for a farm boy."

"Taylor was my grandfather's name. He was a circuit judge for the area."

"Following in grandpa's footsteps?"

"And my father's. He has a law office in Laddonia; well I guess I should say the law office in Laddonia."

"So, what does a lawyer do in the big city of Laddonia?"

"Do you like musicals?"

"What? . . . Yeah, sure. Your father a song and dance lawyer?"

"No, but do you remember that song in Rogers and Hammerstein's *Oklahoma* titled *The Farmer and the Cowman Should be Friends*?

"Yes."

"Well, sometimes it doesn't work out that way and so my dad gets involved. Don't tell Norman Rockwell, but when a farm is passed down from generation to generation, the children can fight pretty nasty to get what they consider to be their fair share, which of course, they consider to be all of it. Now remember, these people own guns, so if my father is not arguing a family lawsuit over daddy's estate, he's defending Junior for aggravated assault. Add to that a number of wills, a few speeding tickets on Highway 54, a divorce here and there, the periodic real estate transactions, and a couple farm boy DUIs; it's not *Perry Mason*, but we've had a good life."

"So, are you going home to practice with dad?"

"No, I doubt there's enough legal drama in Laddonia to feed us both."

"Do you miss it?"

"Laddonia? Sure. It is a small town . . . real small. No grocery store so you have to drive to Mexico or Vandalia to buy a loaf of bread."

"Mexico! That seems extreme."

"It's the county seat a few miles up the road. For Laddonia, the baseball field functions as the town's central nervous system. From April to September most folks are out there about every night except Sundays and Wednesdays. The Baptists make sure those nights are kept open. If you aren't playing a Little League game, you are watching a Little League game or an American Legion game or a men's slow pitch softball game. In the evening as the sun descends and the lights of the ball field come on, parents, grandparents, and neighbors are lounging on their lawn chairs, exchanging gossip and recipes, negotiating farm leases, comparing crop yields, complaining about futures prices, sharing quilt patterns, and talking politics. The toddlers squeal and chase one another. The elementary aged kids play red rover and argue about who is cheating. And the high school boys and girls are preening around one another like mountain goats doing the mating dance in one of those Disney nature movies." Chuckling, he said, "It's a scene, man!"

"Laddonia, Population 500. S-a-a-lute!"

"Somebody's been watching too much *Hee Haw*."

"John Deere or Allis Chalmers?"

"John Deere. No doubt. But how would a Talbots tailored Carolina coed know about tractors?"

"Thank you for noticing. My hometown is not that much larger than yours. You look pretty fit; were you an athlete?"

"O, I played a little baseball, but when you go to a high school named Community R-6, the sports program is going to be fairly limited. Seriously, there were a lot more of those blue corduroy Future Farmers of America jackets than letter jackets. I did grow up with a love for golf, though."

"Golf in Laddonia? Is the goal to aim between the cow patties?"

"Ha, ha. It isn't quite that bad. In Laddonia you have two options. They have a nice nine hole layout at the Mexico Country Club or you could drive over to Vandalia where they have a course with sand greens."

"I've heard of sand traps, but not sand greens."

"Yeah, it's pretty primitive. Greens are expensive to keep up and so some courses have greens that are by no means green and are made of sand. They have a contraption that allows you to carve a track between your ball and the hole. It's a little weird. By the way, where's your home?"

"Mocksville."

"Mocksville? Sounds like a segment on *Laugh In*. 'This week, we mock the urologists with our special guest Sly and the Kidney Stone.'"

"If you don't make it as a lawyer, maybe you can go on the road with Henny Youngman."

"I think he called my agent last week. Did you say your father was a Presbyterian minister?"

"Yes, and I'm a daddy's girl so no preacher jokes."

"By no means. In fact, I've been an elder in my hometown church since I was in high school. There aren't a whole lot of Presbyterians in Laddonia. Well, there aren't a lot of people in Laddonia, but my great grandfather was one of the charter members of Laddonia Presbyterian. I sure do miss those covered dish dinners, though. Tuna noodle casserole . . . "

"With the potato chips crumbled on top?"

"Absolutely. Is that recipe in scripture somewhere? Second Casserole, chapter 3—'For six days you may use Lay's Chips, but on the Sabbath you may only use Ruffles; for it is an offering that is fragrant to the Lord. Thou shalt not substitute Durkee's potato sticks, lest ye die.'"

"And all God's people said, 'Amen.' I think I'm having Jello withdrawals."

Taylor and Tess didn't even notice that the Pit had emptied of students, protesters, profs, and jocks as a cool March evening breeze took the place of a sun-warmed Carolina blue afternoon. Though neither had dated extensively, they were instantly comfortable with one another. The conversation came quite easily, continuing into the night and on through their forty-second anniversary last week.

They both picked up their diplomas that May, were married by Tess' father in August, moved to the Midwood neighborhood of Charlotte, and began life together, rent-free, in an elegantly furnished, stately brick home set among the pines and magnolias.

Filled with antiques, artwork, a grand piano, and a glorious floor-to-ceiling curved window that looked out upon an artist's palette of azaleas, camellia bushes, wisteria and crepe myrtle trees. The home was owned by Tess' Uncle Harold and his friend Bill. They were known to be kind-hearted, exquisitely dressed, inordinately hospitable, the best hosts a party could have. Everybody loved Harold and Bill. That they were gay was typically assumed, seldom discussed, and didn't seem to matter anyway. They were talented, gracious men who had formed a lifelong partnership and it sure didn't appear that they were in any way "destroying the fabric of the American family."

When in her early teens, Tess overheard her father, Jordan, comparing his brother and Bill to an old married couple while they fussed with one another during his weekly phone conversation with them, she intoned from the kitchen table, "They're not like an old married couple. They are an old married couple." Tess had grown up visiting these men and she would never comprehend why Presbyterians seemed so tortured over something that Jesus had never deemed a topic significant enough to broach, not even so much as a mention—"Oh by the way, about the gays . . ." Yes, verses from Leviticus and Romans would adorn placards and pepper sermon manuscripts as the red line *that shalt not be crossed*, but Timothy seemed to have a beef against Tiffany's and Tess sure as hell wasn't giving up the string of pearls her grandmother had given her.

Harold and Bill had graciously opened their home to Taylor and Tess when Taylor accepted a position as a public defender for Mecklenburg County after passing the bar exam. The *old married couple*, cello and oboe principals for the Charlotte Symphony, had been given a two-year sabbatical so that they could play a stint in London's Academy of St. Martin in the Fields. They had framed the letter of invitation from Sir Neville Marriner and hung it in what they called the music room. Both Harold and Bill were understated in demeanor but there was one way in which they certainly fit the stereotype. They both had impeccable taste. And so, Tess and Taylor's first residence was no garage apartment but more of a miniature Biltmore Estate. Taylor commented, "I feel like I should put up velvet ropes around the perimeter and plastic on the sofa so that I don't damage something that costs more than I earn in six months!"

Taylor wasn't into antiques, but he was into golf and Chez Harold/Bill was only a nine iron away from a postcard ready Donald Ross golf course at the Charlotte Country Club. Paradise. Of course, fresh out of law school, that wasn't happening, but regularly on his drive home, Taylor would drive by the golf course entrance, craning his neck to see a sliver of a fairway beyond the grand white edifice of the elegant clubhouse. It was as if he was driving by a Cadillac commercial. You know, the gleaming tail-finned, metallic silver land barge with the black landau top eases around the tulip lined circle drive and out steps Mr. Hart Shaffner and Marx, handing the keys to the valet while stepping around the chrome grille to open the door for some runway model with legs perfectly toned for the camera close-up as she lifts herself from the supple hand-stitched leather seat, her satin Halston dress undulating with the gentle evening breeze. *Coupe Deville—Do it today . . . not "someday."*

Well, someday wouldn't be today for the Parish family, and if it were up to Tess, "someday" wouldn't come at all. Taylor would have to bring his *A* game as a litigator to argue that case. The Charlotte Country Club wasn't integrated and that would probably be a deal breaker. The only people of color were the white-coated waiters, the caddies, the cooks, and the over-broiled debutante moms sipping Mimosas down at the pool. Tess wouldn't want anything to do with that, and Taylor had no interest in the black-tie soirees or the penis measuring men's nights, but it was a Donald Ross course! Turtleback greens framed with grass hollows and swales and beautifully manicured Bermuda on the tee boxes. Oh well, the initiation fee was out of the question anyway and a law degree alone wouldn't warrant an invitation in the first place.

With that thought, Taylor would awake from the daydream and point the hand-me-down '61 Impala toward the house nearby. There was a lawn to mow.

Tess went to teach American History at West Charlotte High as it ushered in a grand experiment in integration of race and class that would serve as a model for the nation until being summarily dismantled by Judge Potter in 1999. Elijah would be a student at West Charlotte in those last years before progress became a dirty word.

Tess taught and Taylor went to the courthouse where he worked in the Public Defender's office. After two years of being buried under piles of files when he wasn't sprinting from courtroom to courtroom to the county jail and back to the courtroom again, Taylor was invited to lunch by an old-school Charlotte attorney named Turner Chambers. Taylor certainly knew of Chambers and had met him once at a bar association event, but did not know him personally, at least not until two minutes into their conversation at Anderson's Restaurant, a landmark Greek-owned meat and two in the shadow of Presbyterian Hospital. Everything from souvlaki to mac and cheese, from baklava to banana pudding was there to seduce you on one of those poster-sized plastic menus with the paper insert listing the specials along with the vegetables of the day.

Turner Chambers was one of those rare individuals who could enter a conversation with a stranger as if he had known him since the second grade. He was so at ease with and unfailingly present to those in his company. Chambers despised what he called "those frat boy assholes," who while shaking your hand, would be scanning the room for someone more important to talk to.

Turner Chambers cut an impressive figure and Taylor stumbled into the conversation, distracted by how closely Chambers resembled the actor Hal Holbrook. In fact, during lunch, some Bubba from Honea Path, SC, in town for his wife's colostomy procedure, came to the table and asked for an autograph, saying, "My wife shore wud 'preciate it. She just loves yor Mark Twain act. You know, I do a little actin' myself." Without missing a beat, Turner responded with a classic Twain quote, "Well, just remember, 'To succeed in life, you need two things: ignorance and confidence.'"

Tall and lanky with bushy eyebrows and elegantly tousled gray hair; he even had that gravelly Southern lilt in his voice that carried you away to a front porch in a Kennedy rocker and put in your hand a tall tumbler of syrupy sweet iced tea. Chambers was live oak, Spanish moss, single malt scotch, and cherry paneled library. He was seersucker in the summer, Harris tweed or pinstripes in winter, khakis on the weekends, and bow ties throughout the year.

It was about fifteen minutes into their conversation that Taylor realized this was a job interview. His palms started sweating, his heart started racing, and he suddenly regretted ordering the spaghetti that the waitress was delivering to the table; probably the worst thing to try and eat during an interview. Of course, I would have ordered Lucky Charms. You can never go wrong with Lucky Charms.

In Luke's account of Jesus going to the house of a leader of the Pharisees to eat a meal on the Sabbath, it says, "They were watching him closely." I'll bet they were. How in the world did a meal come to be considered an essential part of the job interview process? What a nightmare! Granted, it's not so bad if you are the interviewer. In fact, the interviewer may well look upon it as a gracious act. The candidate has made the effort to travel to the interview, surviving flight delays and lost baggage or the drama of negotiating complex directions and unwieldy maps in a strange city while the other drivers point with fingers offering directions that bear no relation to where he or she wants to arrive.

"I'm sure the candidate is tired from travel," the interviewer thinks. "Let's take her out to eat. Let's tempt this young graduate with a feast in an exquisite restaurant. My what a nice interviewer I am."

But if you are the interviewee, the perspective is significantly different. The waitstaff are hovering over you, waiting for you to order from the menu you haven't even peeked at because you are trying to respond to a question about Keynsian economic theory without sounding like that poor teen beauty queen from South Carolina when asked about finding the U.S. on a map.

You would truly like the taste of a Coca-Cola right now, but would ordering anything other than water be a sign of fiscal foolishness?

And speaking of ordering, how can you know what to order? Steak is out of the question. It's one of the more expensive items on the menu, and again, you don't want to be seen as one who would play loose with an expense account. If you order it medium-well they may consider you unsophisticated. If you order it rare, they may assume you are animalistic or too aggressive. And have you ever chewed on a piece of meat that just won't go down? Try and describe your master's thesis while attempting to masticate that.

How about the club sandwich? I love a good club sandwich. But have you ever stopped to think about how wide you have to open your mouth to take a bite out of that? That's a pretty sight to offer someone you've just met!

Of course, when you are in the middle of an interview, you are usually not even hungry as your nerves incite a labor riot in your stomach led by the union of American Abdominal Acid Producers.

How about a salad? It is simple. It reveals a prudence in regard to corporate overhead. You just need to push the big leaves to the side and pick at the rest, focusing on not allowing your fork to exaggerate the sight of your nervous hands shaking. Then when you actually do get hungry after the interview, you can make a late-night run to Chick-fil-a.

But let's be honest, the interview meal is not about the interviewer's altruism and graciousness. Nor is it about your taste buds. The interviewers are watching you. Jesus knew that. Luke's gospel reports, "On one occasion when Jesus was going to the house of a leader of the Pharisees to eat a meal on the Sabbath, they were watching him closely . . ."

They are observing how you comport yourself in a public place. They are watching how you interact with others at the table and with the waitstaff. They notice if you are paying more attention to the basket of sourdough bread than the conversation. They are aware of your manner and your manners. This is not a meal. It is a test.

Perhaps you remember the legend of JC Penney who it is said would always take a prospective employee to dinner and if the candidate salted his food before he tasted it, Mr. Penney would not hire him because he thought it was a sign of rash judgment.

That observation bears the ring of truth, for how we deal with one another in the small things says a great deal about how we deal with one another in the larger things. Even though it could seem a small thing, how you experience the table has a big impact upon larger things in your life.

Elijah would be deeply influenced by the humility of our parents and their love of table fellowship. Though my world was mostly silent, the table at the Parish home was a place of ideas and rich conversation. Gathered around their daily bread, there were no lectures about homework or unfinished chores. The table was a sacred place and from an early age Elijah was included as a partner in the conversation. At the table, Taylor and Tess were careful not to patronize, belittle, exclude, or speak in code. If Elijah didn't understand any of the topics of the day, they would patiently answer his questions in clear, direct terms. Elijah relished those mealtime excursions into a world of ideas, politics, theology, music, and history and would one day refer to the centerpiece of the Parish breakfast room as the Algonquin Roundtable of the South. I heard him say the dialogue was so rich that even the requisite two forkfuls of peas went down easier. One night while discussing the '88 presidential election, there was this brief lull in the conversation, the kind that happens just before you get up to start clearing the dishes, and Elijah pleaded, "Let's keep talking. I don't want this to end."

I, on the other hand, insisted on sitting at the far end of the table, silently devouring all the golf statistics I could find in the daily sports page or dad's copy of *Golf Digest*. Dad told mom that if I obsessed over the horses as much as I obsessed over golf, we'd be living in Hearst Castle. I couldn't wait to get dad to the golf course and Elijah couldn't wait to get mom and dad to the dinner table. Conversation was an art form that came easily to them. In this over-scheduled, hyperkinetic, spend too much time in front of a TV or computer screen world in which we live, people forget the significance of the table and what happens around it.

Taylor would be similarly influenced by the witness and character of Turner Chambers, but at this moment in the lunchtime hustle and bustle of Anderson's Cafe, Taylor was ruing the choice of spaghetti, sure that his quaking hands would leave him wearing the marinara.

Leaning back in the booth, Turner honed in on the unspoken but assumed purpose of the lunch. "I've been watching you around the courthouse. In the midst of the maelstrom, you seem to remain shrouded in a blanket of calm."

"I don't remember seeing you in the courtroom."

"O, I fancy sliding in the back row anonymously to watch every now and then. Don't tell anyone around these parts, but I find it a whole lot more fascinating than basketball, and I sure as hell am not going for a jog when I get a bit of free time. You know, I didn't go into law for the money. No, I went to law school because I love the law. I don't chase ambulances, loose women, or dead ends. I practice law, and though it may sound corny, I think justice is something worth standing up for. I sense that the same is true for you. I've been watching because you are on the front lines, sifting through all the bullshit in pursuit of the truth. You are not a dealmaker. You are not a schmooze, a climber, or an asshole. You are a lawyer. You don't sugarcoat the consequences for the guilty and you just try to ensure the system treats them fairly. But if someone is wrongly accused, you'd shit a brick in front of the Supreme Court in order for your client to be heard. You seem to understand that it's not about you, and in a way, it's not about the client, it's about truth. You a Presbyterian?"

"Uh . . . yes."

"Thought so; something about that whole sovereignty of God, total depravity of man worldview that informs the character of guys like us. You know that you're no more innocent than the convict and neither is the judge. It changes the way you relate to others. You don't brownnose the powerful or belittle the craven. We're all a bunch of cretins, but God loves us anyway. Taylor, I want to work with you. The income will be good . . . damn good, and the benefits, sweet. The occasional big payday will allow you to do pro bono or advocate for someone who's never been given the dignity of a voice. We'll laugh. We'll cry. We'll work harder than hell, but we'll refuse to let work make a sacrificial offering of our families. I met your wife over at the high school. Looks like you married a whole lot better than she did. Whatever you do, wherever you go, don't screw that up. I hope you'll come join me over in Dilworth."

"Wow, Turner, tell me the truth; were you weaned by the mavens on Madison Avenue? I haven't seen a pitch that good since my dad took me to see Bob Gibson in the World Series."

"Damn, that dude could throw some smoke!"

"So can you. I'm flattered and intrigued by your proposition."

"Oh, be careful with that word *proposition*. We've argued cases for a prostitute now and then."

"I've got files for twenty of them on my desk, right now. Some real sad stories."

"I hear ya."

"Turner, I'm certainly intrigued. I know a bit about the reputation and character of your practice and sense that it would be a good fit. But, if you met my wife, you know I'm not going to be more than intrigued until I talk with her."

"Taylor, if you had said yes on the spot, I would have rescinded the offer and wished you well for a career in night court. 'Without counsel plans go wrong, but with many advisers they succeed.'"

"Proverbs 15. A few chapters later, it says, 'If one gives answer before he hears, it is his folly and shame.'"

"Amen." Flagging the waiter, Turner asked, "Dear waiter, how about reheating my friend's spaghetti here? The ask has been made, the mystery has evaporated, and though the deal's yet to be done, I sense his hands are steady enough now to navigate that fork."

"As you wish, Turner, my old friend. And banana pudding?" The waiter's smile and Greek accent were the standard in Charlotte restaurants.

"You know me well."

The courts were closed for Labor Day, so they continued talking into the early afternoon about everything from pitching wedges to pitching hay bales; from cow tipping to tort reform; from Watergate to the immense wisdom of their wives.

Turner Chambers was a legal legend in Charlotte. You weren't going to outthink or outwork him, so most attorneys resigned themselves to fighting for some kind of draw when going against Chambers. He would never be referred to as flashy and never joined his peers in the race for a microphone and a television camera. He was not one to make statements on the courthouse steps and never called a press conference. When asked why, Turner was memorably heard to say, "If I preen for the camera at the end of a day in court, who's going to be watching the news except for Aunt Myrtle who's shelling beans for supper; the housewife who can't hear the TV anyway because the kids are fighting WWIII; and the retired trucker who just wants the news to be over so he can watch Hollywood Squares. So, what's the point?"

Chambers eschewed the corporate towers of Uptown and what he called "their conspicuous falderol." For his offices, he converted a stately Craftsman bungalow on East Boulevard, designed by a disciple of Frank Lloyd Wright; lots of woodwork, beveled glass, Tiffany lamps, and rich leather cigar chairs. When Turner toured Taylor through the offices that afternoon, Taylor was keen on the possibility of having a window. The basement of the Mecklenburg County Courthouse was an environmentally sterile cave that would have made a good bunker in wartime.

He couldn't wait to get home to talk to Tess.

The Impala and the Microbus pulled onto their street right after one another as if it was choreographed, a mini Parish parade down Belvedere. Climbing out of their aging cars, no longer defined by horsepower, but as horses that needed to be put out to pasture, the blessed evening stillness was but momentarily disrupted by creaking of their arthritic doors closing. Playing it cool, perhaps because he didn't know any other way to play it, Taylor lightly kissed Tess and harbored no agenda other than the genuine desire to know how his wife experienced her day.

"So, how's life in the land of Pilgrim's pride? How do we know the Pilgrims were proud, anyway? Didn't they have to put all their energy into staying warm, avoiding sickness, and praying to survive the winter? I mean, can't you hear the complaints in that homeowner's association meeting? 'Who's idea was this anyway? The pamphlet said we were going to the beach, and here we are in the frozen tundra. I want a refund. And let me just say, I think Squanto's wife isn't crazy about us being here in the first place. She gave me a funny look when I passed her a turkey leg.'"

"Well, I can tell you one thing. If Squanto or his wife knew what was coming, they'd have spiked that turkey with hemlock and claimed they were vegetarians."

"So, how is this year shaping up for the students of AP U.S. History? Did Washington really cross the Delaware?"

"He swam across in a pair of grape smugglers. This should be an interesting year. With Watergate we'll have box seats for what future historians will define as an epochal event in American politics."

"You really think a botched burglary is that big of a deal? I'm in the courtroom four or five times a week defending thieves exponentially sharper than those witless wonders at Watergate."

"Taylor, as this thing unravels, I think that relatively unknown office complex could be remembered as the place that brought down a president. So, how was your lunch?"

"Hal Holbrook offered me a job."

"What, hair and makeup? Script practice partner? Eyebrow trimmer?"

"Partner."

"Wow! Didn't see that coming."

"Nor did I."

"Well, congratulations. I may not have seen this coming, but I'm not surprised. Mr. Chambers has an eye for talent and character. So, what are you thinking?"

"That's what I was going to ask you."

"I asked you first."

"I'll be going to my knees in prayer."

"You headed to a monastery? I'm trying to picture you in a brown robe."

"Not really my color, but, we both know this is going to take some deep prayer for discernment. Turner Chambers' reputation is stellar and his practice is the kind of legal work I can see myself doing. It doesn't portend the confinement of corporate law or the narrowness of a specialty. I'd be doing everything from representing a country doctor in a malpractice case; to taking a philandering banker to the cleaners so that it's the ex-wife who vacations in Hawaii; to representing migrant farm workers; to defending churches offering sanctuary to political refugees; to suing the hell out of Jesse Helms if the chance ever presented itself; to drawing on my dad's expertise when siblings wrestle over daddy's business; to, as Turner put it, defending the prostitute every now and then. It's the variety of it all that fascinates me."

"The variety of prostitutes?"

"Okay now, Phyllis Diller, you know what I mean."

"I always did find it interesting that in the Public Defender's office you've had such a good reputation among the ladies of the evening."

"I think it's because I'm the only one who will actually listen to them without staring at their boobs. It took some training, but I think I've mastered it."

"A man of discipline indeed; at least as long as that's the only thing you've *mastered*."

"You're a riot. I told Turner that I was certainly flattered and intrigued, but that I couldn't be any more than that until I had talked with you."

"Wise choice."

"That's what he said."

"Well, forgive me if it sounds like I'm channeling my father, but I probably am. I know what his first question would be. Do you feel called to this?"

"No need to apologize, good Reverend. That's the question that calls for some serious reflection. Are you up for a long walk this evening?"

"Let me change into something more comfortable."

"Funny, I was kind of hoping you'd be saying that later tonight."

"Well, you don't want me to change into that if we're going for a walk."

"I don't know, old man Tyson down the street would get a thrill."

"Well, old man Tyson can just call one of your prostitutes."

"That makes me sound like I should be wearing a fur fedora and driving an Eldorado."

"It's a look. I'll be ready in five minutes."

Tess and Taylor's evening walks tended to take them to that place the Scots call *a thin place*, where the veil that separates earth and heaven is so thin you can almost see through it. During these walks the conversation was surely not incessant. What was said was thoughtful, prayerful, open to reason, and pertinent. The silences allowed the conversation to breathe and it was in those moments that the Spirit of God usually went to work on them, opening the door to the future for them. Interestingly, the Greek word, *pneuma*, is the same word used for spirit, breath, and wind. It's hard to notice the wind when whiling away the hours in a hermetically sealed, artificially air-conditioned family room, dulling all our senses as we stare at what Edward R. Murrow called "lights and wires in a box." However, on those shared long walks through the neighborhoods, parks, or the trails of the Blue Ridge, the wind of the Spirit healed them, moved them, stirred them, and breathed life into them.

Five weeks later, Taylor would be organizing his office on the second floor of a Dilworth bungalow and meeting with Tess and a realtor to close on a four-bedroom ranch in Myers Park. It was a busy but blessed life as Tess taught and Taylor practiced law; as Tess chaired the Christian Education Committee at Myers Park Presbyterian where Taylor served on the Local Benevolence Committee; as Tess prodded, prompted, and pushed the citizens of Charlotte to be a little more cognizant of the needs of the poor and disenfranchised and Taylor finally had the chance to step on the first tee of a Donald Ross masterpiece. They would certainly endure pain with the passing of Taylor's mom in Missouri and Tess' first miscarriage. Three years later they would know the surreal horror of bearing a stillborn child. Periodically, there would be another wave of hate mail opposing their work in supporting issues including school integration and affordable housing. Yet, they would face it all together, prayerfully walking their way through the dark passages and facing their misfortunes with the equanimity of those who trust that God will not abandon them.

Just when they assumed that the possibility of holding a child of their own was fading, the rabbit died, and months later Elijah Lovejoy Parish entered the world; three years after that, so would I. Another two years brought my sister Dina Beth, who always went by D, unless she was in trouble, which was fairly often. "Dina Beth Parish!!!" was a familiar and frequent sound in our home and neighborhood throughout D's childhood and adolescence. She didn't mean to be trouble. Didn't have a malicious cell in her perpetually in motion makeup. Trouble would sneak up on D like Jason on a drunken teen in the midnight woods, and by then she couldn't escape it because she was covered with it. At that point, more often than not, she decided to at least enjoy the ride.

When a couple marries, the occasion marks much more than two individuals coming together. They each bring with them the impact of the generations before them. That they have been shaped, molded, imprinted, and informed by that history will directly influence the way they relate to one another. Elijah says that when a couple comes to him in preparation for marriage, he tells them they need to sit down together one evening and plot out the branches of their respective family trees, penciling in notes of all the twists, turns, triumphs, tragedies, hooking up, splitting up, breaking down, acting out, and downright quirkiness that make up the stock in which they each have been marinated. This is priceless information, not as a warning of what they will encounter at the family reunion, but as insight into the physical, emotional, mental, and spiritual DNA of the person toward whom they hope to articulate the promise, "I will."

As the son of a lawyer, Elijah knows you don't sign contracts with someone you don't even know. Attempting to sustain a relationship without trying to understand the influences that shaped your intended is like taking an exam without having read the book. Of course, everyone knows *that* guy who never cracked a book and didn't make it past the first semester of college before he was back home working at the carwash, and the marriage statistics certainly reveal that more than half of the couples who tie the knot may have put on one helluva wedding party, but never got beyond the cover art of the book jacket protecting the pages that have formed each other.

Elijah's wisdom is found in his understanding of how he is the product of Tess and Taylor in ways far beyond the collision of sperm and egg. He cites the importance of the genealogies in the Bible, which tend to rank high on the top ten lists of excuses people use for not joining a Bible study. "It's so boring! Who wants to sit through a roll call of names?" Well, those genealogies, like the names on your family tree, are so important in coming to understand who you are and how you came to be you. They mark you no less than the maze of lines that form your fingerprint. When my father was given a prescription for a statin to combat his cholesterol, just like his dad before him, the doctor memorably declared, "You can run fifty marathons, but you can't run away from your genes."

The genealogies of the Bible and the branches of your family tree, along with the pages you have already etched in the story of your days offer a treasure trove of information about your makeup, your character, your blind spots, your gifts, your faults, your quirks, your desires, your politics, your beliefs. When the wandering youth or the philandering middle-aged insurance salesman feels so compelled to *go find himself*, just tell him, "Listen up, idiot! You don't have to trek through a rainforest or plant your penis in the nearest Barbie doll to find yourself. Look at the genealogies, the family tree, the victories, graces, regrets and screwups of your misspent youth. It's all there. Listen to the people and the stories that formed you. Listen to the pages you have added to the family tree. It's all there, and in the end, it's not about finding yourself, anyway, it's about being found." *I was lost but now* am *found; was blind but now I see.*

The genealogy at the beginning of the gospel of Matthew chronicles a history of promise making, promise breaking, hate, intrigue, deception, dysfunction and enduring love that informs and shapes Jesus' understanding of the human condition and his particular compassion for the forgotten, the outcast, the outsider, and the broken. It is a witness to a love that refuses to give up on us.

Take the story of Jacob, #3 in the cast of characters highlighted in the genealogy of Jesus. Elijah recently offered this spin on family trees and life struggles by taking his congregation to the ford of the Jabbock River along with the ornery character of Jacob, son of Isaac, grandson of Abraham, the one designated to carry forward the promise of God to his people, that holy hellion headlining *Wrestlemania* long before *The Rock* or Charlotte's own *Ric Flair* were tossing rivals into the turnbuckle. Though Jacob thought he was headed to a reckoning with his brother Esau, God had another foe for him to confront first.

After a week of contemplating family trees, the Rev. Elijah Lovejoy Parish stepped forward to the pulpit on a rainy Sunday morning in early June to read the lesson for the day from the book of Genesis.

Genesis 32: 22-32

22 *The same night he got up and took his two wives, his two maids, and his eleven children, and crossed the ford of the Jabbok.* **23** *He took them and sent them across the stream, and likewise everything that he had.* **24** *Jacob was left alone; and a man wrestled with him until daybreak.* **25** *When the man saw that he did not prevail against Jacob, he struck him on the hip socket; and Jacob's hip was put out of joint as he wrestled with him.* **26** *Then* *he said, "Let me go, for the day is breaking." But Jacob said, "I will not let you go, unless you bless me."* **27** *So he said to him, "What is your name?" And he said, "Jacob."* **28** *Then the man said, "You shall no longer be called Jacob, but Israel, for you have striven with God and with humans, and have prevailed."* **29** *Then Jacob asked him, "Please tell me your name." But he said, "Why is it that you ask my name?" And there he blessed him.* **30** *So Jacob called the place Peniel, saying, "For I have seen God face to face, and yet my life is preserved."* **31** *The sun rose upon him as he passed Penuel, limping because of his hip.* **32** *Therefore to this day the Israelites do not eat the thigh muscle that is on the hip socket, because he struck Jacob on the hip socket at the thigh muscle.*

One: This is the word of the Lord.

Many: Thanks be to God.

Maybe you have had the experience of driving by a distinctive house on a regular basis, a grand old white frame home with inviting front porches and awnings over the windows. Set amongst the towering oaks and beefy magnolias, it is a captivating place, and as you drive by each day you think it would be a wonderful, no a perfect place to live. But maybe at some point you are invited to a party at that perfect domicile and upon closer examination you notice that the floors creak, the windows are rotting at the edges, the porch is slanted, and the whole place could use a good painting. The idyllic image in your mind does not match the reality you see.

You check in to the legendary bed and breakfast, the place you've dreamed about for years. You had to wait eight months for reservations. But you get no sleep in the luxuriant down tufted bed because of the blasted banging of boiler pipes all night long. The gushing magazine ad didn't mention anything about that.

You're tempted each time you walk by the display window and see that outfit, the same outfit advertised in *Town and Country*, the outfit that seems extravagant but looks so good. But when you finally enter that door to be Talbotized, Pradafied, or Gucci-cooed, there is that chance that after the tags have been clipped you will notice a flaw in the fabric. Like the pindot of a spaghetti splash on your starched white shirt or the pink pimple plaguing your nose, most folks won't notice, but you do, and it just eats away at you.

The idyllic home, the perfect getaway, the essential wardrobe addition, no matter what the cost, it will most likely come with a flaw. Such is the nature of things whether we are talking about architectural wonders, consumer products, or family trees.

I've been reading a book highlighting American history and as I've read about some of those legendary families whose names mark many of our schools, universities, and institutions, I am drawn to the conclusion that they were or are just as dysfunctional as the rest of us, the only difference being that they wore more expensive clothing.

If you read much history you will either become mired in cynicism or be pleasantly surprised by how well we have survived, in spite of ourselves. An examination of any family tree will reveal generous helpings of transgression, illicit liaison, bitter rivalries, and ego-sired iniquities. Think of all the shady stories that were discreetly left out of your family histories, the shocking stories Aunt Martha just couldn't bring herself to include when she compiled your family genealogy.

Well, a study of our family tree in the Bible is no different. Look at any of the Bible's genealogies and behind the names you will find the stories that raise eyebrows and evoke snickers. That's why I'm somewhat perplexed when my contemporaries and colleagues pound their pulpits and fill the airwaves with calls for a return to biblical moral values. Are they referring to David and his illicit affair or his conspiracy to commit murder? Are they talking about Rahab the harlot, or are they speaking of Hosea's angst over falling in love with a prostitute, or maybe they are alluding to Solomon's seven hundred wives and three hundred concubines. Most of those characters find their place in Jesus' family tree.

From Abraham to Zaccheus, though at times we will use the term saints, we must always remember that the people of the Bible, like the people of the world, are sinners.

You see, the goal of the Bible is not to reveal the high moral character of a people. Rather, it is to proclaim the power and unrelenting love of a gracious God. Time and again, what we read in the Bible is the story of a God who will not allow our flaws to impede his purpose for us.

Certainly, this is the case when we come to the story of Jacob. You can just imagine the stories from this guy's childhood. I'm sure you've seen the brand and model of this child before. Just the mention of his name would lead a room of adults to shake their heads. "My, my, my." Isn't there always one at a birthday party? You know, the kid who pushes the other kids out of the way, the one who steals the presents out of the birthday girl's hands, the one who sticks his fingers in the icing before the cake is cut. Rounder, scoundrel, scamp, contemptible, conniving, scheming, selfish, rotten brat. That's Jacob. Think Eddie Haskell, only more devious. Ferris Bueller with an attitude.

His name means, "heel grabber," alluding to the story of his birth, when Jacob was grabbing the heel of his brother Esau in an effort to get out of the womb first. His growing years were marked by the time he conned Esau out of his birthright and later conned his poor old blind father Isaac into giving him the blessing that was meant for Esau. Do you think Esau friended his brother on Facebook?

When this flimflam artist became the victim of Laban's con, Jacob turned around and managed to take about everything poor old Laban had ever possessed, including both of his daughters who became Jacob's wives. Jacob, the godfather of identity theft, could enchant you with his smile while stealing your passwords with his sticky fingers.

Well, you don't live that kind of life without creating some animosity in those whose lives you have trampled. So you can imagine that Jacob was a bit tense about an appointed meeting with his brother Esau. What would Esau do? Was the con man about to get his comeuppance?

As only Jacob would, he sent his wives and his servants out in front of him. You know the old saying, "I'm behind you all the way." Yet, while Jacob had placed some insulation, a human shield between himself and Esau, Jacob, the trickster, the con man, was now vulnerable and alone.

And so it was, that fateful night by the ford of the Jabbock River, that Jacob was confronted by a stranger. "Jacob was left alone," the writer tells us, "and a man wrestled with him until daybreak." It is a curious encounter. We can't really identify this mysterious wrestling opponent, the scholars can't either, but history and tradition have given us the sense that in some way, Jacob was wrestling with God.

That seems abundantly strange to us. A wandering livestock herder shouldn't be talkin' trash and trading take downs with the "Immortal, Invisible, God only Wise." How can the human contest the Divine? This is way beyond David and Goliath stuff. We are speaking of the One whose word alone transformed nothing into a universe. You wanna mess with God? "I brought you into this world, I can take you out."

In a wrestling match between Jacob and God, it seems to me that the Vegas oddsmakers couldn't make those numbers high enough even if Jacob managed to bribe the judges, which I'm sure he would have attempted.

What does this mean? It is a strange story. And yet, it is a story that at some level resonates with us, speaking to our own struggles with the One who formed both molehill and mountain. While I'm no match for that One who set the stars in the sky, I certainly know of those times when it feels as if I am wrestling with God. I read many of the Psalms and I can tell that the writers feel as if they are wrestling with God. I hear your stories and what I hear is that faith so often seems to be a wrestling match. The Apostle Paul even speaks of it in terms of a boxing match.

We want what we want and we want God to want what we want and, well, God may have something else in mind. Wrestling.

We see what we see in the world and we question what God is up to, failing to consider that God is certainly questioning what in the world we think we're doing. Wrestling. Relationship involves wrestling. And anyone who has ever put knee to floor and face to heaven knows the experience of grappling with God.

You will note in our story that Jacob's unnamed foe gives him, along with a limp, a new name, Israel, which, get this, means, "strives with God." It is the name that Jacob's children, that God's people, that we will bear. For by the grace of Jesus Christ, we, too, carry forward the promise of Jacob/Israel. "The promise is for you, for your children..." Peter proclaims. Those who strive with God. If we're honest it still fits us, doesn't it?

If you've ever wrestled with relationship, you know what it means to be bruised. It may have been your heart rather than your hip that was thrown out of joint, but life and relationship will inevitably bring about a certain amount of limping. And yet, somehow, as we limp along through the wrestling match that is life, there is or there can be the experience of great blessing in it all.

We learn in this story that the blessing is not because of what you have done. Rather, it is because of who God is. Jacob/Israel, far beyond his deserving was blessed and so are we.

One consequence of having a heart, mind, and will is the inevitability of grappling with God. But think for a moment about what is happening in that experience. The Creator of tomorrow cares enough to confront you today. The love of the Almighty for you is such that he is willing and patient enough to confront you today. You may be bruised. You are certainly changed by the exchange. But in the end you are blessed.

Think of the young adult who after surviving all the teenage wrestling matches with her parents discovers an unforeseen gratitude that they cared enough to confront her. She felt so bruised at the time (remember the slouch, the lip, the attitude, "I wear black because my life is so dark!"), but now facing tomorrow, she knows she's been blessed. The God with whom we strive is also the God who blesses us and places us on the same path that mixed bag of sinning saints has traveled before us. Jacob's story can't be denied at Jesus' family reunion, which we call Sunday worship. All those characters travel with us as we journey to wherever it is that Christ is leading us. That path that may cross through the valley of darkness and the veil of tears and leave us with a limp; but will eventually lead us home, and you know what they say about home. When you knock on that door, they have to let you in. Amen.

———————————————

Cain, Abel, Esau, Jacob, Rahab, Rachel, Panina, Gomer, David, Jesus, Peter, Saul, Lois, Eunice, Jordan, Adele, Zachary, Tyler, Myrtle, Alexandra, Tess, Taylor, Crazy Uncle Billy, Elijah, Zach, D, Hannah, Xani, and baby Nathan. Wherever Elijah goes, he carries those names and countless others with him. Following my death, they went with him to Westminster College in Missouri, Union Seminary in Virginia, and to the foothills of North Carolina where this summer he enters his sixth year of ministry. He can no more deny the combined impact of those stories on his worldview than he can deny the scar that cuts through his left eyebrow. The family tree is who he is. Its roots, branches, and leaves extend further than he can imagine. The tree shapes his character, nurtures his faith, and certainly informs his ministry. To deny it is to be shackled by it. To comprehend it and see it through the eyes of Christ is to know the enduring, redeeming, sustaining, and freeing love of God.

Elijah Lovejoy Parish ponders the governing impact of the tree every time he walks through the shadow of the noble oak that stands sentry in the cloistered garth separating sanctuary and fellowship hall at the St. Martin Presbyterian Church of Edinburgh, North Carolina.

2

Summer

HOT. SEARING, SWELTERING, SMOLDERING, sizzling, stick-the-tongs-in-me-and-get-my-fat-ass-out-of-this-deep-fryer hot. In the South, people are wont to lament on sticky, summer days, "It's not the heat; it's the humidity." Nonsense. It's the heat and the humidity. Many years in Edinburgh, summer begins in early May and ends in late September. The shower following a run at dawn is useless because as the towel glides over your tush, you can feel drops of sweat emerging from your pores and carving the Catawba River down your back. If the house was empty, the shades weren't open, and the neighbors couldn't see, you'd go stand buck naked in front of an open freezer so you could at least get your boxers on without them sticking to your legs.

Hot. On sizzling summer Sundays following the benediction when Elijah exits the sanctuary and pint-sized vestibule to greet worshippers outside, his black robe becomes a furnace funneling heat to his pits, pecs, back, bellybutton, thighs, knees, and calves. By the time Miss Gertrude finishes her excruciatingly exhaustive weekly dissertation on such subjects as her recent bunionectomy, Elijah is soaked from the knot of his Brooks Brothers tie to the tip of his Gold Toe socks.

Summer arrived early and angry this year. By the first of July, it was hard to find a blade of grass that hadn't applied for hospice care. Even the rich folks in the Barton historic district with their manicured, irrigated lawns were fighting a losing battle with fungus and grub worms. And you should have heard them holler when the city invoked water restrictions. "Restrictions? Not until you pry the sprinklers from my cold dead hands!"

Some of them kept on watering anyway and paid the fines. I can just hear my Aunt Myrtle, dripping with Southern sarcasm. "Well, bless their hearts. They must need that water because they are just sooo special!"

Oh, if they only knew that the agenda of the city council that evening would include a proposal from the fire department to cancel the annual fireworks display at the fairgrounds. Of course, it didn't have a chance of passing. This is the South. Robbing a redneck of his firecrackers could spark a cherry bomb jihad.

Under the torrid sun of mid-afternoon, Elijah climbed out of the beloved silver Jeep his father had handed down to him upon his graduation from seminary. Elijah loves that Jeep more than a preacher is supposed to love any inanimate object, and often when polishing or washing it, he will sing the line of an old country song, "She said me or the car; between us you must choose. And I cried all the way to the bus station; I hate she had to lose." On this afternoon the Jeep had transported Elijah to the parking lot of the town's public housing complex in order to meet the daughter of long-time church member Josie Ellerbe. Thirty minutes earlier Shania had called Elijah crying, one decibel shy of hysterical.

"You gotta come and meet me outside momma's apartment. We hafta go tell her that Sam's been kilt."

"Shania?"

"Yeah, Sam got hisself kilt on his motorcycle last night! Get on over there and we'll meet ya."

The parking lot at the housing complex was a griddle and Elijah was a hamburger waiting for someone to slap a piece of cheese on him. Sizzling summer days lead you to envision that God's dream job was to be a short order cook. White t-shirt with his cigarettes rolled up in his sleeve. White paper cap with black stenciled letters spelling out *The Divine Diner*. Grease-stained apron and a Brooklyn accent suggesting a diet of unfiltered Marlboros and black coffee. "Oahder up!!"

About the time Elijah realized that his earlobes were dripping, a battered, sun-bleached blue minivan with one hubcap and a cracked windshield careened into the parking lot. The passenger door swung open, allowing a Big Gulp cup to fall to the pavement, a quart of Sun Drop forming a puddle that looked like pee.

"Shit! . . . They better give me a free refill. That damn Mexican didn't put the cap on right. Shut up, kids! Stop yer hollerin'! I gotta talk to the preacher here."

Shania never did make it to the cotillion, but she had seen the inside of the county lockup where she and her brothers Sam and Frank were regular customers. "Damn Frank! You do look good in orange!" DUI, Disturbing the Peace, robbery, larceny, bad checks, fraudulent welfare applications, public drunkenness, battery (that was usually Shania), shoplifting; the Ellerbe kids had sampled about everything on the menu that didn't involve a bullet. Oh, how they had tortured their mother through the years. The Edinburgh Scotsman, the local paper, could have run a regular Stupid Crooks article featuring only the Ellerbes. Sam had just recently been released after serving a three-year sentence for auto theft and burglary. Get this, he hot-wired a Taurus and later that evening used the owner's iPhone to have a pizza delivered to his trailer. When there was a knock on the door, he pulled out a ten and opened the door only to greet the sheriff's deputy instead of the expected pimple-poppin' delivery guy.

"Sam, you should have this memorized by now. Heh. Heh. Well, maybe that's not feasible for you. You have the right . . . "

"Feasible? O hell! Is there gonna be a fee for this?"

As they loaded him into the back of the police cruiser, Sam shouted to the deputy, "Hey, can't we wait for my pizza?"

Shania's latest adventure was a questionable worker's compensation claim at the leather factory that had just hired her over in Lenoir. Feigning a back injury from a slip in the bathroom "witnessed" only by her cousin, she somehow conned the insurance company into a $30,000 settlement. She thought she had won the lottery but within ten days had blown the majority of it on cocaine. Then, while she was waiting for her disability application to be reviewed, she actually said the following to her wheel-chair bound, public assistance dependent, food-stamp receiving mother: "My babies ain't got no shoes. If you don't give me a hundred bucks to buy 'em some Nikes, I'm gonna call Social Services and send 'em away, and you won't see 'em no more." Lord, how they torture that woman.

Frank was scheduled to get out of his fourth stint in rehab the next day, and no one had informed him about Sam, either. So, there stood Elijah and Shania in the public housing parking lot, separated by a puddle of Sun Drop that looked like pee, the kids screaming in the back of the minivan.

"Trace won't give me back my Game Boy!"

"Shut up ya little turd!"

Elijah couldn't help but shake his head, wondering what in the world the Psalmist had been drinking when he sang to the Lord, "what are human beings that you are mindful of them, mortals that you care for them? Yet you have made them a little lower than God, and crowned them with glory and honor." A little lower? Glory? Honor? Seriously?

"Oh, preacher, I can't believe it. I can't believe it. He's been kilt. My brother's dead. You gotta tell my mother. I can't do it. It'll kill her. You gotta do it. It'll kill her."

Elijah's first thought was that the Ellerbe kids had been trying to kill their mom their whole lives. "Shania, I'm so sorry for your loss. What happened?"

"Like I tooold you, it was a motorcycle wreck. He had just stopped for a few beers with his buds, and when he left it was dark. He couldn't see too good out there on Brown Mountain Road, well, because of the buzz, you know, and course, the headlight was busted. He took a corner too wide and was hit by one of those big Cadillac, ah hell, whaddya call 'em, SUVs. There weren't nuthin the EMTs could do. Sam never took to wearin a helmet."

"Well, I know it's a shock. I'm sorry. Let's go talk to Josie."

"Ok. Shit, you think I oughta leave the kids in the car?"

"Shania, it's up to you."

"It'll be hard on them."

"I suppose it will." Though Elijah noticed they didn't seem to be suffering too bad so far.

"Lemme have it, Dickhead!"

"O yeah? Kick my butt."

"Hah! You hear that, Little Dickie, Ha! Ha! I luv sayin' that! Little Dick here told me to kick his butt! Why, I'd be glad to! Ha! Ha!"

"You know I meant kiss!! You know I meant kiss it."

"Trace! Dickie! I'm gonna kick both your butts if you don't simmer down!"

Meanwhile, Robbie Gallimore, Shania's common-law husband, was sitting silent in the driver's seat picking at the little balled up bits of deodorant in his armpit. Elijah chuckled to himself. "A little less than God? Seriously?"

Stepping away from the sizzling pee puddle, Rev. Parish and the bereaved sister walked toward Josie's apartment. With each step, Elijah was turning over in his mind the different options of how to tell a mother that her son was dead, but when he opened the door, Shania knocked him into the door jamb as she ran into the apartment wailing, "They kilt Sam!! The bastards kilt your little boy!!" Elijah hadn't considered *that* option. Shania collapsed into the lap of her shocked mother, causing the wheelchair to lurch backward, dumping Shania with a loud thump on the linoleum floor. "Shit, Mom! Didn't you have your brakes on?"

You know how you can tell that a toddler is about to bust a lung screaming when there is that momentary pause between injury and squall? Well, there was a brief silence in that corner of the housing complex before the bleating began. A deep guttural moan ascended into a glass shattering shriek. "They killed my baby! They killed my baby! Why me, Lord? Why him?" Not to be outdone, Shania joined the chorus and for a brief moment it sounded like they were hollering in harmony. If Elijah would have jumped in a third lower, they could have had a nice little trio. Instead, he pulled a chair from the kitchen and sat down until the storm petered out. Taking a cue from the hockey referees over in Raleigh who would stand back from the melee until the protagonists were wearing down, Elijah had learned the folly of introducing rational discourse to a raging storm.

Waving her handkerchief in front of her face like the white flag of surrender, Josie sighed, "Whew! I'm hot. Preacher, how about pouring me a glass of Coke? I'm feelin' a little dizzy."

As Elijah went to the freezer and pulled out one of those ancient ice trays to fill the Mason jar glass, Shania stroked her mother's hand and told her what had happened.

"Well, Mama, Sam was out drinkin' and tokin' last night. Preacher, he has to do this to ease the pain in his back, what with the arthritis and all. But J.D. said he wasn't willin' to crash on the couch like he sometimes does. So, he jumped on that old rice rocket with the busted headlight and headed up Brown Mountain Road. He went a little wide on a corner and hit some big-ass-rich-bitch SUV. J.D. said the medallion on the grill left an imprint on his forehead. Ain't that weird? 'Cause Sam always wanted an Escalade, you know. He wouldn't wear no helmet, so I guess you could say he was dying to get an Escalade. I was thinkin' on the way over here; maybe we could sue that driver. J.D. said her name was Maggie Bost and that she's some kind of lawyer. They was comin' back from some hoity-toity concert up in Boone. I bet they got deep pockets. You think we ought to sue 'em? You figure we got a case?

Elijah tried to look contemplative as though he was seriously considering her question, but this is what was going through his mind: "Let's see, a convicted felon, without a license or headlight, driving in the dark on the wrong side of the road, all while under the influence of Pabst Blue Ribbon, Jack Daniels, and marijuana runs into a car, and his sister, who has a record, wants to sue the driver, who happens to be the local district attorney returning to Edinburgh after a chamber orchestra concert at Appalachian State. Yeah, that oughta work."

"Well, Shania, now is probably not the best time to pursue that conversation. Let's let your mom process things, right now."

Josie chimed in, "We got a lawyer in the church that can sue people, right?"

"Well, yes, but he's out of the country right now. So, maybe we can look into that later. I am so sorry for your loss and I want you to know that the people of St. Martin are here to walk with you through this journey."

Elijah began to walk Josie through the steps of planning a funeral and burial, but became distracted, losing his train of thought when he witnessed something for which seminary never prepared him. Shania fell into a velour Lazyboy, popped the lever, stretched out, unbuttoned her jeans and unzipped her zipper as she let out a big sigh. Well, she didn't actually have to unzip her zipper. It was under so much pressure that it sort of acted on its own.

"Whew!! That's better. I been wantin' to do that all day. These jeans right near choked me. I think they shrunk."

"Shrunk?" Elijah thought to himself. "It's not the jeans that are the problem." Rappers are always talking about *junk in the trunk*. Well, Shania's junk had escaped the trunk and expanded all the way around to the hood. "Yet you have made them a little lower than God, and crowned them with glory and honor." Seriously?

"You sure we shouldn't go ahead and start that lawsuit? My trailer could use a new deck."

———————————————————————

There is a voyeuristic element in the work of a pastor, not the salacious porn-addicted/peephole in the robing room variety of the preachers who look disheveled and creepy as detectives lead them on a perp walk, but the rare combination of privilege and burden that pastors are given occasionally to peek behind the superficial Sunday morning masks of the "I'm fine—aren't we successful—lookin' like an ad for Ralph Lauren—my what a beautiful family" members populating the pews. Looking upon the gathering crowd in the period before the organ prelude, were it not for the pews and stained glass, you could easily mistake the gathering for a cocktail party at the club, sans booze.

Yet, when Elijah looks out from the pulpit of St. Martin Presbyterian, he knows that the golden-haired, strong jawed, Hugo Boss draped radiologist in the third row is having an affair, and that this week he will basically tell his beautiful wife that her life as a Norman Rockwell painting is over. He sees the fortysomething couple, sitting stiffly in the back row, who sat in his study last week literally screaming at one another. He sees the single-mom over on the left who was just diagnosed with pancreatic cancer and has never felt so alone in all her life.

He knows that the tall bass behind him in the choir loft is floundering following retirement from the police force and that his wife fears he is contemplating suicide. He knows that the young couple with the newborn in the front row is overjoyed, overwhelmed, sleep deprived, and close to

comatose. He knows that the usher handing out bulletins and passing offering plates has a 19-year-old son who will make a court appearance this
week facing a charge of vehicular manslaughter after texting, drinking, and
running a red light in Chapel Hill, killing a respected Chemistry professor who was walking through a crosswalk after a late night in the lab. He
knows the couple that winces each time there is a baptism because of their
inability to have children.

He knows the teacher feeling buried by paperwork and butchered by
budget cutbacks. He knows the architect whose firm was forced to close. He
knows the nurse facing foreclosure. He knows the shy 11-year-old who just
moved to town and is scared to death. And he knows approximately two
women and three men who stay at the office until late at night, not because
of the workload, but because the thought of going home suffocates them.
He knows the fiftysomething couple that left their jobs to open a coffee shop
on the courthouse square who are anxious and terrified. And he knows that
this is the way of life and these are the people of Christ's church.

For the most part, Hollywood is clueless when it comes to faith in
general and the church in particular. Apparently, the sole direction given to
actors cast to play a pastor consists of the following: "Put on a clerical collar and act like an idiot." Pastors are portrayed as clumsy, dimwitted dorks
(a la Mr. Bean); or embezzling, philandering blinged-out con artists (a la
Elmer Gantry); or snake-handling hillbillies a few synapses short of a brain;
or power obsessed politicians and pedophiles manipulating those around
them through fear, intimidation, and abuse (a la Philip Seymour Hoffman).
Certainly, there are real life examples to be found that match the labels, but
the default setting for film scripts seems to be that all preachers are frauds
and all worshippers are gullible fools; as though intelligence and faith
are mutually exclusive.

Those who worship and those who shepherd them are at times bril-
liant, broken, caring, cold, selfless, selfish, deeply insightful, and foolishly
blind. The difference between those who worship and those who mock
them may be that those who worship confess at least the possibility of a
God smarter than them, are therefore open to mystery, and find a way
to live with the paradox of a loving God and a broken world. That sober-
looking 16th century voice of the Reformation, John Calvin, said that,
"There is no worse screen to block out the Spirit of God than confidence in
our own intelligence."

Faith isn't about gullibility. It is about humility. Faith is about acknowledging our mixed motivations, mercenary machinations, our manipulative
master plans. Faith is about understanding our utter dependence upon

that divine something or someone outside of ourselves in order to give our selves in relationship.

So, when the worshippers gather at St. Martin Presbyterian Church in Edinburgh, North Carolina, they congregate not as the callow casualties of fraud, but as real people with real faults, real fears, real problems, real potential, and real hopes for the future in spite of their sometimes wavering faith in a sovereign God.

St. Martin was established by Scottish immigrants in 1784 in an area that marked the transition between the Piedmont and Foothills of North Carolina. The town of Edinburgh itself was an outgrowth of the church. Presbyterian churches are not regularly named after saints because in the Reformed Tradition, all members of the kirk (the Scottish word for church), past, present, and future are considered saints. However, this particular saint meant something to those early settlers.

St. Martin in the Fields, otherwise known as St. Martin, bishop of Tours, was first a soldier. Born in what is modern-day Hungary in the early 4th century, he was the son of a veteran officer in the Roman army. While parents today repeatedly have to drag their kids to church, at the age of ten and against the wishes of his parents, Martin went to church on his own and enrolled as a candidate for baptism. Yet, before he would follow through on that process, he was required, as the son of an officer, to join the Roman army. While stationed in Gaul, the territory that would one day be called France, Martin was traveling toward the city of Amiens when he came upon a beggar three threads away from being naked. Martin instinctively took out his sword, cut his own cloak in two, and gave half to the beggar. That night, Martin had a dream in which he saw Jesus wearing that very cloak and saying to the angels, "Here is Martin, the Roman soldier who is not baptized, he has clad me."[2] When Martin awoke, he determined that he could no longer be a soldier of war. Instead, he would be a soldier for Christ. He was soon baptized and would eventually become the Bishop of Tours.

The story of St. Martin's compassion had an important influence on Columba, the abbot who was instrumental in taking the Gospel to Scotland and further into Europe. It was Columba who established an abbey in 563 on the small island of Iona off the west coast of Scotland.

2. Sulpitius Severus, *Life of St. Martin*, translated by Anderson Roberts, New York, 1984, quoted in Wikipedia.

Jumping forward over 1200 years, three Scots who found their way to the North Carolina foothills had once been to Iona and were moved by the story behind the ancient cross of St. Martin, which continues to stand sentry in front of Iona's Abbey. So, when it came time to name the fledgling congregation in the wilderness of rolling hills that would become Edinburgh, it was proposed by those Iona pilgrims that the church be called St. Martin Presbyterian Church.

Well, as is typical of most Presbyterian decisions, there was an argument, or what we like to call a debate. Some folks wanted the church to be named *Smokey Ridge Presbyterian Church* while others insisted on *St. Martin Presbyterian Church*. There were motions, calls to order, amendments, amendments to the amendments, points of order, two calls for a division of the house, and a failed effort to table the motion in order to form a task force to study the matter. Finally, someone with half a brain stood up and called the question, which is a fancy way of saying, "Will y'all just shut up and let us vote, for Chrissake?" The majority voted for St. Martin as the name for their new church, and Martin's witness continues to influence the congregation's outreach to the town of Edinburgh.

The collection of Scots who established St. Martin and then Edinburgh had come to the area from Charlotte, Cornwallis' hornet's nest. The Revolutionary War was now over and it was time for former soldiers to find a way to support their families. The area was rich with hardwoods and one of the settlers had a vision. Seamus McArthur had served as a captain in the militia of General William Lee Davidson, but prior to the war McArthur had worked as an apprentice for Thomas Affleck, a Scottish cabinetmaker in Philadelphia.

A cabinetmaker surrounded by hardwoods would share the joy of a linebacker surrounded by prime rib. Seamus knew how he could put those resources to work. Rather than just stripping the land and selling the timber, why not treat the forest like a farm that, continuously replenished, would provide a regular supply of choice hardwood for finely crafted furniture. Thus, the McArthur Furniture Company was born and still maintains a significant influence in Edinburgh. The heirs of Seamus McArthur have not yet failed to take the torch of the previous generation and carry it forward. They have been able to weather wars, depressions, and recessions without abandoning their roots in Edinburgh, never wavering in their commitment to the community. Spencer McArthur Smythe is the current CEO, accepting the position when her brother Mark retired last year. Like Mark, Spencer has a keen mind and a generous spirit, though competitors, vendors, and suppliers know her to be a tough negotiator. They also know you cannot outwork or outsmart a McArthur. Elijah says that there is probably not an elbow that hasn't touched a McArthur table nor a fanny that hasn't flopped in a McArthur chair in the lower forty-eight.

Seamus McArthur was the first clerk of session for St. Martin Presbyterian, and he designed and supervised the construction of the first sanctuary. When that sanctuary fell victim to a fire in 1902, his great, great grandson, John McArthur, served as the chair of the building committee for what is St. Martin's current sanctuary, an artfully crafted merging of stone, wood, and stained glass. Mark McArthur is the current clerk of session and his sister Spencer chairs the community outreach committee and also served as the head of the search committee that brought Elijah to St. Martin. The McArthurs' influence is significant, but could certainly not be categorized as a form of power politics. Unassuming, wise and . . . invested, in the best sense of that word; these adjectives would characterize the involvement of the McArthurs.

St. Martin Presbyterian Church:

- Membership—315
- Average Worship Attendance—220
- Budget—We're not Baptist, but we get by.

The church administrator had developed such a ritual of bringing a new bottle of Maalox with her when she arrived for work after her annual Christmas vacation that Elijah started wrapping a bottle and placing it under the Chrismon tree in the foyer outside the church office. The Maalox was a totem announcing the impending arrival of the deadline for the annual statistical report required by the denomination. Yikes!

> Lizard's leg, and owlet's wing,
> For a charm of powerful trouble,
> Like a hell-broth boil and bubble.

—William Shakespeare, *Macbeth*

Tamara Perry, the church administrator, pictured Shakespeare's witches when thinking about denominational bureaucrats and their vexing statistical fetishes. The reporting procedures did not jibe with the church software, and so it seemed to her an annual exercise in futility as she manually recalculated number after number in order to answer their questions with St. Martin's statistics. Tamara was hyper-organized, ethical, possessing an eye for detail and a dry wit. So, it wasn't the minutiae of statistical work that infuriated her so much as the knowledge that a good percentage of churches fudged the statistics.

"I've been to that church before and they don't have that many people attending even if you count the stiffs in the cemetery out back! I don't know where they get these numbers from . . . Well, maybe I do. 'Hey preacher! What should I put for attendance?' 'O, I don't know, say 300.' Bull! And look here, last year's report says they had 800 people enrolled in Sunday School! Are you kidding me?"

St. Martin is not the sole outpost of Presbyterianism in Edinburgh, nor is it the largest. This is not surprising, given the Scottish roots of the community. The largest Presbyterian Church renamed itself five years ago and is now called The Intersection. It seems that a recent trend in the church marketing business is to remove any symbols that would lead one to believe he or she was entering a church, and for God's sake, don't call it a church, as if the uninitiated and unaffiliated will innocently assume they are entering a warehouse for a rave or an office park for an eye exam or a movie theater to catch the latest Bond flick. Even the banners announcing an upcoming theme could be easily mistaken for an ad highlighting the *Twilight* saga. Steeples, crosses, hymnals, organs, and Sunday school are taboo, not cool, out of touch. Instead of sanctuaries, stained glass and the Apostles' Creed, the emphasis is on concrete floors, theater seating, black walls, exposed roof trusses and air ducts, drum cages, Stratocasters, and enough wiring to rival the White House Situation Room.

At The Intersection, a former Disney Imagineer has the funky job title, the Technonerd, and he manages the massive control board that can make the gathered crowd sense they are in an Amazon rainforest, a desert wilderness, mid-town Manhattan, the Hollywood Bowl, or the set of *Saturday Night Live*. The light shows, video montages, and special effects can be a little overwhelming. The first time they used the smoke machine, around a hundred people stampeded the exits, thinking that the stage was on fire. The emphasis at The Intersection is on being hip, though they would never use that word. My use of it is clearly a sign of being a relic of the past, which, when you think about it, is exactly what I am.

Anyway, whatever you call *hip* today is what they are. The staff wear those trendy gray gas stationesque buttoned shirts that are a size too small and have their names on those patches embroidered in red with a white background. The Lead Pastor has meticulously tousled hair and favors thin v-necked t-shirts that accentuate his sculpted pecs, deltoids, and biceps. He spends $400 on jeans carefully crafted to look well-worn and are tight enough to display taut buns and a cyclist's thighs. On one wrist he wears a braided leather cord along with a couple of colored bands promoting the hottest trends in the world of causes; and on the other wrist is a metal watch the size of a hubcap that costs about as much as a late model Buick. Worshippers swoon when they hear his name, and he is escorted from the darkness to the illuminated stage by a coterie of linebackers from the local high school, there to keep the cheering crowd at bay and point their LED flashlights down the aisle so that Teacher Tim won't trip in the darkness. The only thing missing is one of those glimmering capes that James Brown used to wear in concert.

The Intersection was founded by a dynamic, charismatic former Campus Crusade leader along with a group of members from St. Martin who were troubled by trends of inclusivity and what they perceived as a virus of biblical interpretation within the mainline church. With other disgruntled Presbyterians across the land, they were in the process of leaving the denomination and forming another, The Resolute American Presbyterian Church (RAP).

For some reason, Elijah was not troubled or intimidated by The Intersection. He did find the name curious, because it was nowhere close to an intersection, but was located on a large parcel of donated land on the outskirts of town. He also found it ironic that the church's marketing strategy was all about being trendy and accessible while the church's theology was decidedly exclusive and hyper-focused on who's in and who's out in the great up yonder. They used code words and terms like *authentic faith, genuine spiritual experience, true believer*, and the message was clear—the folks at St. Martin were deemed far from the kingdom of God. However, what made Elijah laugh each time he drove by the Intersection, was the incongruity of what they called *guests* entering their *worship experience* to hear the Word of God proclaimed and being handed earplugs by the ushers because of the volume. It brought to mind Jesus' words, "Hearing they do not listen."

The only thing separating The Intersection from the typical suburban megachurch was the absence of the mega. This is Edinburgh, and you don't find mega-anything in Edinburgh except for maybe the family size pizza at Rotino's over on the courthouse square. The dream of a megachurch in Edinburgh was less an act of faith and more a failure to understand basic math. If every man, woman, and dog in Edinburgh went to The Intersection, they would still struggle to recoup their investment in electronics and audio-visual equipment, not to mention the demands of a pastor who wanted to emulate the lifestyles of his suburban counterparts down in Charlotte. So, there were cracks forming beneath the surface of seamless Sunday spectacles at The Intersection as the elders of the church attempted to introduce Teacher Tim to a spreadsheet.

Finances at St. Martin are solid, but of course, Elijah and Teacher Tim do not live in the same neighborhood. Yet, that was fine with Elijah, who didn't have the stomach for living lavishly on the cliff's edge overlooking bankruptcy canyon. There were rumors making the rounds about Tim and Carlotta Sigmon, as rumors are wont to do in places like Edinburgh.

Rumors are to small towns what no-see-ums are to the beach—prevalent, inescapable, and irritating as hell. In the weeks before Elijah was introduced to the congregation of St. Martin, it was rumored that he was a woman from Scotland that had served in the RAF. When his resume became public, the people didn't mind the gender error so much as the fact that he wasn't a jet pilot. They thought that element of cool might attract new members or at least make for great party conversation. "I'll bet your preacher doesn't travel at Mach 1." Elijah, however, is not a fan of heights.

The rumors floating around Tim and Carlotta like an unfortunate cologne were a tad more salacious. Carlotta, tall, long legged, olive skinned, flowing locks of burnt sienna, could not claim a Tuscan pedigree, though she relished fabricating that illusion. Much to her dismay, Carlotta's given name was Charlene Clontz and her hometown was the exotic locale of Waxhaw, home of the Outlet World of Wood—cheap furniture and lots of it. She never broke the four-digit barrier on her SAT, but she makes up for it with street smarts, rural route style.

Strikingly sensual in appearance, Charlene/Carlotta had been trading on the wrapping God had given her since grade school. After landing a spokesmodel gig with the Outlet World of Wood, she became a regular welcome sight on local commercials, standing with that "I get off at eleven" smile in front of Maytags, Kias, Lazy-Boys, and Hyundais. One submission to the Charlotte Observer's Comment Column read, "They can tax my tush and take my job as long as I can see the World of Wood Girl on TV each morning." Well, the rumor up the road in Edinburgh had Carlotta intersecting with NASCAR rookie Flip Forest, who had earned his nickname after surviving a terrifying wreck on a dirt track over in Elm City. Steve Sigmon, a local dentist and cousin of Teacher Tim told the Rotary regulars at his table last week that he had seen Tim and Carlotta angrily shouting at one another in the parking lot of the Lonesome Pine Steakhouse out by the interstate, and he added that they weren't reciting scriptures. Yet, whether Carlotta's affair is factual or fabricated, a growing number of people would tell you that Tim has had an extramarital affair for years . . . with himself.

Elijah just rolled his eyes when the rumor arrived at his Tuesday evening Bible study, and driving home that night he found himself feeling sorry for them knowing how the self-involved so often self-destruct. Obsessed with image and captive to the desire to acquire, the capacity for relationship corrodes. It is hard to love another when you are so in love with yourself. This squall of hubris becomes a raging storm when you factor in the adulation of others. The fatal flaw that sends so many public figures tumbling down from the lofty heights of their Potemkin image is an inclination to believe their own press. And so it is that Paul advises, "For by the grace given to me I say to everyone among you not to think of yourself more highly than you ought to think, but to think with sober judgment."

Maybe Teacher Tim and his tight t-shirts are headed for a crash at The Intersection because his series of sermons on sacred marriage bear little resemblance to the reality of his life with Carlotta. Cousin Steve doesn't seem hopeful. He said, "I wouldn't be looking for a peaceful resolution. Carlotta may not actually be an Italian woman, but she can sure fight like one." With that, the guys at Rotary laughed with prurient glee.

Elijah, however, felt bad for all the people in the path of the coming storm. Of course, he knew a healthy percentage of the members at The Intersection, many of whom had once been members of his congregation. A congregation that allows itself to be as enamored of the pastor's family photo as a nun brought to her knees by the stations of the cross, is inevitably devastated by the specter of infidelity. Though they no longer worshipped and served together, Elijah still felt emotionally tied to his former members, and he was saddened by the thought of the pain that would soon infect their spirits. And yet, the irony was not lost on Elijah that these faith-filled folks left St. Martin over a question of sexuality never spoken of by Jesus, but would soon be embroiled in an issue of sexuality codifed in the Ten Commandments and even expanded on by Jesus.

The Baptists and the folks over at the Church of God relished the idea of garnering the righteous remnant from the fiery pileup at The Intersection, knowing that the lexicon of worship and style they shared in common with The Intersection contrasted markedly from the worship and style of St. Martin, even though the name *Presbyterian* would be found somewhere in the wreckage.

Pulling into his driveway, Elijah said a brief prayer for Tim, Carlotta, and all those gathered at The Intersection, and he gave thanks for his marriage to a woman who was his best friend long before she was his wife.

Hannah Swenson Parish was standing in front of an open freezer, fanning the cool burst of air toward her glistening face. Eight months pregnant and feeling like a walking furnace thanks to an Edinburgh summer that bore scant similarity to its sister city across the Atlantic, Hannah still radiated an unpretentious, naturally athletic beauty in spite of her present misery. Her desperation was obvious to Elijah because he knew that the frugality of the farmer's daughter wouldn't normally allow her to hold the freezer door open for more than a nanosecond. Yet, at this moment her head was so far into the freezer that she didn't even notice him entering the back door.

"Is Admiral Perry closing in on the North Pole? If you stick your head in there any further, you may run into him."

"Oh, hey E, I didn't hear you come in."

"Hot enough for ya? You look a little flushed."

"Ya think?"

"Why don't I get an ice pack and we can sit down and I'll hold it on the back of your neck?"

"Nothing could sound more romantic to me right now. Madison won't be bringing the kids back for another half hour. She insisted on taking them along with the dog to the park and then feeding them supper over at their house."

"The pitter-patter of little feet."

"Pitter-patter? More like an EF 5 tornado!"

"Yes, we are overdue for a weekend away. Mom called and suggested that she could come up for a couple of days so that we could escape to the beach house."

"I do love your mother."

"We could head out after church on Sunday and come back on Wednesday morning. Of course, next week will be pretty crowded at the coast." In the Carolinas, it was once the rule that all the mills, plants, and manufacturers shuttered their doors the week of the Fourth resulting in a mass migration to the beach. Thankfully, Elijah's parents had a cottage at Wrightsville Beach and not Myrtle Beach. Wrightsville would be busy but Myrtle would be Ground Zero, a melee of mullets, sleeveless NASCAR t-shirts, beer-bellied-bikini-broads, tramp stamps, and Confederate bumper stickers. The air would be choked with the unforgettable smell of sweat mingled with cheap beer, cotton candy, coconut oil, and dead fish. Every surface you touch at Myrtle Beach leaves you feeling like you had just rubbed your hands with a glazed donut. Compared to that, Wrightsville is Kauai.

"Who cares about the traffic? I doubt that I'll leave the back porch."

Collapsing on the rugged old leather couch, a hand-me-down from the judge's chambers of his great-grandfather, Elijah slowly introduced the ice pack to the back of Hannah's neck, hoping to soothe and not shock with the sudden chill.

"You are the best husband."

"I doubt that, but you're stuck with me."

They sat there resting, the silence only interrupted by the occasional observation of some item in the day's newspaper. The letters to the editor usually contained at least one comment worthy of a look of incredulity accompanied by a chuckle at the loopy logic and incivility underlying a majority of public discourse. "Those idiot liberals on the school board ain't never gonna convince me they can teach my kids anything." The Edinburgh Scotsman clung to a curious editorial policy promising to print every letter to the editor as long as it wasn't profane. Thus, as a form of entertainment, the letters in the Scotsman ranked second only to the Gaelic Movie Theatre on Courthouse Square.

The rare stillness of a summer evening, a time usually regimented by the nightly drill of dinner—bath—bed, was a serendipitous luxury that Elijah and Hannah embraced, so comfortable in the company of each other, just as they had been for nearly their entire lives.

Elijah and Hannah came together as toddlers during Vacation Bible School at Laddonia Presbyterian Church and little had separated them ever since. Growing up, Elijah spent every July and most Christmas breaks in Missouri at the gentleman's farm of his grandfather. Hannah Swenson, the quintessential farmer's daughter, grew up on a huge working farm adjacent to the Parish place. The youngest of four children and the only girl, Hannah learned early on how to take care of herself. Quiet in nature, strong in character, inquisitively intellectual, lithe, athletic, and quick, Hannah could outrun and outwit her brothers by the time she reached the second grade, and she would never let them catch up. Hannah won the sprint every year at May Day Play Day and would earn a scholarship to run hurdles for the University of Missouri. She showed cattle at the 4H fair, could toss her share of hay bales, was the class salutatorian and wore the tiara reserved for the homecoming queen.

To just glance at Hannah invoked enchantment and to see her run was observing art in motion. Seeing her in a dress, grown men grew giddy. Everyone saw her beauty, yet no one remembered to inform her. Minimal makeup, bereft of bling, Hannah preferred jeans and hand-me-down cotton oxfords outgrown by her brothers. She kept her distance from the mean girls crowd, and was entirely uncomfortable around the high drama of high school relationships. She was always friendly but never needy. Disarmingly serene, in her house Hannah was the calm Monet lily in the midst of the chaos of a testosterone churned pond. She demurred at the advances of the local guys, not out of snobbery or prudishness, but because even before they were ever officially an item, Hannah's heart belonged to Elijah.

Even on that first day of VBS, they were so at ease with each other. The tornado of preschoolers swirling around them failed to disrupt the serenity of their partnership as they constructed a barn out of Lincoln Logs. Their fathers, Taylor Parish and Beau Swenson, were lifelong friends, a gift that would be passed down from generation to generation. Beau and Taylor played Little League together, golfed with one another, cruised the A&W over in Mexico together, plowed and harvested fields together. It wasn't until college that they didn't ride to school together.

Taylor went to Westminster for History and Pre-Law and Beau went to Mizzou for baseball, Ag Econ, and a future on the farm. When Taylor, Tess, and crew vacationed at the beach, the brood of Beau and Lisa Swenson often joined them. When Beau and Lisa planned a trip to the Grand Canyon, the Parishes came along. And when Lisa was diagnosed with breast cancer in '96, Tess spent the summer at her bedside, singing hymns with her and praying with her as she held her hand the day she died. Three months later, on the morning following the car wreck that took my life, Hannah was on a plane to Charlotte, and her presence was a needed balm for the whole family through those first dark days. Two summers later, when Hannah called Elijah the evening after each had received their high school diplomas, tearfully relaying her fear that depression and alcohol had thrown Beau into a deep dark pit with no ladder, Taylor and Elijah drove through the night to help Hannah and her brothers get Beau the care he needed at the hospital over in Columbia.

The families were close, but Elijah and Hannah were closer. In their elementary years they covered every square inch of acreage on the farms, racing one another, riding bikes together, building forts together, fishing together, playing hide and seek when the corn was high, swimming in the Parish pool, playing ping pong in the Swenson barn, sitting next to one another in the pew at church, and even playing on a little league team together. And when they weren't burning calories, they would sit under a shade tree and read or flop on a family room couch and watch *101 Dalmatians* for the 101st time. As toddlers they talked mostly about tractors and ice cream, but as they grew their conversations grew with them. There were few topics that didn't make it to their roundtable. They talked about how much they loved *Seinfeld* and how much they hated *Saved by the Bell*. They'd hike out to the middle of a field in the dark of a rural night away from street lamps and house lights. They would lie on their backs, point to the constellations and ponder the size of the universe. Then they'd run back to the house in order not to miss the first skit on *Saturday Night Live*. They lamented the genocide in Rwanda, dissected wealth in America and poverty in sub-Saharan Africa. They wrestled with the meaning of the Trinity and debated the playoff chances of the Cardinals. They laughed, they cried, they prayed. Each could produce a list of people they could call friends, and yet, neither felt the adolescent obsession to hang out with them.

It was the third inning of a bantam league game at the Laddonia ballfield when the platonic became romantic. To this day the debate continues over who initiated that first kiss a few yards outside the left field flagpole.

"Hey, I was just turning my head away from a mosquito and the next thing I know, she's got her lips on me."

"You kept leaning in and shying away like some kid who can't find the courage to jump off the diving board. Finally, I just got tired of waiting. If I hadn't acted when you leaned over once more, you'd still be out there hemming and hawing on top of that picnic table, and by God, I wanted to get home before winter."

Just a few weeks into their breath mints addiction, Elijah and Hannah would enter their freshman year at high schools separated by 900 miles of Interstate, U.S. Highways, and county roads. When a blushing Elijah timidly stuttered the news to his parents that Hannah was now his girlfriend, Tess inquired, "You mean she wasn't already? Taylor, I think the phone bill is about to blow up." E-mail hadn't debuted, the country had not yet been digitized, books still had pages, and text was only a noun. So, Hannah and Elijah honed their writing skills, kept a supply of stamps, and looked for jobs so they could contribute to the phone bill.

When it came time to act on the college acceptance letters, Hannah followed through on her letter of intent to run the hurdles for the University of Missouri, majoring in elementary education and Elijah followed in the footsteps of his father, grandfather, and great-grandfather, majoring in history at Westminster College. Tess secretly hoped he would choose a school closer to home but did not protest the inevitable. That the two colleges were only a half hour apart instead of 13 hours undoubtedly sealed the deal. Hannah's brothers liked to torture the pair by mimicking Bubba Gump. "[Hannah] and me was like peas and carrots." Given the baggage those movie characters carried around, along with the fact that neither Hannah nor Elijah liked peas and carrots, the young couple didn't take kindly to the comparison. Loved the movie. Not crazy about the comparison. After all, their relationship could never be called star crossed. It began with ease in Vacation Bible School and it was no less so as they rose from the leather couch to greet their children when Madison's car pulled into the driveway.

First came Joab the chocolate lab, leading his people to the promised land through the back door. Then came Xani, short for Alexandra, four years old and named after Hannah's aunt, and Nathan, two years old and named after Elijah's favorite prophet. "You are the man!" Of course, Nathan's indictment of King David was far more courageous and had a far greater impact than the banal bravos unleashed from golf's galleries whenever Tiger Woods swings his mighty club. It was yet to be seen whether Nathan could perceive and speak truth to power with such clarity. He at least needed to be potty trained first.

Following the giggling (Xani), squeeling (Nathan), and slobbering (Joab) through the door was Madison Smythe, the daughter of Spencer and Tom, a rising junior at Edinburgh High School. She started as a babysitter but quickly became a member of the family. A beautiful young girl, more interested in books than proms and cheerleading, Madison adored Hannah, who had been her mentor during Confirmation, and when Hannah saw her run so gracefully after a stray soccer ball in the backyard while playing with Xani, she recruited Madison to run hurdles for the high school where Hannah happened to be the coach of the track team. Madison dreamed of being an elementary school teacher, and when Hannah wasn't coaching track, she was teaching second graders at Macallan Elementary School. Elijah thought it ironic for a school to bear the name of a treasured Scotch whiskey. "What's next? Jack Daniels Preschool? Guinness High School?" However, the school was named after a scion of one of Edinburgh's original immigrants who was the county's first superintendent.

Each August, Madison would ride with Hannah every day to help set up the classroom for the year.

Beaming as Madison followed the three little stooges into the house, Hannah said, "Oh Madison, that was such a wonderful gift of time and rest you provided us. Thank you. Can I get you something to drink? I picked up a bottle of your favorite Wink at the Food Lion today."

"That's tempting, but I have to get home and pack. Remember, we're headed to New York City for a few days."

"Oh, that's right. Have a wonderful trip and enjoy *Crazy For You*. I heard Matthew Broderick is great."

Gathering the little ones in a big hug, Madison said, "Ooooh, I'll miss you, but I'll be back in time for church on Sunday. Save me a seat in your pew."

Later that evening after the kids had been put to bed and Joab had been walked, Elijah and Hannah sat down for a late night supper of leftover baked spaghetti, the most underrated of gastronomic delicacies; something about allowing the meat sauce to marinate the pasta for a day and then lathering it with grated cheese and reheating it. Bliss.

While they ate, Elijah replayed the encounter with the Ellerbe clan and when he offered a verbal portrait of Shania setting her ample belly free from its zippered prison, Hannah laughed so hard, her iced tea came out of her nose.

"The visitation is tomorrow night and there will be a graveside service on Thursday outside of Old Fort."

"Do you need me to get a babysitter so I can go with you to the visitation?"

"That's not necessary. It could be entertaining, but Josie would certainly understand that you needed to stay with the kids."

"I wish I could ride with you to the graveside, but I have that doctor's appointment on Thursday morning."

"Yeah, I'm real sorry about the timing of this. I should be taking you to the appointment or at least coming home to watch the kids. Josie insisted on scheduling it before Frank could go on another bender."

"Oh, that's no problem at all. I'll bet D.A. could come and ride herd over the kids until I get back."

"She is ever the angel in our midst."

There are four types of funerals in Edinburgh. The first had become the custom at St. Martin. The graveside or columbarium service comes first, followed by a memorial service in the sanctuary, after which the family receives visitors in the fellowship hall with food and punch provided by the bereavement team. There's a comforting orderliness in first acknowledging the reality of death with the graveside and then celebrating the resurrection at the memorial service. Elegantly tailored dark suits, cap toe shoes, white shirts, pastel ties, sleeveless black dresses, strings of pearls, simple black heels, and expensive clutch purses. That's what would adorn the pews with most of it being provided by Trad's Place. Trad and Tipper Thompson were tasteful clothiers that had found a niche in providing the wardrobe for mill executives, furniture barons and the trust fund heirs, lawyers, physicians, furniture designers, and hospital administrators.

These memorial services were formal, relatively brief, and organ blessed. There were prayers, scripture readings, a thoughtful homily offering thanks for the life and witness for the love lost, a celebration of resurrection reality. The receptions served as a homecoming for Edinburgh's diaspora of grown children out conquering Wall Street, making their way through graduate school, working for the banks in Charlotte, or leading Outward Bound expeditions out West.

The second type of funeral is an old ritual that endures particularly in the rural South. The visitation is always the night before the funeral and always takes place at the funeral home. The funeral directors open the doors to the soft light of the air-conditioned lobby where you join the line of the deceased's friends, co-workers, neighbors, and fellow church members stretched down the long hallway toward the receiving room where family members form another line, often greeting strangers they have never met and will never see again. In the waiting line everyone tries to maintain a mien of solemnity while craning their necks to see an acquaintance to whom they give the universally recognized sober and subtle nod. There is conversation but it is muted and if there is laughter it is stifled. The visitors

file by the open casket and the family, expressing their sorrow and awkwardly saying how nice the breathless body looks. Upon offering condolences to
the departed's second cousin once removed, they break into conversation
clusters. If they do not know enough people to work the crowd, they file out
to the parking lot where they overhear those conversations that leave the
dead in less than the best light.

"You know, she never did pay her share for those flowers the office gave
the boss on her birthday."

"Oh hell, I heard he didn't retire. He was fired for making a pass at
Darla when Steve was out of town."

"Did you hear how she died? Choked on a meatball over at Geppeto's
in Newton. Seems strange since everyone knows she was bulimic."

"He was such an ass. Mert certainly has a place reserved in heaven for
stickin' with that man all these years. I'm not so sure he's getting' good news
up at the pearly gates. I heard Mert's already scheduled a trip to Vegas."

The following day's funeral could be at the funeral home or in a sanctuary. The dress code is more Penney's and Dress Barn than Brooks Brothers
and Ann Taylor. They'll sing *How Great Thou Art* and follow that with at
least three eulogies; and if it's a Baptist Church, the preacher won't let the
occasion pass without an altar call.

"I was there last week in the hospital when Johnny invited Jesus
into his heart so I know where he is today. Where will you be? Don't wait
and be late."

Of course, after all the words are said and the solos are sung, you'd still
have to say that the primary ingredient is the food—more ham, chicken,
potato salad, baked beans, and bundt cake than a warehouse could hold. To
Elijah, it seems ironic that the primary response to someone's demise is to
clog the bereaved's arteries with cholesterol.

The third type of funeral is unparalleled in artistry, atmosphere, excellence, and energy and it is experienced in the African American church. A
whole team of elegantly robed preachers, music that will send spirits soar-
ing, messages that bring forth both tears and rapture, wide open emotions,
and food that tastes so good you'll wanna shout, "Damn the calories! Full
speed ahead!!" Elijah said that he never felt so inadequate as a preacher than
when he was asked to participate in an African American funeral. He said,
"Those guys are major league, and I will always be in the minors."

And then, there's the fourth type of funeral, for which Elijah was gird-
ing himself on Thursday morning. If Wednesday's visitation was a prequel,
Thursday's graveside would be a Three Stooges festival of nonstop nyuks.
Walking across the parking lot Elijah surmised that if the local police were
smart, they would have set up a dragnet blocking all the entrances, because

there had to be a fistful of outstanding warrants congregating inside. However, when he looked across the street and saw the unmarked car sitting under the maple tree, he knew someone had deduced this grand opportunity before he had. Elijah wondered whether there would be anyone left to attend the graveside in Old Fort. He was disappointed to see that the morticians weren't scanning mourners for weapons as they entered.

"Evening, preacher."

"This should be interesting."

"Should be? I'll guaran-damn-tee it. Pardon me Rev."

"No worries, I think you hit the nail on the head."

"Jimmy wanted me to let you know you could ride with us tomorrow if you'd like."

"That's kind of you, but I think I want my wheels so I can get out of the way before the knife fight starts."

"In that case, maybe I want to ride with you. You'll find Josie back in viewing room #2."

"Thanks, Ray."

Suddreth's was the last independent funeral home in the county. All the others had been swallowed up by the big national conglomerates; yet another blow to small business. Jimmy Suddreth was determined to hang onto the business he inherited from his father Jack. The business went back four generations. Jimmy didn't fit the stereotype of the tall, deathly thin, Bella Lugosi-looking mortician with the bass clef voice. Jimmy had been a linebacker at Clemson and had as much personality as he had muscle. Though he was Episcopalian, he knew the St. Martin facility better than Elijah did. He would switch out pall and paraments without having to ask where to find them, and he repeatedly had to tutor Elijah on how to override the program on the sanctuary's thermostat. Jimmy had played high school football with Amos, the church sexton, and once, they confessed to Elijah about breaking into the church periodically during their teens to throw craps down in the furnace room.

Jimmy and Elijah had become friends at Rotary where they ritually sat at the back table mocking those zealous Rotarians who had attended one too many Dale Carnegie seminars, their smiles too plastic, their khakis too pressed, their speech too stilted, their handshakes too formulaic. Getting cornered in conversation with them was akin to getting thrown into one of those animatronic displays at Disney World. Elijah and Jimmy refer to themselves as the Rotary Rebels, their civil disobedience seen in their refusal to sing the Rotary song: R-O-T-A-R-Y! That spells Ro-ta-reee. The one time they were called out on it, they would chime in: "R-O-T-A-R-Y! Sounds like hell to me."

Elijah had his misgivings about the whole funeral industry, but Jimmy was a good guy trying to keep a small business open.

With an impish grin, Jimmy shook Elijah's hand. "You'd better keep your hands on your wallet when hugging the bereaved."

"I hear ya . . . though they might be tempted to say the same thing about you."

"Riiight. Like they are gonna pay their bill on time."

"Yeah, if you didn't get anything up front, you won't see a dime."

"I learned that lesson long ago. I managed to get the last $500 out of Shania's *settlement.* That girl and her brothers were *Dumb and Dumber* in school and it's just gotten worse over the years. Their combined IQ can't be more than sixty."

"Well, you've heard about their father and you know poor old Josie. As they say, two fifties don't make a hundred."

"Ray told me your thoughts on a knife fight. I'd have to agree. Look at 'em. You can't make this stuff up. Just be glad the funeral's not at the church. You'd be saying goodbye to a couple of computers and the silver communion ware."

"Now thank we all our God."

"We still riding Saturday morning?"

"I'll meet you at the church parking lot at 7:00."

Three things Elijah and Jimmy shared in common: a love of football, torn ACLs, and a passion for cycling. Elijah had been a promising running back in high school on the radar of a number of colleges until his junior year, when he tore both his ACL and MCL as his West Charlotte Lions were being soundly spanked by Richmond County in the playoffs. Football was done for Elijah at that point, but during rehab he had taken up cycling and was hooked. Jimmy tore his ACL at Clemson, but advancements in surgical procedures allowed him to return to the lineup. Even so, his cycling during rehab made him a bike addict, too.

Speaking of addicts and rehab of a different sort, when Elijah entered the viewing room he was surrounded. The air reeked of stale smoke and alcohol. Absent the casket you could have mistaken the gathering for a Friday night at a biker bar. There wasn't a tie to be seen in the room. For that matter, there was not a collared shirt in the room either. Sam's corpse would win the best dressed award and he was wearing jeans, a new Metallica t-shirt, and a leather vest. Someone had placed a bottle of George Dickel between his arm and ribs.

Elijah was outfitted in his regular visitation outfit: blue blazer, gray tropical wool slacks, white starched oxford button down, repp striped tie, and black Cole Haan loafers. He stuck out like a wildebeast in a pride of lions. It was but a moment when he heard a familiar voice behind him.

"Hey preacher, you see the bottle of Dickel I slid into the casket?"

"Yes I did, Frank. Yes I did." Rehab didn't take. Obviously Frank had purchased multiple bottles of Tennessee whiskey. Elijah just wondered where he found the money. He later heard that it was the money Josie had set aside for an honorarium for Elijah.

" I jus' figured Sam shouldn't take this next journey without somethin' to keep him warm. Hell, I couldn't put no live hooker in there, and Sam was partial to George Dickel."

Elijah, was speechless, not because of Frank's logic, but because Frank had obviously let out a muted but potent fart and Elijah was afraid to breathe for fear he would pass out.

With strained voice as he was running out of breath and making his escape, Elijah proffered his condolences. "I'm . . . sorry . . . for-your-loss-please-know-you-are-in-my-prayers."

He was stepping away as fast as he could when he heard Shania's boy, little Dickie, exclaim, "Oooooh, someone farted! Was that you preacher?"

Danger, danger! Panic wrapped in a heart attack and lathered with humiliation! "No, Dickie, I'm sure it wasn't me."

"Well, thank the Lord, cause that stink could choke a skunk. Hey turd brain! Stop messin' with Uncle Sam!" Trace was leaning over the casket trying to fold Sam's knuckles to make it appear as though he was giving everyone the finger.

"Shut up, microdick! You ain't the boss of me. Hey, look at this! George Dickel Whiskey! Look, they named a whiskey after you, ya little shit!"

Elijah jumped out of the way of Shania who was in full sprint across the room, her arm raised to swat at Trace who took off as Shania chased him, circling the room three times with Trace screaming, "Child abuse! Child abuse!!" The third time around the room Trace knocked over a flower arrangement and then ventured too close to Robbie Gallimore who stuck out his arm, clotheslining the boy, who was now sprawled on the ground with Shania kicking at his behind.

"How dare you embarrass me in front of Sam's dead body. How dare you mess up that flower arrangement. I was hopin' to sell those for good money."

Thankfully, Josie was blissfully unaware, over in the corner fast asleep in the electric wheelchair the church had purchased, her head leaning to the side, a drop of drool landing on her breast.

Elijah quickly slid toward the exit and out of the corner of his eye could see Jimmy and Ray howling with laughter in the background. Shaking his head, Elijah could only wonder what the morrow would bring.

The morrow would bring a Shakespearean Tragic Comedy, or more precisely, the continued comedy of the Ellerbes and an unforeseen tragedy that would again impress upon Elijah that faith is a gift and not an accomplishment.

Wearing what he calls his marrying and burying suit, a charcoal gray number purchased when one of the national chains was having a 70% off sale, Elijah jumped in the Jeep and headed west toward Old Fort on I-40, that endless ribbon of highway that in thirty-five hours could land Elijah in Barstow, California. Thankfully, Elijah's drive would only take him less than thirty minutes, but those twenty miles would be among the most scenic of the entire route, ferrying him from the foothills to the base of the Black Mountains which stand nobly as sentinels overlooking the Catawba Valley River Basin. The drive presents a paradox, though. You are on the interstate because you want to get somewhere with haste, and yet the bewitching grandeur and increasing clarity of the mountain range as you drive west is a siren tempting you to pull off and revel in the view.

Elijah does pull off at exit 72, not as a tourist but to officiate at a graveside service, and with the Ellerbes, the essence of *officiate* is altered. Arriving in Old Fort before the funeral cortege, he pondered ditching the suit for the stripes of a referee. His Jeep meandered down the main street toward the cemetery on the edge of town. The mountains to his west are sometimes called America's front porch. If that's the case, then Old Fort is the rusted Pontiac on blocks in the front yard. There had been a downtown when the train would stop to unload and pick up passengers before the country abandoned trains for the interstate. Today commercial buildings sag, paint peels, and tenants turn over as entrepreneurial dreams have the life choked out of them. The most thriving business in town seems to be the Hardees that serves those who accidentally wander off the highway, and even that business is known more as a place parents stop to let their children pee before dropping them off at Camp Grier, a rustic Presbyterian summer camp found outside of town.

The service was scheduled for 11:00 a.m., but until 11:45 it was just Elijah and Ray from the funeral home. They took refuge from the heat in Ray's black Cadillac and debated the virtues of the St. Louis Cardinals versus the Atlanta Braves. When they saw the body and the mourners driving up the road, they got out and walked to meet the mortuary limo. Jimmy stepped out first and Elijah offered that sly grin that silently inquires, "Where in the hell have you been?"

Jimmy shook his head in disgust, muttering, "Just don't ask. Just don't ask." Leaning close so that no one but Elijah could hear, he continued, "I'll tell you one thing, though. I've been around this business a long time, but this is the first time the bereaved has asked me to stop at the convenience store so that she could buy a case of beer. They've been guzzling since we left town."

Elijah smiled and whispered, "There goes the rest of my honorarium."

Trace and Little Dickie popped out of the back seat, high-fiving one another. "That was so cool!! Wait till our friends hear that we've been riding in a limo!"

"Yeah! I can't wait till somebody else dies so that we can do that again!"

With that, they ran to the green Suddreth tent and were pushing open the lid of the casket until Ray put the kibosh on them.

As the funeral party walked toward the tent, Robbie Gallimore, Shania's paramour, ambled over behind Elijah, startling him.

"Whew, Robbie, didn't see you there!" Immediately, Elijah realized how ridiculous that sounded. Robbie topped 350 pounds."

His usual vacant expression had been replaced by what looked like fear. "Preacher, how long is this thing going to last?"

Elijah was nonplussed because he had never heard Robbie speak and he had known the family five years. "Well, Robbie, it will be fairly brief, an opportunity to give thanks to God for Sam and the promises that not even death can take from us."

"Yeah, whatever, just as long as it goes no more than, say, fifteen minutes."

"I think you are safe with that."

Shania was unusually silent. It wasn't grief, though. Rather, she seemed nervous, skittish, distracted; looking over her shoulder the way a child would when walking through a cemetery at night. As Ray wheeled a glassy-eyed, heavily medicated Josie into place, Jimmy walked over to Elijah who was standing outside of the tent.

"I think we're good to go."

"Aren't we missing someone?"

"Frank's not coming. Robbed the ABC store last night. Came in asking for some boxes for packing, and when the clerk went to the back to gather a few, Frank grabbed a case of Jose Cuervo and bolted, and well . . . remember this *is* Frank Ellerbe . . . the moron looked straight into the security camera. When the sheriff's deputies arrived and looked at the footage, they spontaneously howled in chorus: 'FRANK!! You da man! Woo Hoo.' They decided to wait ten minutes before they raided Sam's trailer, where Frank typically crashed for a bender. They wanted him to enjoy his last drink for a long time, because even if it's cheap whiskey, twelve bottles would constitute a felony, and Frank got his third strike four innings ago. So, I think everybody's here that's comin'. By the way," pointing to the casket, "the head's on that side."

"I've never understood why y'all always insist on telling us that. What's the significance?"

"To be honest, I don't have a clue. I grew up hearing my daddy say it, and so when I joined the business, I started saying it, too. Anyway, pray a good one. It's showtime."

"Your piety is unsurpassed."

Elijah reflexively looked at the sky, hearing the telltale sound of a helicopter hovering low. It appeared over the trees, circled the cemetery, and vanished over the ridge. He thought it curious, but not strange enough to delay the matter at hand any longer. Yet, before taking his place at the head (or was it the foot?) of the casket, Elijah paused to offer a silent prayer.

> O God of immeasurable, unbounded, and eternal love,
> in the midst of the storm of our lives,
> you remain as the peace which passes all understanding.
> So, in the midst of this family's chaos, grant them peace;
> and help me to remember that I am no more worthy of your
> grace and care than they are. Though my abilities are limited,
> use me as an instrument of your grace. Grant them strength for
> today and hope for tomorrow;
> for whether we live or whether we die, we are yours through
> Christ our Lord. Amen.

As a result of Christ's self-offering on the cross, when we gather at the grave, there are no winners or losers; there is no distinction between the titan of industry, the homeless poor, or the tyrant on the family tree. There are only children of a God whose love, manifested in Christ, will not let them go. Elizabeth Clephane, the 19th Century Scottish hymn writer, born and buried in the other Edinburgh across the pond, wrote one of the more eloquent witnesses to this truth in a beloved hymn that seekers and disciples sing during Holy Week:

> Upon the cross of Jesus
> mine eye at times can see
> the very dying form of One
> who suffered there for me;
> and from my stricken heart with tears
> two wonders I confess:
> the wonders of redeeming love
> and my unworthiness.
>
> —Elizabeth Clephane, *Beneath the Cross of Jesus*

No one would deny that the Ellerbes are what Southerners call *a hot mess*. Yet, Elijah knows that at some point, anyone watching from the front row of our lives and probing our deepest thoughts, could say the same about him, could say the same about all who are born into this world. When a church member inquired how Elijah could speak of heaven's promise among those who spent their lives raising hell, Elijah quoted that renegade, redneck, whiskey sippin', erudite Baptist preacher, Will Campbell, who when pressed to articulate the Christian faith in ten words or less, said, "We're all bastards but God loves us anyway."[3]

Who are we to limit the reach of God's love? That task is above our pay grade. God had not abandoned the Ellerbes any more than God would abandon the Psalmist—"Where can I go from your spirit? Or where can I flee from your presence? If I ascend to heaven, you are there; if I make my bed in Sheol, you are there. If I take the wings of the morning and settle at the farthest limits of the sea, even there your hand shall lead me, and your right hand shall hold me fast. If I say, 'Surely the darkness shall cover me, and the light around me become night,' even the darkness is not dark to you; the night is as bright as the day, for darkness is as light to you."

In my brief earthly sojourn before the car wreck, I never told anyone that I loved them; never *invited* Jesus into my life; never consciously acknowledged the presence of God. I just wasn't wired for that connection. I memorized and would recite the Apostles' Creed, the Nicene Creed, and all the other creeds in worship, yet without comprehension. Memorizing words was a breeze; attaching meaning and context to them was nigh impossible for me. Did that disqualify me from God's embrace? From Christ's grace? It is only now that I understand Augustine's description of the sacraments of baptism and the Lord's Supper—an outward and visible sign of an inward and invisible grace. Thus, in ways I could not possibly comprehend, God's Spirit was at work within me so that what I could not perceive at the time, I now know fully, even as I have been fully known. So, why would I, Elijah, or anyone else think that we could draw conclusions about the Ellerbes when God has not?

It is this understanding of grace that prevents Elijah from feeling any duplicity in affirming the promise of the gospel beside the graves of those whose lives we perceive to be a repudiation of the gospel.

Elijah resolutely stepped under the green canopy of the Suddreth tent and proceeded to read scripture—"I lift up my eyes to the hills; from where will my help come? My help comes from the Lord, who made heaven and earth;" to offer prayer—"May Josie and this family be given your grace in

3. Campbell, Will, *Brother To a Dragonfly*, New York, Continuum, 1977.

these challenging days, comforted by the vision of a kingdom where all that is broken will be made whole;" and to commend Sam's body to God's care— "Earth to earth, ashes to ashes, dust to dust; Blessed are the dead who die in the Lord, says the Spirit."

Elijah noticed that Shania remained distracted throughout the proceedings, more fearful than mournful, but she did keep her pants zipped. Following the benediction when Elijah stepped forward to greet the family individually, Shania and Robbie bolted before he could get to them. They were running, five hundred pounds bounding down the hillside; and before anybody realized what was happening they jumped in the front of the limo, shifted into drive, and took off. Jimmy threw aside the flower arrangement like a linebacker slapping aside a wide receiver on the way to a tailback and sprinted across the lawn, hurdling gravestones as if they were fallen blockers. Old instincts die hard. He needn't have worried about the new Cadillac, though. Before Bonnie and Clyde made it to the praying hands statue at the south entrance, a swarm of black SUVS, Crown Vics, and gun bearing officers in blue windbreakers appeared out of nowhere, surrounding them. There was nowhere for the dynamic duo to go, and so they clambered out of the giant getaway car with their hands in the air. Even the black helicopter reappeared and landed across the way. The windbreakers on the officers and the letters on the copter gave away what was going down: DEA.

The woman in charge, Special Agent Harper, exited the helicopter just like in the movies, ducking down beneath the whirring rotors as she jogged over to where Jimmy was bent over, hands on knees, sucking eggs. He could ride a bike over a hundred miles, but a full on hundred-meter sprint sent him to the precipice of passing out. As he gathered himself, Special Agent Harper explained to him what was transpiring. Then as quickly as she came, she climbed back in the helicopter and disappeared over the horizon. In like manner, the swarm of agents wasted no time getting out of there. As they loaded a handcuffed Shania in the back seat of an SUV, she shouted, "Somebody, take care of my babies!" The babies didn't know whether to be terrified, distraught, or thrilled. A social worker recruited for the sting, gathered them up, promising to stop for ice cream, and explaining that they would be taken to a safe place while their parents were working things out. That they had seen their mom in handcuffs before seemed to mitigate the panic. One too many Xanax became a blessing for Josie. She was knocked out, snoring like grandpa after a Thanksgiving feast.

Jimmy was shaking his head as he walked up the hill to Elijah.

"Special Agent Harper asked me to extend her apologies to you for disrupting the service. That was not their intention, but when Butch Cassidy and Sundance tried to make a run for it, they had to act."

Elijah raised his arms offering an expression of inquiry. "Soooo?"

"Robbie Gallimore may be the silent type, look like a halfwit, and in need of an oil drum of deodorant, but he's not stupid. He's been operating the biggest meth lab in the Southeast for three years. He's the brains and Shania is the muscle. They have $2.5 million hidden somewhere up in those hills."

"Josie?"

"She's doesn't have a clue. Thought they were surviving on unemployment, food stamps, and whatever they could squeeze out of her, which is mostly true. Robbie was smart enough to not let Shania spend any money. He just wasn't quite quick enough. They knew the feds were closing in and they were planning to bolt for South America tomorrow and open up a lab there. That explains why this had to go down today."

"The boys?"

"Grandfather Home up in Banner Elk."

"We have some folks that volunteer there. I'll ask them to connect with the kids."

Looking toward Josie, "It's a good thing she didn't follow the instructions on that bottle of Xanax. She would have had a stroke and died right here."

"I suppose you're right. Let's try to rouse her and deliver the hard news. Josie can be a hangnail at times, but she's got a good heart, and my Lord, how her kids have tortured her through the years."

Upon waking Josie up, they knelt beside her, slowly and softly explaining the events of the day. She sobbed but did not wail, more despairing than distraught, more resigned than outraged. She, too, had seen Shania in handcuffs before. Josie seemed comforted to know Trace and Little Dickie would be safe at Grandfather Home. She knew she couldn't handle them or provide for them. Elijah promised to drive her up to see them, once they were settled in. Robbie and Shania would be provided for by the prison system. Jimmy said he would take Josie back to her apartment and Elijah said he would check on her that evening. He then offered a prayer and watched as Jimmy carefully rolled her back to the limo.

Ray approached to shake Elijah's hand and Elijah observed, "Look at that, Ray, you work for a good man."

"I sure do. Of course, so do you."

"Hmmm, I can't debate that."

Walking back to the Jeep, Elijah was surprised that it was already two in the afternoon and it dawned on him that he was drenched with sweat. Quickly, upon opening the door, he turned the key and cranked up the air conditioner, abundantly thankful he had invested in rebuilding the AC in early spring. When he picked up his phone, he saw that he had six missed calls and two urgent texts. Elijah was careful not to carry his phone with him when leading worship ever since Clara Forbes' funeral two years ago when the sound of Dave Matthews' *Ants Marching* filled the sanctuary during the Call to Worship. Before he could silence the ringtone, the aggressive thumping of the drum was combining with the shrieking pulse of the soprano sax, heralding the start of a day. The head of Ina Forbes, Clara's sister, jerked to attention as if a stained glass window had crashed to the floor. Crimson faced, Elijah raised up from fumbling with his phone, and looking out to the gathered congregation, he saw Jimmy in the back pumping his arms like he was Jay Z.

After the service, Jimmy couldn't resist, "Loved the special music today, Reverend."

"Oh my gosh. I won't live that down anytime soon. They'll remember that long after I'm gone; more than any sermon I preached."

"Congratulations, Elijah. You are now a legend."

Back in the Jeep, Elijah was pondering the sudden rush of messages. Six calls and two texts. That seemed strange to Elijah. "What is this? It's not like I'm one of those campaign directors with three cells going at once." The first text suddenly robbed the car of oxygen. It was from Hannah and had come mid-morning. "Elijah, D.A. is taking me to the hospital. I'm okay but there is a problem. When you finish at the cemetery, can you come to the hospital?"

The second text, which had come an hour after the first and then two hours before he read it, stopped his heart. It was from Hannah's doctor, one of her closest friends and an elder at the church. Jane's text read, "Come to the hospital when you finish the funeral. I'll be straight with you: Hannah will be fine. Baby is in trouble. We're doing what we can and praying, too."

Elijah shifted into drive and passing by the inelegant statue of praying hands, he offered the only prayer his troubled mind could come up with, Reinhold Niebuhr's profound all-inclusive prayer long associated with AA: "God, give me the grace to accept with serenity the things that cannot be changed; the courage to change the things that should be changed; and the wisdom to distinguish the one from the other." Elijah continued with the equally powerful, but lesser known second stanza:

> "Living one day at a time,
> Enjoying one moment at a time,
> Accepting hardship as a pathway to peace,
> Taking, as Jesus did,
> This sinful world as it is,
> Not as I would have it,
> Trusting that You will make all things right,

If I surrender to Your will,
So that I may be reasonably happy in this life,
And supremely happy with You forever in the next.
Amen."

—*Reinhold Niebuhr*

Remembering that the area, still abuzz with what would come to be known as the Redneck Cartel Sting, was blanketed with all manner of law enforcement vehicles, Elijah resisted driving with complete abandon down the interstate. Yet, regardless of how fast he drove, each mile seemed like a hundred. He made one phone call.

"T . . . " Choked suddenly with emotion he couldn't voice another word, a silence that rends the heart of the listener. Tess refused to have her kids call her *Mom*. She said it made her sound matronly, and by God, she'd grow old gracefully, but she would never be matronly. So they settled on "T," but don't let the informality of the moniker lead you to think that Tess was one of those suburban moms who, clinging to her fading youth, dresses like she's still 17 and tries to be her child's best friend. They may have called her "T," but Tess was *all mom*, and would always retain their respect, admiration, trust, and love.

"Elijah? What's wrong?"

Composing himself, "It's Hannah and the baby. Hannah will be okay, but they say the baby is in trouble. I'm on my way to the hospital now." Immediately, the memory of her own dark day when the doctor uttered that terror inducing word—stillborn.

"I'll be there in an hour and a half, and Elijah, drive carefully and hold Hannah tight. Be strong for her. I love you."

"Thanks T, love you, too."

Arriving at the hospital, he ran into the ER where Karen, the charge nurse and a neighbor who lived two doors down, pointed him toward labor and delivery while saying, "Room 222. We're all praying for you."

Outside the door to Hannah's room, Dr. Jane O'Malley was talking with a nurse. Strawberry blonde tresses, runner's physique, inquisitive mind that abhorred the unturned stone whether discussing diagnoses or theology, her words were always matter of fact but gilded with compassion. Dr. Jane and Hannah were usually training for a triathlon when Jimmy and Elijah were riding bikes around Lake James. Dr. Jane and Jimmy, both divorced, had been dating for close to two years. It was assumed by all that they were headed to the altar, but both had been wounded badly, Dr. Jane by an abusive husband and Jimmy by a former Clemson Rally Cat dance team member from Atlanta who couldn't or wouldn't adjust to the constraints of life in a small town. She escaped with the weatherman at WSPA down in Greenville-Spartanburg. Elijah liked to razz his friend about the cliché of a linebacker—dance team pinup romance.

Following their routine Saturday morning outdoor adventures, the endorphin foursome, as they called themselves, would ritually gather, along with Madison and the kids, at the Lakeside Diner for a late breakfast. The Parishes knew that their friends both wanted children and assumed it would just be a matter of time before they set a date for a wedding.

Seeing Elijah, Dr. Jane motioned for him to step away with her to talk privately.

"Hannah is fine physically and we both know how tough she is emotionally. We had to do a C-section so she'll have to stay a couple of days, but she'll be fine."

"Thank God. The baby?"

"She just couldn't make it."

"She?" Elijah felt as though he had been hit with a medicine ball shot from a cannon.

"Yes, a girl. I'm so sorry. Hypoplastic left heart syndrome. The main pumping chamber of her heart was just too small, underdeveloped. Just didn't have the horsepower to get blood to the body. Increasingly, we are able to do surgery or even a transplant, but in this case her condition was so acute that before we reached surgery, she had died."

"Was it because she was premature?"

"Possibly or at least partially. We don't really know. One recent study pointed toward seasonal or environmental factors and with the early and sustained heat we've had . . . Bottom line, we can't say and that sucks."

Though slipping into the limbo of loss and shock, Elijah had not yet shaken the role of the pastor. "Jane, sometimes, more often than we'd ever admit, life and death just happen in spite of our efforts to outsmart the mystery of creation. Do not beat yourself up. I am so grateful for you and that Hannah was in your care. She's going to need you now, more as her friend than her doctor."

"I love her deeply and I respect her so." Tearing up, she concluded. "I just hate to see her hurt. I hate to see the both of you hurt."

The pastor and physician embraced briefly, neither one being big huggers, and together they entered Hannah's room. Hannah's eyes connected with Elijah's and her Midwestern stoic resolve melted, her tears quickly forming rivulets on her cheeks as with a sudden summer shower. Elijah sat down on the edge of the bed, pulling her close, and ducking their heads into the confluence of neck and trapezious, they quietly wept. After a few moments the couple sat up straight. Hannah dabbed her eyes and with the subtle laughter of embarrassed awkwardness, chastising herself, "Oh, let's pull ourselves together, girl."

In the room with Dr. Jane were D.A. and Tamara. D.A., always able to play the role of mother, caregiver, shepherd, or sheriff, depending on what was needed, gave the marching orders. "Well, she needs her rest, so let's get out of here. Hannah, honey, I love you."

"You're an angel, lady."

"Now let us away."

Even Elijah stood up to leave. He made it a habit to obey D.A.'s instructions.

"Not you kid. You've got some nursing to do."

"Yes ma'am."

Tamara, ever the organizer asked, "You want me to call Spencer and Madison?"

Hannah said, "No, let them enjoy their weekend in New York."

Looking to Elijah, "Your mom?"

"She's on her way."

"Who should I call about Sunday? I'm assuming you won't be there."

Elijah's eyes searched for Hannah's. With their marriage being preceded with a twenty-year courtship, they could carry on an entire conversation without a word.

Hannah answered Elijah's question for him. "He'll be there."

Jane asked, "You sure?"

Elijah answered, "Yes. If I can't stand in the pulpit this Sunday, I probably shouldn't stand up there at all. I may get a sub for next week so we can go down to the beach, but this Sunday, I need to be there. The same is true for us that is true for the Ellerbes, God bless 'em. 'Whether we live or whether we die, we are the Lord's.'"

Before D.A. could grab everybody by the scruff of the neck to make her exit, Elijah inquired, "Would you all indulge us for just a moment? My mind's a bit fuzzy, right now, and I'm about prayed out for today, but would it be okay if we sang the Doxology?"

"Absolutely."

"You bet."

"What a marvelous idea."

They circled the bed, held hands, and led by Tamara's angel voice, they sang.

> Praise God, from Whom all blessings flow;
> Praise Him, all creatures here below;

Praise Him above, ye heav'nly host;
Praise Father, Son, and Holy Ghost.

D.A. and Tamara exited leaving the doctor and couple. Jane asked Elijah the question he sensed was coming. "Do you want to see the baby?"

Again, Elijah's eyes locked on Hannah's. It was uncanny. After touring real estate the day they arrived in Edinburgh, they had committed to make the offer on their house without a word. They just looked at one another.

Elijah nodded and Hannah voiced what their eyes had communicated. "Yes, that would be good. I'm glad we can share this together."

While they waited for the nurse to bring the baby, Jane observed, "That thing you do with your eyes kinda freaks me out. It's like some kind of Vulcan mind meld."

"Consequence of being together since we were in diapers."

"Speak for yourself, dude. I'm thinking I was already potty trained."

"Could be. You were always a step quicker than most folks. Xani is just like you." Like the coyote in *Roadrunner*, his eyes jumped out of his head. "The kids!!"

"Relax, they are with Megan."

Megan MacIntosh, child of the church, armed with a secondary education degree from Presbyterian College, was hired by the church three years ago to be the youth director after working two years with Young Life followed by a year on staff at Camus, part of Scotland's Iona Community. There she worked with youth groups gathered from tough life circumstances in Glasgow. Following that, she toured the states for a couple of years with a Celtic/bluegrass trio she formed with a couple of Scottish colleagues she had worked with at Camus. Rave reviews, but they eventually tired of the road. Megan missed the mountains and the Scots were homesick for the isle of Mull. The youth at St. Martin loved her. Xani and Nathan idolized her.

"I'll text T and maybe she can pick them up when she gets into town."

The nurse entered with a tiny pink bundle. Taking the bundle in her arms, Hannah breathed deeply in the same way she did in college when the starter ordered, "On your marks."

Upon opening the blanket Elijah and Hannah were whelmed with a paradoxical mixture of sorrow and wonder. The rivulets reappeared on both of their cheeks, yet even with the sharp pain of loss, they were awed by the majesty and beauty of God's creation. The psalmist's prayer flooded Elijah's mind, and he softly prayed, "I praise you, for I am fearfully and wonderfully made . . . My frame was not hidden from you, when I was being made in secret, intricately woven in the depths of the earth. Your eyes beheld my unformed substance."

"Look at her toes. So . . . beautiful. Her eyelashes . . . stunning. Oh, I love her and miss her already."

Elijah reached over and stroked her head. "Feel the fuzz on the top of her ear. It's . . . incredible. Incredibly sad and incredibly wonderful."

"Do we give her a name?"

"I don't know, maybe a name we just keep to ourselves, our private memory of this . . . I don't know . . . hallowed moment. Something we keep for ourselves and maybe share with the kids one day. 'Whether we live or whether we die, we are the Lord's.' We have to hold onto that when the dark fog threatens."

"Talitha cum."

"Hannah, that's perfect. A powerful reminder of resurrection. Talitha cum."

Talitha cum. "Little girl, get up." In Mark 5, it is written:

"While he was still speaking, some people came from the leader's house to say, 'Your daughter is dead. Why trouble the teacher any further?' But overhearing what they said, Jesus said to the leader of the synagogue, 'Do not fear, only believe.' He allowed no one to follow him except Peter, James, and John, the brother of James. When they came to the house of the leader of the synagogue, he saw a commotion, people weeping and wailing loudly. When he had entered, he said to them, 'Why do you make a commotion and weep? The child is not dead but sleeping.' And they laughed at him. Then he put them all outside, and took the child's father and mother and those who were with him, and went in where the child was. He took her by the hand and said to her, 'Talitha cum,' which means, 'Little girl, get up!' And immediately the girl got up and began to walk about (she was twelve years of age). At this they were overcome with amazement. He strictly ordered them that no one should know this, and told them to give her something to eat."

Elijah and Hannah would find enduring comfort through the years in the image of the risen, living, and ascended Christ calling out to their child in the mystery of God's kingdom, "Little girl, get up."

Hannah softly sang from a verse of the hymn her mom would sing to her when she was little and frightened, the same song they sang at her mother's funeral.

"Here I raise mine Ebenezer;
hither by thy help I'm come;
and I hope, by thy good pleasure,
safely to arrive at home . . . "

— *Come, Thou Fount of Every Blessing*, Robert Robinson

They said their goodbyes as Dr. Jane and the nurse returned to the room.

"I talked with Jimmy. Elijah, you've had quite a day."

"It was definitely one for the scrapbooks. Hannah, I'll tell you all about it when we get down to the beach."

"Jimmy asked if he could help with anything."

Elijah and Hannah looked eye to eye again.

"I'm thinking about a small, private gathering at the columbarium the morning after Hannah's released, keeping it on the down low. I'll read a couple of scriptures, we'll sing the hymn together, offer prayer and commit the ashes.

"That's all I need to know. Jimmy will prepare things. What's the hymn?"

"*Come Thou Fount*"

Jane looked to Hannah, "Your momma's song. I remember. What about your dad and brothers?"

Hannah sighed. "There's no need for them to come all the way out here. We'll go out there sometime later this summer, probably sooner than later. We'll call Dad later this afternoon. I'll call my brother first so that he can be there when I call Dad. I hope this doesn't become a thing . . . "

"Alcohol?"

"That and depression, yeah."

"Tell your brother to get him to a meeting."

"Yes."

"Shifting from doctor to friend to elder, I've been asked to ask you if you would like a meal."

"Not necessary. I guess it's inevitable, but not necessary now."

"Your call." And looking intently at both of them, "Get some rest."

As Hannah handed the bundle back to the nurse, she whispered, "Peace, Talitha."

Elijah added, "The Lord bless you and keep you, little girl."

Jane and the nurse made their exit, closing the door tight behind them. Elijah turned off the lights, pulled the curtain around the bed, and through her tears, Hannah whispered, "This is so hard."

"Yes it is."

"E, you said all the right things a preacher would say; you didn't punch a hole in the wall, never have; you were calm, almost sedate, offering only witness to what I know is your deep and profound faith . . . but . . . how do you really feel?"

"Conflicted, maybe. On the one hand, I feel like Bill Buckner in Game 6 of the World Series. Extra innings. Two outs. He's playing first base. Slow rolling, easy grounder comes to him. He could have taken his cap and picked it up. Inning would be over. Rolls right through his legs. It was right there. He had it. It was right there." Choking with emotion, "She was right there. And then she wasn't. I had the same feeling that day in the ER when they told me my brother Zachary was dead. We were just driving to my sister's little league game. I wasn't distracted. I was paying attention . . . and out of nowhere . . . He was there and then he wasn't. When I read those angry psalms in the Old Testament, they are lashing out at God, at their enemies, lashing out at anyone and anything. They are in that dark place where you'd throw a fit over everything. The ice cream is too cold and the water is too wet. I know what they are feeling. You are totally right. This is hard, and I think the hardest part for me is to see you hurting. Nothing slays my spirit more.

"On the other hand, I'm laying here with you, holding you, and . . . I'm so grateful, grateful to the point of joy that you are healthy and here."

"E, I have loved you my whole life, and I don't want to sound corny . . . "

"Corny as Kansas in August?"

"You know not to use the word Kansas around me."

"You Mizzou folks won't quit fighting the Civil War. Anyway, forgive me. You were saying . . ."

"I was saying, I don't want to sound corny. I do know the sun will come out tomorrow, the sun *will* come out tomorrow. I believe that and yet it all seems so dark right now. The images are rolling around in my head like one of those newfangled electronic billboards on the highway. There she is, insisting that she wear her full-length princess costume on the day we take her to Cinderella's Castle at Disney. There I am, acting the fool, screaming like a crazy woman as she's gliding over high school hurdles. There you are, all robed up and trying to hold it together as you walk her down the aisle and perform her marriage cer . . ." A swell of emotion constricts her throat as tears puddle at eyelids' edge. "It all just seems so dark. Do you ever feel that . . . God's not listening?"

"Sure. Dark night of the soul. Christ felt that absence on the cross. Mother Teresa felt it on the streets of Calcutta, and we both know I'm not in their league. Of course, I suspect that a majority of the time, it isn't God that has turned a deaf ear, but me."

"So, what do you do?"

"Pray again."

"Pray again?"

"Yeah, even when we think our prayers are getting thrown out by God's spam filter, we keep at it. At some point it may finally dawn on me that prayer isn't about getting what I want. I'm always forgetting that prayer isn't nearly as much about my laundry list of complaints and perceived needs as it is about relationship. It is about listening. It is about losing the obsession of self, so that we may grow in gratitude for those signs of where God's presence is evidenced. It is about looking for signs of where God is at work."

"E, you know I'm not asking you as a theologian, I'm asking you as a dad who just lost a baby before even seeing her breathe."

"O Lord, I believe; help my unbelief."

"Scripture? That's still a preacher answer."

"Guess so. Everything about this blows. I don't know, maybe I keep praying to remind myself that I'm not God. Times like this call me back to what Barbara Brown Taylor said about God's answer to a suffering Job's laments. Job questions God's sense of justice. However, God's answer doesn't speak to the issue of justice, but omnipotence. Taylor says, 'As far as I know that is the only reliable answer human beings have ever gotten about why things happen the way they do. God only knows. And we are not God.'[4] My story, and I'm sticking to it, is that primarily, prayer is less about getting answers explaining suffering and more about finding the strength to face the suffering. But it still stinks, and my primary worry now is you. To have carried that child for eight months . . . Where are you?"

A contemplative pause separates his question from her response. "Oh, I'm here. In shock a bit. It's going to take my body and mind some time to figure out the sudden change of circumstances. You know how they say that following an amputation the amputee can still feel the lost limb? Still feel pain in the place where there is no there? I still feel her, E. I know what has happened. I know that her body will be cremated very soon, and yet, I still feel her growing, kicking, moving inside of me. The light shines in the darkness. I know that. I know that. I just feel like I'm on the other side of the dark chasm, and I'm not quite sure how to get to the other side to grab on to it. The light may come tomorrow, but today is for the darkness. But I don't feel alone. When you came in the room earlier, I felt this sudden surge of peace. To be honest, the emotion was as much relief as it was grief. I am so grateful for you."

"I know I'd be lost without you."

Soft giggle. "Yes, you would."

A nurse entered to take vitals and Hannah asked if they could hold off on visitors, nutritionists, housekeeping, etc. for a couple of hours to sleep. Vital signs being normal, the nurse turned off the lights and put a sign on the closed door.

Elijah said, "At least we don't have to worry about the preacher showing up."

4. Brown Taylor, Barbara.

"Well, preacher, you feel so good next to me. I just hope this isn't your method of pastoral care for all your parishioners."

"Well, you know the Widow Waechter is pretty hot in her bathrobe . . . No, you're my only girlfriend, and when I say only, I mean only . . . ever. You know, I was probably the only kindergartner involved in a long-distance romance. I knew a good thing when I saw it, and I've been hanging on for dear life ever since."

With that they held onto one another as they had in so many ways since they were toddlers as sleep quickly freed them from the weight of the dark cloud.

They didn't awake until the darkness of the room was equaled by the growing darkness outside. The door had opened sending a wake up call of light and with the light was Tess following the nurse who had returned again check vital signs.

Elijah stood up, hugged his mom tightly and stepped aside so T and Hannah could commune. Ever since Hannah's mom died, Tess assumed that role, pursuing it, as with so many things, firmly and deeply. The death had left Hannah isolated in a testosterone test tube of a house populated by a father and his three sons. Tess was a lifeline for Hannah, calling her several times a week, flying her to Charlotte to shop for school, taking her to New York City to see museums and musicals, teaching her Adele's treasured recipes that she could cook for herself to escape the steady diet of T-bones and potatoes preferred by the cattle jockeys. Elijah was Hannah's confidant, but Tess was her consigliere.

"T, what time is it?"

"9:00 p.m."

"O my . . . the kids."

"Don't worry, they are in bed and Taylor's on grandparent patrol. Elijah, you head home and I'll spend the night here with Hannah."

"But . . . "

Tess, could stop anyone mid-sentence with just the slightest waving motion of her hand. Taylor always joked that he could use her in court when the opposing lawyer was giving his closing argument.

Hannah, always a much better caregiver than care-receiver, interjected, "T, you don't need to feel like you have to . . . "

There went the hand again. "You may have some female things to handle that the preacher boy won't be much help with. Also, I'll cover the calls from the farm and the church. Elijah, did I hear you're still preaching Sunday?"

"Yes."

"Well, I guess you've got a little work to do. We'll be okay for the night. Why don't you come up mid-morning and we can change shifts."

"E, she's a wise woman, and I do want you there when the children wake up in the morning."

"Yeah, dang it. It's not that T has to be right. She just tends to be right. Dad taught me that before he taught me how to stand up to pee."

Driving home, Elijah stopped at a convenience mart to get a Yuengling for his father and a Pepsi for himself. He looked in the children's rooms. They were so quiet, so peaceful, so unaware of the squall that overwhelmed their parents. The nightlights offering the softest glow to their cheeks, Elijah knew it was true; the light does shine in the darkness.

He sat down with his dad at the kitchen table to talk and sip.

Taylor, was multi-lingual in that he could instantly shift from the patois of the Missouri farm-boy to the learned lexicon of a traditional Southern attorney. I can't say which of the two dialects dominated his dreams, but he knew how to speak according to the context.

"Kinda sucks, doesn't it?" Farm boy it is.

"I heard that." Attempting whatever patois Elijah had gleaned from Hannah and her brothers.

"Your great grandfather, Judge Parish, liked to tell the story of the time he was preparing to give the sentence to a farmer convicted of assault and battery after beating up a neighbor for taking a drunken drive on a tractor across his vegetable garden. Judge asked the convicted man if he had anything to say before receiving his sentence, and with a gravelly and decidedly country voice, he growled, 'I feel like a cockroach on a cowpie being stepped on by a passing mule.'"

"Shit happens?"

"Exactly. The judge laughed so hard he reduced the sentence from thirty days to ten."

"The delicate balance of grace and law."

"Your Uncle Billy called. He had a message for you, and I quote, 'Suck it up. Don't be a pussy. Drink a beer and move on.'"

"Ever the philosopher. How's the corn faring?"

"He said they need rain or your cousins will be dropping out of college and eating Beanie Weenies all winter." Uncle Billy is Taylor's younger brother and the two are as identical as Atticus Finch and Ricky Bobby. Where Taylor is cerebral, Billy doesn't probe much deeper than ESPN and the Weather Channel. Where Taylor is methodical, steady, and patient, Billy is impulsive, unpredictable, and 100 mph all the time until he crashes. Taylor is a '65 Thunderbird with the top down on the Pacific Coast Highway. Billy is a '69 GTO flying by a Buick on the wrong side of the yellow line. He always manages to beat the oncoming pickup, but you can't help holding your breath. Taylor is one bottle of Heineken with an appetizer. Billy is a six-pack of Bud and a bag of Cheetos. But Billy has a good heart and will *go to the mattresses* for you without hesitation. He teaches agriculture at the Vo-Tech school and tends the family farm. His wife Carla is as sweet as a cinnamon bun and nurses at the Audrain Medical Center. They have twin girls who are sophomores at Mizzou, one studying to be a nurse, the other hopes to go to law school.

"We need to get out there to see them."

"Maybe we can all go out together before the wives have to go back to school."

"That will be good for Hannah."

"Spencer called. She and Madison are taking an early flight back from New York on Sunday. She's planning on making it back to Edinburgh in time for church . . . and she wants me to represent the company in the lawsuit if you don't have a problem with it."

"Her cousin?"

"You guessed it."

"Take the case. That man's going to be the death of her, and while he's at it, me too."

Sean McArthur IV, the wild child of Sean McArthur III, is a legend in his own mind and a legend in a much different way among those who remember him as a youth. His peers claim he had been the go-to guy for drugs in high school. His parents, rebels in their own right, divorced and little Sean migrated back and forth between their addresses depending on who had tossed him out last. A 1.3 GPA, four school suspensions, three DUIs, a hit and run charge, and assault with a deadly weapon. The last one required an attorney from New York to keep him out of the High Rise, the state youth correctional facility outside of Morganton, a monolithic 16-story pile of bricks, mortar, steel, institutional green paint, chain links and razor wire. Locals call it the North Carolina School for Felony. If you weren't a recidivist criminal on the way in, you were on the way out, armed with a B.S.S.S.S.—a Bachelor of Science in Scamming, Scheming, and Stealing. The people of Edinburgh hoped Sean wouldn't wind up there because he'd be a tenured professor by the second day.

Sean, drunk and stoned, was showing off a hot beretta pistol to Robbie Gallimore's daddy and accidentally shot him in the shoulder. The day he was let off on a technicality, he drank a fifth of Seagrams 7 and ran his Jeep Wrangler into a tree. Finally, the perpetually volatile parents threw up their hands and told him he couldn't stay with either of them, but could shack up in their cabin on the north side of Lake James. Can you say brier patch? It was a party around the clock. In the next six months he managed to get two girls pregnant, bribing them both to get an abortion. When the next conquest had a negative pregnancy test, they decided to celebrate with fireworks . . . inside the cabin. A fire started and they took off in Sean III's Chris Craft without calling the fire department.

Military School!!! That lasted three months before he was kicked out and while hitchhiking back to Edinburgh he took cover from a thunderstorm in a Pentecostal church during Wednesday night services. That's where he "found Jesus." Elijah decided not to engage him in a debate about whether it is we who find Jesus, or, in keeping with the Reformed tradition, it is Jesus who finds us. "I was lost but now am found . . ."

Well, with the Lord firing his engine, Sean IV Jesus roared back into Edinburgh like Billy Sunday, he of the *Sliding Home for Jesus* legend. He was determined to pull his hometown out of "the immoral sludge of liberalism." His daddy had died of cirrhosis, courtesy of Wild Turkey and his momma died from a combination of bitterness and lung cancer, thanks to Sean III and two packs of Pall Malls a day.

So, Sean IV had a stack of cash, two historic homes, and lots of time to save the morally stunted people of Edinburgh. But he wouldn't have a lake cottage, would he? He quickly married Bethany Power, the daughter of the pastor of Little Creek Apostolic Tabernacle and the first girl he had impregnated a couple of years before. In seven years they produced seven children. Yet, instead of joining his "baby momma's" church, the church he usually attended, he held onto his membership at St. Martin, supposedly because of the family heritage, but more likely to torture Elijah and his first cousins, Mark and Spencer. Sean IV lobbied unsuccessfully to get St. Martin to leave the denomination saying it had abandoned Christianity for liberalism. He repeatedly accused Elijah of subverting the Gospel and fraternizing with the "homos, Mexicans, and welfare addicts." Whenever Elijah heard Sean's voice in the hallway at church, it took all his strength to resist hiding under his desk.

"The lawsuit" against Mark and Spencer was over what he called disputed shares of company stock. The McArthur corporation had bought back the stock from Sean III around the time of Sean IVs bonfire at the lake. Now, nine years later, Sean IV was claiming the Lord had told him those shares were rightfully his, ignoring the fact that Sean III had been paid the market price, money Sean IV was now using to sue his cousins for the stock.

"Dad, do you think he has a case?"

"I'm afraid that's irrelevant, Elijah. He's lawyered up pretty good, and if nothing else, they can make a mess for Mark and Spencer just to shake him off their legs . . . Oh, D called also, she's withdrawing from the tournament in Canada and will be heading here in the morning."

"Dad, she doesn't need to do that. I mean, this whole thing stinks but it's no cause for a shout out to the family cavalry."

"That's what I told her, but she insisted on being with family this weekend. It's been a rough week. The New York Post, page six, claimed she was having an affair with the daughter of Governor Jablonski. D's never even met her, but the paparazzi posted a photo of New York's first daughter at the Women's U.S. Open last week, and some jerk tweeted that she and D were leading a lesbian summit."

"It's a good thing Jesus didn't say that the idiots shall inherit the earth. How can the event of two gay people being on the same piece of real estate constitute an affair?"

"I worry about D. She's strong and smart, but fragile, too."

"Maybe the two of you can commune out on the golf course this weekend."

"I'm sure we will. I'll probably ride back to Charlotte with her tomorrow night and come back early Sunday morning. You were never infected with the golf virus."

"O, I love the game. The timing has just never been right."

"Timing?"

"I stepped away from golf as a kid because I knew that Zach needed that time with you and you needed that time with him. When Zach died, D was just beginning to show signs of a special talent. You needed that time with her and she needed that time with you. Then came college, marriage, seminary, St. Martin, and parenthood. I just never got back to it. Oh, I sneak out to the course about six times a year. Hannah and I have talked about golfing as the kids grow older. Someday, I could envision us taking a golf trip with you and D. Someday."

"Someday soon . . . The good Rev. McPheeters called. He and Adele wanted me to tell you that they hold you in their prayers."

"I know they will."

"When I told him you were still planning to preach on Sunday, he said, 'Of course he is. Why wouldn't he?' He seemed surprised that I would suggest that there could be another option."

"Old School."

Taylor headed to bed and Elijah headed downstairs to his study. He loved this house, a simple, compact, but well-appointed three bedroom, two bath brick ranch with a walkout half basement that had been finished as a study. The previous owners must have known a marvelous wood craftsman because the place was fully outfitted with plantation shutters and crown molding. The tasteful, clean white cabinets of the kitchen were accented with statuary marble countertops. The only reason Elijah and Hannah had been able to buy the house was that they moved to Edinburgh just after the housing bubble burst. The study was the clincher for Elijah. Built-in bookshelves of richly stained cherry hardwood covered almost every available wall space. A large bay window looked out to the side yard and the neighbors' meticulously entrancing landscaping. Living in a furniture town and belonging to a lineage of lawyers made furnishing this slice of heaven a breeze.

Another lawyer's leather couch and matching cigar chair and ottoman came courtesy of Turner Chambers, who was redecorating his office. The leather-topped writing desk had been his grandfather's and the classic black swivel-tilt McArthur chair came as a housewarming gift from Spencer.

The hour was late, but Elijah's eyes were wide open for now, and the Keurig on the shelf would supply the caffeine when necessary. By the light of the desk and the screen of the laptop, Elijah went to work, setting aside the sermon he had been writing and starting with a new scripture.

Sunday morning dawned bright and cool, as long as you consider 70 degrees cool. In any case, a storm had bustled through town, turning down the temperature setting on the oven, ending the tyrannical reign of suffocating humidity and exiling it to the sandhills at least for the day. Whereas Saturday had been a day for brimmed hats, sunglasses, spf 60, and looking away from the glare of the heat lamp, this Lord's Day welcomed whipped cream clouds set against Tar Heel blue, drawing eyes upward to the mountains and sky, suddenly, pleasingly released from the shroud of haze that had rendered them invisible just a day earlier. The summer oven had failed to remove all color from the church grounds. Regal purple blooms on the crepe myrtles and butterfly bushes, the British racing green sheen of magnolia leaves, along with the well-tended and freshly watered flowers in the huge pots guarding the garth offered echoes of the Psalmist. "This is the day that the Lord has made. Let us rejoice and be glad in it."

Hannah was to be discharged from the hospital early that afternoon, so the Parish clan filled a pew similar to a number of the native multi-generational families interspersed across the sanctuary. The church was filled, which was unusual when summer sirens beckon potential worshippers deeper into the mountains or down to the coast. Some were present because they were always present, worship marking their identity no less than their names. Others were here searching for light in the darkness, possibly their own, or maybe Hannah's loss raised within them those questions of purpose and causality that always follow tragedy. Others here were analogous to NASCAR fans weathering the heat, the deafening roar, and the nightmarish traffic jam in the chance that they would witness the big wreck, a pileup of fiberglass, flames, and engine parts, leaving drivers to point fingers, slug jaws, and kick groins. Would the preacher break down during the sermon, gripped by grief and revealing the bitterness that chokes faith?

Looking out upon the diverse crowd during the prelude, the mixed motivations that brought the worshippers here didn't trouble Elijah. He was just grateful for the fellowship of the saints. Following the anthem, Elijah slowly stepped forward to the pulpit, pulled the chain on the lectern lamp, removed the paper clip from his manuscript, and looked out upon the church family assembled inside the stacked flagstone walls and Willette stained glass. Apart from Hannah, Xani, and Nathan, it was the most beautiful sight he had ever seen. He was home.

"Let us pray . . ."

"Our Scripture readings for the day are found in the book of Job and the epistle of First Corinthians. Let us open our hearts and hear the Word of the Lord."

Job 19: 23-27

23 *"O that my words were written down! O that they were inscribed in a book!* **24** *O that with an iron pen and with lead they were engraved on a rock forever!* **25** *For I know that my Redeemer lives, and that at the last he will stand upon the earth;* **26** *and after my skin has been thus destroyed, then in my flesh I shall see God,* **27** *whom I shall see on my side, and my eyes shall behold, and not another. My heart faints within me!*

1 Corinthians 10:13

13 *No testing has overtaken you that is not common to every-one. God is faithful, and he will not let you be tested beyond your strength, but with the testing he will also provide the way out so that you may be able to endure it.*

One: This is the Word of the Lord.

Many: Thanks be to God.

Expectation—operating under the conviction that something will take place, an unbroken line between cause and effect. You flip the switch and expect for a light to come on. You turn the key or press the button and expect the engine to fire, the radio to greet you with the voice of Bruce Springsteen or Carl Kasell. You open the wrapper of your favorite candy bar and expect the familiar pleasure to greet your taste buds.

Anticipation—what marks the period of waiting before that which you expect to happen. Anticipation may be colored by hope and joy as you await the arrival of a relative coming for a visit, or your anticipation may be tinted with anxiety and dread as you await the arrival of a relative coming for a visit.

Expectation and anticipation, together these synonyms dominate our waking hours and fuel our emotions. I expect the water in the shower to be warm, the paper in the driveway to be on time and dry, the wi-fi to be working, the cereal to be in the pantry, the shoes to fit, the watch to offer the right time, the car to be in working order, the roads to be passable. Simultaneously, I anticipate the mood of the morning meeting, the taste of the baker's bread at lunch, the welcome exertion and mind-clearing anesthetic of a late afternoon ride on my bike, the joy of conversation that accompanies a dinner out with friends.

Expectation and anticipation. A trip to London last year offered me the opportunity to leisurely walk along the city streets one morning while all around me the world was hustling and bustling, dashing and darting on its way to work. Our hotel was near Charing Cross, one of the busier tube stops in that part of the city, about a block from Trafalgar Square. A giant glob of humanity was spilling out of the tunnel doors like ground beef out of a meat grinder—government officials in Savile Row suits, shop clerks in uniform, messengers in sneakers with their cloth valises, the clean lines and smart tailoring of designer outfitted women powering their way through the glass ceiling to the halls of power, negotiating the terrain in heels as quickly and deftly as ballerinas en pointe. It was a wondrous sight. The time was too early for the teeming of tourists and so it was a rare opportunity to see the great urban center on its way to work.

As I pondered where they were headed and what they would be doing, it struck me that each scurrying pedestrian had established routines requiring that expectations be met. The Oyster card would work, giving them access to the tube, the trains would be on time, the umbrellas would pop open with the push of a button, the coffee would come as ordered from Costa, the daily rumor in the office, the shifting piles of files on desktops, the dependability of one colleague along with the characteristic foundering of another—every person rushing by me was operating on the assumption that a litany of expectations would be met.

At the same time, each commuter harbored a variety of emotions in anticipation of some event or encounter. It could be the excitement of looking forward to a weekend in the Lake District. It could be the ping-ponging of nerves in anticipation of a blind date. It could be the gut-rumbling anxiety of an upcoming job interview. It could be the fear of what the CAT scan will reveal. It could be the embarrassment rising in anticipation of the inevitable encounter with the person who has just broken your heart. Expectation and its cousin, anticipation, are as much a part of our days as the air we breathe.

But . . . what happens when our expectations are not met and our anticipation is disrupted?

Many of you are aware that it has been a tough week in our house. For the last eight months our lives have been influenced by the expectation that the pregnancy would proceed without complication and the anticipation of the incomparable joy and sheer terror that accompany a baby's birth. Thursday, it was determined that our expectations would not be met and that our anticipation was without warrant. We would not experience the shalom of observing an infant at rest and we would not luxuriate in the feel of a baby's cheek against our own. I will not hold her hand as we walk into school on the first day of kindergarten. Hannah will not cheer her on as she glides over hurdles. We will not watch her receive her diploma, witness her wedding, or hold her child.

So, what is one to do, think, or say when expectations are cut off before they can bloom and hopeful anticipation is replaced by heart-rending grief? Certainly, our spirits have been laid low and dismantling the crib and changing table will produce more tears than sweat. Packing Xani's hand-me-downs into boxes and returning or donating shower gifts so that others may benefit from them will slow the dissolving of our grief. Sorrow draws us inward, but we must not fail to look outward, acknowledging that our loss is no more significant, no more visceral than losses you have known, losses that have added lines to your faces or silence to your homes. Indeed, we have come out of this week relatively unscathed. Hannah is healthy, Xani is looking forward to Vacation Bible School, Nathan is anticipating his next bowl of Cheerios, and we are surrounded by the grace and love of an abundantly caring church family. I believe we have enough casserole and cake to weather next winter. This death will not diminish the gratitude we owe for blessings received.

And yet, you know and I know that the pain death invokes is real. The specter of death persists as the subtext for an alarming percentage of what we do, how we live. Did you know there are 17.5 miles of corridors in the Pentagon and that the Department of Defense employs over 3.2 million people? The fear of death looms large and influences everything from missile silos in South Dakota to the single aspirin your cardiologist recommends you to take each morning.

Death has the power to make us mute, and if not mute, death may even seduce us to curse God. Brought low by the death of those he loved, the loss of all he possessed, the scorn of those around him, not to mention the plague and pain of a body blighting disease, Job laments, "You lift me up on the wind, you make me ride on it, and you toss me about in the roar of the storm. I know that you will bring me to death, and to the house appointed for all living. Surely one does not turn against the needy, when in disaster they cry for help. Did I not weep for those whose day was hard? Was not my soul grieved for the poor? But when I looked for good, evil came; and when I waited for light, darkness came."

Too often in the face of evil, like a hiker desperately reaching for a hand hold as she helplessly slides down the steep slope of a rock strewn hill, we grasp for anything we can hold onto, and we'll say things like, "It's God's will," "Everything happens for a reason." Not only are such statements not helpful; most of the time they are simply not true. Friday evening, a well meaning nurse's assistant uttered those words that are as erroneous as they are ubiquitous. To be honest, I take them to be a poor interpretation of a verse from our text today. Wanting to be helpful she pulled me aside to tell me she was praying for us and to remind me that, "God will not give you more than you can handle." I smiled and thanked her, but I wanted to scream, "Are you kidding? From the day we were conceived to the day we're sucking oxygen in the Hospice unit, God gives us more than we can handle. It's called life!" Yes, each morning we wake to more than we can handle. The folly of humanity is living with the illusion that we can somehow handle, manage, or control life. We just weren't wired for that. The Psalmist proclaims the truth we resist throughout life. "I lift up my eyes to the hills. From where does my help come? My help comes from the Lord who made heaven and earth."

We weren't made to handle life. We were created for relationship with one another and with God. Our part of the deal was to understand we'd be crazy to think we could manage it on our own. Life is precarious and even on the most mundane of days I cannot say with any surety that my expectations will not be blown to bits. You cannot tell me that everything happens for a reason, for some things just happen. It is the nature of life in a finite world. There will not be an identifiable reason to explain everything that happens. Part of the wonder of life is the mystery of it all—joy lining up with tragedy, triumph, injury, healing, dark valleys and high mountains in the table of contents of life's owner's manual. Cliched attempts to explain the trials we endure will never suffice. I know it can't be said that God needed that child more than we did, and the question of whether this loss was God's will is far above my pay grade.

I believe it was William Sloane Coffin who once said something that is both true and enduringly helpful. It went something like this. Any time we perceive God's love as less than human love at its best, we are mistaken.

So, there are many things we can't say or shouldn't say in the face of suffering or death. What we can say and what the cross of Christ communicated is that there is nothing we will face that God will not endure with us and nowhere we will go that God will not travel alongside us. That is what I glean from Paul's counsel to the Corinthians. "No testing has overtaken you that is not common to everyone. God is faithful, and he will not let you be tested beyond your strength, but with the testing he will also provide the way out so that you may be able to endure it."

God may not test us beyond our strength, but the life God gave us most certainly does, every day. This text is not about God playing chess with our lives, capriciously making decisions about the piano hanging over our heads. Rather, this text points to the reality that one thing we all share in common is that we shall suffer, and Paul is wise enough to know that faith is not a way to evade suffering, but instead is the way through the suffering. "God is faithful . . . with the testing he will also provide the [path] out so that you may be able to endure it."

Following the death on Thursday, we were given a private moment to hold our baby, to feel the soft wisps of hair on the top of her head, to marvel at the artful shape of her tiny hand. The hardest thing I have ever done was to hand that beautiful but lifeless body back to the nurse. And yet, the solace that sustains us is that as we wept, commending her to God's keeping, God was there, weeping with us. I do not know what to expect tomorrow. I am not privy to the knowledge of why Thursday evolved as it did. But sustained by the love of God through Christ our Lord, I can say with Job, "For I know that my Redeemer lives, and that at the last he will stand upon the earth." Amen.

3

Fall

SPRING GARNERS TOO MUCH credit for the regeneration of life. Sure, April's azaleas, cherry blossoms, and tulips reawaken senses dulled by the gray skies and barren limbs of winter, and yet, on September Saturdays, the garden center at Lowe's is teeming with the same motivated lawn zealots you would find there in March. Pallets of pansies, carts of chrysanthemums, wagons lugging fifty pound bags of grass seed, fertilizer, lime, and mulch; it's Macy's at Christmas, Louisville on Derby Day, Capitol Hill's Mall on the Fourth of July.

Yes, fall's arrival is trumpeted by luminous yellow poplars, Clemson orange maples, and passionate red oaks as carotenoids and anthocyanins elbow their way past the chlorophyll so they may have their turn in the sun's spotlight. Less renowned but equally vivid is the greening and growth of fall fescue. Mowers rumbling around the cul de sacs almost can't keep pace with the sudden burst of growth and a walk through a freshly mown lawn leaves shoes colored like a St. Paddy's Day parade.

Fall is the growing season. In the South, you plant trees, shrubs, and grass seed in the fall rather than the spring as the cooler temperatures encourage root systems to grow strong and the specter of summer heat will not void your toil; and it is not just the grass that is growing as students ascend grade levels while setting aside jeans that no longer touch shoe tops to take to the crisis ministry donation bin.

In like manner, St. Martin springs to life in the fall with the return of Sunday school classes, committee meetings, increased worship attendance, and the reappearance of well-intentioned families trying once again to make church a habit.

The rhythm and routine of fall afforded Elijah and Hannah the chance to find their footing on the fulcrum balancing loss and life. Once again, they were able to claim this truth drawn from the Confession of 1967—"Life is a gift to be received with gratitude and a task to be pursued with courage."[5] Though given the green light to pursue another pregnancy, Elijah and Hannah were talking about holding steady with two for the time being, grateful for both the joy and challenges provided through Xani and Nathan. This would be the first year of preschool for Nathan and the last for Xani, so while Hannah headed out in the early morning darkness for Macallan Elementary, the Parish household quickly devolved into the chaos of a disturbed anthill as Elijah scurried around the house corralling, coaxing, begging, and bribing the two ricocheting electrons into clothes, to the Cheerio bowls, astride the commode, in front of a toothbrush, and into car seats. You know that Army commercial with the narrator gloating about the soldiers doing more before dawn than most folks do all day? He obviously didn't have young children.

Elijah refused the offer of a finely crafted McArthur couch for his study at the church, because by the time he managed to get Xani and Nathan settled in preschool, he'd be too tempted to take a nap.

A late September morning dawned crisp, cool, and clear. As Elijah walked from the preschool across the campus to the church office, he noticed that the leaves on the trees in the garth had started to turn and that the Bradford pear on the corner of the church property was already suffering the onset of male pattern baldness. Entering the office, Elijah immediately sensed a chill issuing from Tamara's desk, which typically signaled an exasperating encounter with a representative of the local St. Martin chapter of the Church Whiner's Society. However, the exaggerated roll of her eyes revealed an irritation beyond that provoked by the usual suspects.

Through clenched teeth, she said, "There's someone waiting for you in your office." Elijah had no appointments scheduled that morning, so he didn't know whether to be intrigued or terrified. The source of Tamara's annoyance was revealed as soon as he stepped through the door jamb to his study.

"Tim?" Though Elijah now knew the root of Tamara's pique, a second mystery quickly stood in for the first. Why in the world would Teacher Tim be standing in Elijah's study perusing his bookshelves? Their encounters in

5. *The Confession of 1967, The Book of Confessions*, PCUSA.

the last three years had been limited to a community Thanksgiving service, a brief conversation in passing in the clergy parking area at the hospital, and one of those awkward greetings men exchange while standing at the urinals in the men's room prior to a Presbytery meeting. There wasn't any animosity. The two pastors, curiously enough, did not share much in common and stood apart from one another on the spectrums of politics and theology. Honestly, while Elijah was suspicious of Teacher Tim's motives and goals, Teacher Tim rarely acknowledged or considered Elijah's presence or relevance.

"Your library is very different from mine."

"Is that so?"

"Who in the world reads Barth in the 21st century? And these other writers, Nouwen, Niebuhr, Buechner, William Sloane Coffin, Barbara Brown Taylor—it looks like a bibliography for the hospice bound mainline church. No wonder the Presbyterian Church is shrinking. You've got to be more entrepreneurial. Where are the books on strategic planning, visioning, principles of business management? You need Jack Welch's book and Jim Collins' *Good to Great*. You want people to be reflective, thoughtful, deep. It ain't happenin' in case you haven't noticed. I'll bet you couldn't get fifteen people in your church to read these books. Heck, most folks can't pronounce erudite, much less spell it, and even less understand it. You ought to go with me to the John Maxwell conference coming up in Atlanta. All of you "pastor-theologians" are going to get covered with cobwebs if you don't lighten up on the reading and warm up to the idea of a marketing strategy. Just sayin'."

"I'll keep that in mind, Tim." It takes a lot of discipline to speak in a pastoral tone when your gag reflexes are tempting the half-digested residue of your Raisin Bran to assault your mouth. "So, what can I do for you?" Even as the words passed his lips, Elijah wished he could retract them. People like Teacher Tim abhorred the idea of others assuming they had the upper hand in a conversation.

"Well . . . we came in . . ." Up to that moment, Elijah hadn't noticed Carlotta standing over in the darkened corner of the study, which is incredible, because Carlotta was certainly dressed to be noticed. Elijah silently nodded to her, tamping down the impulse to shout, "Holy cow!" Heels that required a ladder to step into; jeans painted onto legs that stretched all the way from here to there; and a tank top so tight, bystanders would fear she could either suffocate or die from a boob explosion. Carlotta was leaning decidedly to the left on the JLo—Katharine Hepburn scale, and as if they were waged in a contest for constrictive clothing, Teacher Tim was wearing a black v-neck that would have fit him in the second-grade and tush touting jeans that cost more than Elijah's marrying and burying suit. It struck Elijah that there must be a correlation between the tightness of clothing and the level of vanity. The tighter the threads, the greater the worship of self. Elijah wondered if it was the constriction of Tim's t-shirt that made his hair stand on end. No, it must be the gel.

"Um . . . we came in to see if you might have a couple of resources that we could use." Bible school curriculum? Folding chairs? "You're from Charlotte, right?"

"Yes."

"Your daddy's a lawyer down there, isn't he?"

"Yes."

"With discretion being paramount, what if someone was looking for an attorney who . . . um . . . has some expertise in family law and mediation, on the QT, of course. This is a delicate situation."

"My father does some of that, and he certainly is familiar with a number others who know the ins and outs of mediation, separation, and divorce. I can give you his number and give him a heads up if you'd like."

"Um . . . Thank you. And would you also have a referral for a marriage counselor in Charlotte? Again, discretion is the key. We certainly couldn't see someone local."

"Yes, I could give you a brief list of therapists and pastoral counselors. One of them is just down from my father's office on East Boulevard. Another one is across from SouthPark Mall. However, I do find it interesting that you asked for the lawyer before you asked for the counselor."

"Well, it's a tough time. You know, I try to be the forgive and forget kind . . . "

Cutting him off mid-sentence Carlotta, heretofore silent, entered the conversation with a fury. "Forgive and forget, my ass!! You act like I'm the only one playing Twister in thy neighbor's house, ya rat bastard!!

"Now Carlotta, I'm sure the good reverend here doesn't want to hear about your adventures . . . "

"My adventures!! Hell, you brought that tramp into *my* bed. At least I went out of town to find some form of intimate pleasure. Teacher Tim . . . Ha! They ought to call you Tiny Tim."

The bulging vein in his neck signaled that Tiny Teacher Tim was about to blow a gasket, but you've got to give him credit, he managed to keep the lid on. Though his anger equaled Carlotta's, he knew he had to play this right. Elijah had just rotated off the Committee on Ministry of the Presbytery, and while the COM seeks to be merciful, they still take a pretty dim view toward infidelity. If your ordination isn't rescinded or charges aren't brought against you, you'll at least be forced to leave the church you are currently serving. About the only way to avoid an imbroglio was for the accused to "renounce the jurisdiction of the church," setting aside his or her ordination to avoid the humiliation of the church court. Honestly, Teacher Tim didn't give a hoot about what the Committee on Ministry thought, but he knew timing was of the essence here.

"We've taken enough of your time. Thank you for the referrals." Tim rose, motioning for Carlotta to exit with him. His embarrassment was apparent but it was not enough to supplant his ego. "You know, we've called a congregational meeting for the first Sunday in October to vote on leaving the denomination." A number of congregations are leaving the Presbyterian Church because of the recent vote providing a loophole for congregations and presbyteries open to the ordination of faithful leaders regardless of their sexual orientation.

"Yes, I was sorry to hear that." Believe it or not, Elijah truly meant that.

"It is tragic, but you know, I just can't agree with you on the whole question of homosexuality and ordination; and I know that it won't be long before you're sanctioning gay marriage. My folks won't stand for that, and quite frankly, I think the Bible is pretty clear about that . . . 'Therefore shall a man leave his father and his mother, and shall cleave unto his wife: and they shall be one flesh.'"

"Hmmm. So Tim, what does the Bible have to say about adultery? Divorce? Bearing false witness? Seems I recall that the words, *thou shalt not*, are in there someplace."

"Hey, I can confess to a little youthful indiscretion, but..."

"Youthful indiscretion? A youthful indiscretion is when a six-year-old pockets a Snickers at the grocery store when his mom isn't looking. A youthful indiscretion is when a teenager leaves a flaming bag of poop on your doorstep and rings the doorbell. Tim, you're what? 33? You gave up the get out of jail free card for youthful indiscretions when you were given the right to vote, and certainly by the time you walked down that aisle and said, 'I do.' I don't care if you were hungover at the time."

"How did you know I was hungover?"

"Lucky guess."

"Hey, I don't need a sermon from you, and what do you mean by implying that I am bearing false witness?"

"Tim, I hope those referrals are helpful for you. I hope there is room for reconciliation for the two of you, and if not, I pray that you will find healing as you seek separate lives, but I'm not so dull that I can't see a strategy that works to your benefit here. If your affairs were exposed and you have to face the Committee on Ministry, you're done here. Toast. Adios. However, if your congregation votes to leave the denomination, then you are no longer under our jurisdiction and this new fledgling Presbyterian group isn't yet equipped to adjudicate the misadventures of your tool. Why, you will have the freedom to craft a story that makes divorce seem like the heroic thing for you to do, freeing you to do more for the kingdom of God."

Carlotta chimed in, "I think he's got your number, Tiny Tim."

"Carlotta, he doesn't need your approbation, and don't think for a moment that you'll be able to seduce him. Stick with Mr. NASCAR."

"Asshole."

"You can take the girl out of Union County, but you can't take Union County out of the girl."

"Well aren't you the sophisticated redneck. I guess you forgot you were raised in the same shithole as me. And while we've got the preacher here as witness, let me make it clear that if you bring that whore into my bed again, I'll cut it off. I swear to you, I will . . . cut . . . it . . . off."

At this point, Elijah was hoping they weren't packing weapons because he didn't want his office to hereafter be called *The OK Corral.*

With embarrassment elbowing itself back onto the stage with ego and sensing Elijah's rising anxiety, Teacher Tim said, "I'm sorry if we made a scene. It was kind of you to see us."

"Tim and Carlotta, I know that there are many areas where Tim and I will forever be locked in disagreement, but I want both of you to know that I mean it when I say you are children of God and nothing will change that. You will remain in my prayers, and if I can be helpful, please let me know. And also know that everything said here will remain confidential."

"Well, we may have set up camp in different places theologically, but I believe you to be an honorable man. That's why I felt we could come to you."

Carlotta silently nodded her head in agreement and Elijah walked over to open the door of his study for them, and there, standing in front of Tamara's desk was Sean McArthur IV. On so many levels, Elijah was thinking, "Crap!!" But, before he could close the door, Sean moved toward him just as Tim entered the doorway.

"Whoa! What a surprise! I didn't expect to find a real preacher here. Tim, how the heck are ya!" Sean found it impossible to speak without an exclamation point. "I hope you came over here to teach this boy how it is supposed to be done!"

Seeing Tim's face turn white with the fear of exposure, Elijah interjected, "Sean, it's always good to see you. I guess you have met Tim and Carlotta." Of course, he knew that they had more than met. Tim and Sean met for lunch once a week and whenever Sean wasn't worshipping with his father-in-law over at the Church of God, he was worshipping Tim with his hands raised high at the Intersection, and that's not a typo, it was Tim he was worshipping. "They were kind enough to come over to talk with me about the curriculum for Vacation Bible School."

"Well, that's nice, but Tim, I hope you can help him with more than kiddy programs. You need to teach him how to preach the gospel! Preacher boy, you could learn a whole lot from this prophet. Tim, I know y'all are votin' in a couple of weeks. I'm behind you all the way."

"Sean, I trust that the Lord will show us the way. Always good to see you."

"God bless you and your smokin' hot wife."

Elijah thought, "My Lord, it's Ricky Bobby!"

Actually, Sean creeped Carlotta out. At the local high society events, she felt like he was always staring at her.

Elijah managed to bring this little lovefest to a close. "Tim, thanks for your help with our 'kiddy program."

"Um . . . you're welcome."

As they exited, the human exclamation point barged past Elijah into his study, unannounced and without appointment or warning, of course. Elijah smiled as he saw Tamara reach for her bottle of Maalox. He turned and went in to face the fire.

"So Sean, how are you faring these days?"

"Listen, let's just skip the small talk so I can cut to the chase, toot sweet."

Elijah felt like he was entering a scene from some film noir classic. "Okay Sean, what's up?"

"Let's be honest here. I don't like you, see? I don't feel like you're a real Christian. You're not baptized in the Spirit and I'll bet you've never even spoken in tongues."

"You know, I don't think Calvin ever did, either."

"You're a wise guy, besides. And I don't like wise guys."

"Well, Sean, I'll confess that along with Solomon I've prayed that God would give me a heart of understanding."

"Well, you aren't Solomon, are you?"

"I should say not. I have one wife and Solomon had 700 wives along with 300 concubines. I also surely don't possess his bank account."

"Well, you sure didn't get the wisdom either. I just don't trust you and your liberal, humanist brain."

"Sean, do you even know what a humanist is, because I don't."

"All I know is that it isn't Christian and the word always seems to be cuddled up against the word liberal. So, you must be in the neighborhood of it."

"Sean, why do you use the word 'liberal' as if it is an expletive? Is it because of the concern for the poor? Is it because of the call for equality or justice? Is it because of an emphasis on peace or compassion? I mean, isn't the primary thrust of liberalism basically what Jesus tells us in Matthew 25? 'For I was hungry and you gave me food, I was thirsty and you gave me something to drink, I was a stranger and you welcomed me, I was naked and you gave me clothing, I was sick and you took care of me, I was in prison and you visited me . . . Truly I tell you, just as you did it to one of the least of these who are members of my family, you did it to me.'"

"Don't quote scripture to me. I know my Bible, just as I know you are leading this flock away from the core biblical family values!"

"To what biblical family values are you referring? Could it be Solomon's 700 wives and 300 affairs? Or maybe you are talking about Cain killing Abel because Dad liked lamb chops more than green beans? Would you be thinking about David's conspiracy to murder his mistress's husband and the fact that a case could be made to charge David with sexual assault? Or possibly, are you pondering the rape of Tamar by her brother Amnon, which led to Absalom's revenge, not to mention his attempted coup against his father? To what biblical 'family value' are you alluding?"

"Don't you dare try to wiggle your way out of this. You know what I'm talking about. God created Adam and Eve, not Adam and Steve!"

"Well, Sean, I'd have to disagree with you there. If God created Adam and Eve, and Steve shows up, then I believe God created him, too."

"You liberals are all the same, trying to hide behind the ethic of love, using that as an excuse for everything."

"Now Sean, the Bible does say that 'God is love, and those who abide in love, abide in God, and God abides in them.'"

"I told you not to quote scripture to me, like I don't know what's in there. And another thing, I don't have a problem helping the poor, as long as they deserve it."

"Sean, our whole faith is based on receiving a love that is not deserved. If you know your Bible, then you've read where it says, 'For by grace you have been saved through faith, and this is not your own doing; it is the gift of God - not the result of works, so that no one may boast.'"

"Well, I'm here to tell you that you certainly have no reason to boast. You're preventing these people from following the truth about Christ. And my point today is this: I expect you to call a congregational meeting so that we can vote to leave the denomination like the folks at The Intersection."

"Sean, I'm sorry, but that is not going to happen. We have held forums and classes on the issues. We have met with anyone who wants to talk about it. The Session has expressed its clear support for the denomination. We may not all agree, but we're here living together, and we're not leaving the denomination. The clerk of our Session will tell you the same thing."

"Who's that?"

"Your cousin, Mark."

"I'm not speaking to him right now, but I'm not giving up. This isn't over yet."

"Sean, it never is. The journey to the kingdom of God is a long one."

"Well, let me leave you with this thought. I know two churches and two preachers in town that are a lot closer to the kingdom of God than you are."

"As we say here in the South, 'Bless 'em, Lord.'"

Seeing he wasn't going to shake Elijah from his calm demeanor and bait him into a shouting match, Sean stormed out, Elijah collapsed in his chair, and Tamara poked her head in to ask, "Would you like me to put a contract out on him? I know people."

"I know you do. No, Tamara, Sean's what you call a *hot mess*, but he's God's hot mess just like the rest of us."

For Xani and Nathan during the school year, mornings meant preschool at the church and afternoons of adventure at Mrs. McKee's. What an incredible woman! She was 62 going on 25, and no one in Edinburgh could match her energy or zest for life. Catherine McKee's husband, Ben, had died of a heart attack twelve years ago, but rather than letting her tears drown her, she allowed them to water her spirit, bringing her back to life. When someone you love dies, there is a yawning chasm that opens up before you, and like the rock climber without a rope, it is easy to lose your footing and slide in. St. Martin was the rope for Mrs. McKee. She didn't attend worship the first few weeks after the funeral; couldn't imagine entering that sacred space without Ben, and yet she knew she couldn't live without St. Martin. Feeling herself being pulled down to the point that her eyes were becoming too used to the darkness of the chasm, Catherine knew it was time to pull on the rope. So, one Sunday morning, she looked in the mirror and sensed a voice. "Get it together, girl." The words passed through her lips and the sound of the voice was hers, but if you ask Catherine, she will tell you it was the Holy Spirit talking. She managed to pull out a special dress her late husband had given her, got in the car, marched up the church sidewalk, entered the sanctuary . . . and froze.

The last time Mrs. McKee had stepped into that space, was the day of Ben's memorial service. It seemed the whole town was there, but she had never felt so alone. That loneliness enveloped Mrs. McKee once again with her first step through the doorway separating narthex from nave. With one hand, Catherine could count the number of times she had attended worship at St. Martin without Ben. Where would she sit? She hadn't considered that and sitting in the pew she had shared with Ben for so many years was out of the question.

Sensing her panic, John Thomas, a local attorney, rose and stepped over to Mrs. McKee.

"Why don't you come and sit with me and Margaret? It would be our joy to celebrate worship with you."

That would be the final tug pulling Mrs. McKee out of the chasm and she hasn't stopped running since. That August, after 24 years out of the work force, Mrs. McKee, decided to put her degree in early childhood education from Agnes Scott to good use, taking on a class of frisky four-year-olds in St. Martin's preschool. The children adored her in the same way every child in her charge has adored her over the past 12 years. Eventually, the people of Edinburgh forgot that Mrs. McKee's first name is Catherine. That first year, one of the children started calling her Momma McKee, and now, that is the sole name by which she is known in town. Momma McKee is regularly to be found on the floor with them, listening to their stories, celebrating their Lincoln Log architecture, perfecting the sound of a tractor with her lips as she *plows the fields* with them, reading them stories she has written about a child explorer which allows her to transport them to all the exotic places she has traveled. Her laughter is medicinal and her joy is infectious. Momma McKee was a painting of flowing skirts, colorful scarves, and trendy eyeglass frames accenting the elegant drape of her auburn hair, pinned halfheartedly with a stylish clasp, incorrigible wisps always falling across her face. It all gives her an air of urban sophistication.

When Momma McKee approached Hannah with a proposal to keep Xani and Nathan at her house after preschool each day until Hannah was finished at the elementary school, Hannah squealed with delight, and Hannah is not known for squealing. The afternoon care program down the street had not been the best situation in previous years. Securing the services of Momma McKee was no less a coup than landing the number one pick in the NFL draft.

When you stepped into Momma McKee's quaint white frame one-story Victorian, you instinctively looked for a ticket booth because you would swear you were entering the National Geographic Museum: a striking medley of oriental carpets; a hand-carved coffee table from Cairo; a blue floral porcelain temple jar from Guangzhou; a Chinese Chippendale cabinet from Shanghai, a Meiji period silk tapestry from Yokohama, soapstone carvings from

Nyamarambe, Kenya; a large pewter St. Martin's cross on a pedestal of Iona marble; Native American paintings from Tulsa and pottery from Santa Fe.

Her son, being a pilot for United, opened the door to the world for Momma McKee, and she had taken full advantage of his benefits in the previous twelve years. Her next planned conquest was Croatia on the back end of her biennial pilgrimage to Ben's ancestral home in Ayr, Scotland and the abbey on the isle of Iona. Momma McKee speaks four languages and possesses the adventurous spirit of one who can be comfortable from hostel to five star hotel, and is especially enriched by the new friendships that form when receiving the hospitality of people she has never met. Consequently, the guest room of her home has welcomed foreign friends from seventeen different countries.

Going to Momma McKee's ranks higher than going to the park for Xani and Nathan. Nature walks out at the state park on Lake James and exploring the world through the photos in her scrapbooks, Momma McKee has sparked an adventurous spirit in Xani and is well on the way to lighting one in Nathan. Walking up the sidewalk to Momma McKee's each afternoon, Hannah is excited to hear what bird or wildflower the kids have discovered and to what country Momma McKee has taken them. If quizzed, Xani can tell you about the Maasai, Hutu, and Tutsi tribes; she knows that Hindus refrain from cheeseburgers; she can count to ten in French, Spanish, Russian, and Mandarin; she can point out Nepal on the globe; and she can identify the look and sound of an Aboriginal didgeridoo.

"Mommy, Mommy! Did you know that in Italy, pepperoni is a pepper, not a meat?"

Xani's daily travelogue had its impact upon Hannah, the country girl who had never been outside the country, and thus, a girls' trip was being planned by Momma McKee, D.A., Dr. Jane, Spencer, Madison, Tess, Hannah, and Xani. The destination would be the next Women's British Open where they would join up with D, cheer her on, and travel to Edinburgh following the tournament. When Elijah was apprised of the trip, he remarked that he was sure they would survive the journey, but he wasn't so sure Scotland could survive them. The planning for the trip was evolving into a monthly book/film/confab club where elaborate meals would be prepared based on the setting of the book they were reading or movie they were watching. So, one month it could be the biscuits, fried chicken, and butter beans of Harper Lee's Maycomb, Alabama, and the next month they might be gathered around the qalibi palao, qorma lawand, and naan of Khalid Hosseini's Kabul, Afghanistan. Elijah was not invited, but was entitled to leftovers which he gladly received depending on how exotic the menu stretched. Haggis was out of the question and Elijah made them promise they would never read *The Story of the Andes Survivors.*

The Virtual Traveling Sisterhood of Edinburgh served as the sorority of friends Hannah had missed out on along the rural route near Laddonia where she often felt engulfed in a vat of Y-chromosomes. It has allowed her the grace of unbroken connection so unlike the many acquaintances in our lives who are more like runners linked but briefly by the relay baton on the track. There is a diversity and devotion within the circle of friends that is rare outside of the church and is made possible through the love of a God who desires relationship with and for all his children.

It is a profound joy for me to experience their deep friendship vicariously, a joy I could not know during the disconnected days of my sojourn on earth. In life, I was not wired to understand the worth of friendship, but now, as I look upon those I love, I cannot comprehend how one would survive without it. Humorist Arnold Glasow said, "A true friend never gets in your way unless you happen to be going down."

A few years ago when D was bouncing around on the mini-tours of women's golf, she lived in, or at least had an apartment near one of those white-knuckle urban expressways which are frightening to navigate and terrifying to enter. The entrance ramps were insanely short. You had about the length of grandpa's Buick to merge into the chaos of crazed motorists racing to work. The entrance ramps were so short that they had signal lights. Signal lights! No, not the tri-colored signal light that calmly ushers traffic through a busy intersection. These were more like the signals that launch Funny cars down the drag strip. When that light turned from red to yellow, you had better floor it or you'd have Dominoes delivering you a pizza before you had another chance to enter the expressway. It was crazy! Presbyterians were genuflecting as they pulled onto the ramps.

Well, as my sister tells it, the light switched from red to yellow and she floored it . . . but the driver in front of her did not. Bumpers crunched, radiators burst, fiberglass flew, headlights shattered. In the stress of the moment, she jumped out of the car to see if the other driver was okay, and like any conscious motorist in the big city, she locked her door; only the keys to the car were still in the ignition and the motor was still running, or should I say whining and wheezing at that point. It was then that a patrolman arrived, requesting licenses and suggesting that my sister pull her car to the side of the ramp, both of which were not going to happen anytime soon. That's when my sister broke down, though I can tell you she would survive.

The sun would rise the next day, but her story prompts a question. Whom would you call in that situation? When you manage to push the wrong button and life dumps a big ol' load of fertilizer on you, whom are you going to call? You lock your keys in your car. It isn't until after you enjoy the expensive meal that you realize you left your wallet in yesterday's pants. You have to get to the ER after slicing into your finger instead of the tomato and your spouse is out of town. Your date left you at the nightclub without transportation. The security man escorts you to the door on the day of the layoff when you realize that you rode to work with your supervisor. Whom are you going to call?

When humiliation visits, when trauma turns your day upside down, when embarrassment takes you captive, and you are not in a position to just "suck it up," and dealing with it yourself is not an option, the search engine in your brain comes up with two lists: the people you will call for help and the people you pray will never know. Whom would you call?

Someone said, "A friend is one who comes in when the whole world goes out." We like to fool ourselves with the illusion of independence, but life has a way of occasionally confronting us with the reality of God's observation in Eden's garden; it is not good for us to be alone. No matter how much you may want in the name of liberty to reject that notion, the truth remains that we need one another. Sooner or later, the words we most need or want to hear are: "I'll be right there." A friend is one who loves you more than his precious calendar. So whom would you call?

With his disciples gathered around him, Jesus says, "This is my commandment, that you love one another as I have loved you. No one has greater love than this, to lay down one's life for one's friends. You are my friends if you do what I command you. I do not call you servants any longer, because the servant does not know what the master is doing; but I have called you friends, because I have made known to you everything that I have heard from my Father."

Jesus reveals what prophets, priests, and wisdom writers had affirmed or at least hinted at before him, that the whole human enterprise on this little orb was predicated on the notion that God desired relationship and desired those he created to experience relationship. And so it is that before we even graduate from our Pampers, we're prodding our parents with the question of when that little towheaded neighbor can come over to play.

It doesn't matter whether you listened to your music on a Philco, a jukebox, a hi-fi, an eight track, or an iPod when you were graduated from high school and were asked what you enjoyed, what was important to you, there's a good chance you said what almost every other graduate has said in some dialect or another through the generations: "hanging out with friends." Time and again, that is what our adolescent hearts claim to be important to us.

The value of friendship is such that God himself chose to get in on the action. While Jesus occasionally went off to be by himself, more often than not, when a day of teaching and healing was done, he was hanging out by the fire with his buds, which drove the rules-driven, religious types batty! "Why do you eat and drink with tax collectors and sinners?"

Can't you imagine Jesus' caption in the Nazareth High School yearbook? Dislikes: Church yard sales. Likes: Barefoot waterskiing and . . . hanging out with my friends.

The value of life is experienced through the friendships with which we are blessed. "I do not call you servants any longer, because the servant does not know what the master is doing; but I have called you friends, because I have made known to you everything that I have heard from my Father." Isn't that what is affirmed when someone relates what is special about his or her friendship? "I can tell him/her everything." We allow our dear friends past the veneer of our public persona. They learn who we really are, and miraculously, don't run for the exits. The friends we trust are the ones who have seen us at our worst without finding us contemptible.

Who will hold the cold cloth to your head when the porcelain altar beckons? Who will listen to your rant without waving you off? Who will celebrate your victories, large and small, without jealousy, or worse, indifference? Who will be pained by your pain when failure finds you? Who will tell you the truth in love? Who will listen to you and truly hear you?

The good news of the Gospel is that through the power of the Holy Spirit, Christ reveals himself in the friends by which your life has been graced and who also serve as an answer to these questions. Whom would you call when you're in trouble? When the bottom falls out of your day? When you're too embarrassed to call anyone else? When you wouldn't want to experience something without them? Just as we yearn to hear the words, "I'll be right there;" we also yearn to be able to say the words, "I don't know what I would have done without you."

One of the enduring images of friendship to me is from the day I died in the accident. The first person Tess called when she and my father received the heart ripping news was Belinda Ferguson, the mayor of Charlotte. Belinda, a respected banker and former chair of both the Charlotte Chamber of Commerce and the Mecklenburg County Republican Party had met Tess through a women's circle meeting at Myers Park Presbyterian Church. When it came to politics, Tess and Belinda agreed on . . . nothing. They consistently cancelled out each other's ballots and by October on election years they found it beneficial to maintain cell phone silence and sit on different sides of the sanctuary each Sunday. Yet, when Belinda's husband had open heart surgery, Tess was in the family waiting room holding Belinda's hand. When Tess tore her Achilles, Belinda coordinated our meals for a week.

These two strong personalities disagreed and argued about so many things, and yet they never questioned the faith of each other and always viewed one another as the dearest of friends. As soon as Belinda got the call from Tess on the day of the accident, she dropped everything and arrived the emergency room just as the ambulance was unloading. Belinda cancelled an appearance at a party fundraiser, skipped a city council meeting, and ignored a call from the Governor when his number showed up on the caller id of her cell phone. She sat with Tess and Taylor through the darkest days of their lives, her presence a knot for them to hold onto at the end of their rope.

The power of friendship breaks through politics, pettiness, race, class, bad behavior, dementia, and the ever-shifting winds of culture. A true friend abides the darkness with you and couldn't enjoy a party if you weren't invited.

Hannah's mirthful band of intergenerational friends, emerging from their shared faith and connection to the church, provided an indispensable source of strength, wisdom, support, and light. What a privilege it would be for Xani to grow up in the company of these women of strength. And yet, when sickness compelled Hannah to make an offering at the porcelain altar, there was really only one person she wanted holding her head and wiping her brow with an ice-chilled cloth. It is the same person who had held her hand at her mother's funeral, at their wedding, and at the birth of their children. She relished the fellowship of the Glam Globetrotters Society of Edinburgh, but her drive home was marked by the cheerful thought of sharing the highlights of the gathering with Elijah. To be married to your best friend is to be doubly blessed.

Having spent the day driving the van for the older adult group on their annual trip to Little Switzerland so that they could see the fall leaves at their peak, Elijah was sown into his favorite chair and ottoman, remote in one hand, Nathan napping on his lap, and Joab dozing at his feet. If the Cardinals could put away the Nationals tonight, they'd win the pennant and be headed to another World Series. He was zonked. Something about navigating a van with fourteen septuagenarians and octogenarians in your ears offering directions, commentary, questions, and complaints, can be more exhausting than a century bike ride. He didn't even have the energy to cheer when Yadier Molina hit a two run homer in the bottom of the third.

The familiar silhouette of Hannah's Honda Pilot swinging into the carport did manage to rouse Elijah from his stupor.

"Daddy!"

"Hey there, Pocahontas!" Obsessed with the Disney movie, Xani had insisted on dressing as Pocahontas for the approaching ritual of Hallow's Eve. Hannah had outdone herself by pulling together a remarkable costume out of a giant piece of cheesecloth, a turquoise necklace, and a small leather hair band. The monthly meeting of the Glam Globetrotters had gathered this night with a theme of Halloween, so costumes were the order of the day. Elijah may have been worn out, but he quickly woke up when Hannah came in dressed as Pebbles from *The Flintstones*.

"Yabba Dabba Do!!!"

"O hush, I had all of that cheesecloth and didn't want to spend any more money, so I made this."

(Gulp) "Well I hope you'll keep that around, if you get my drift."

"Hold on there, big boy, we still have to get these kids to bed; and anyway, your mom will be here in a little while. We left early so that Pocahontas, our little Iowa, will be ready for preschool."

"Iowa?

"Middle school geography class. Did you know that Iowa's name comes from a Native American word for 'sleepy ones'?"

"Sorry, we didn't learn that in 'Myuhs Park,' the southern word for pretension . . . So, what ghoulish delights and eerie tales were on the agenda tonight?"

Xani had the answer for that. "Daddy, they talked about a raven, a big black talking bird. Listen, 'Quoth the raven nevermore.' Madison taught me."

"That's great, Xani. 'What this grim, ungainly, ghastly, gaunt, and ominous bird of yore meant in croaking 'Nevermore.'[6] The haunting tale of lost love. Lenore sure did a number on him, didn't she?"

"Yeah!" Xani didn't know what she was agreeing to, but it sounded good.

"So, Pebbles, whatcha got in that bag there? Brontosaurus burgers?"

"No, we supped on candy corn, pumpkin pie, pumpkin chili, and jack-o-lantern oranges, and creepy monster sliders. The chili is fantastic. Momma McKee brought it. And everybody loved T's oranges. She carved the peel just as with a pumpkin, spooned out and chopped the pulp, and then mixed it with chopped apples and grapes, putting it all back in the shell. It was great."

"It all sounds good."

"Have you eaten? I brought you some leftovers."

---

6. Poe, Edgar Allen, *The Raven*, first published in 1845.

"I had a big lunch up on the mountain along with more helpful instruction and pointed direction than a pastor could ever want. I know it was more than I ever wanted."

"Ah yes, the Roaring Retirees."

"Wonderful people. Amazing life journeys. Incredible record of service to God, country, and community. But Lord, they do get worked up over the most inane things: my shortcut is better than your shortcut; the dearth of condiments at the restaurant; the service at the country club is unacceptable; the absolute refusal to admit that their computer/iPad/phone woes could be due to user error; it's too cold in church; it's too hot in church; the children are too loud; the preacher needs to speak up. You know, Sunday isn't Sunday without Ernastine Walker complaining to me about not being able to hear, and every Sunday, there she is in the back row refusing to use one of the hearing devices. And today, Brenda Bost went on a fifteen-minute tirade about how the government just needs to get out of our lives and she has been receiving Social Security disability checks for fifteen years! I have to admit, I love them, well, at least most of them, but they sure can be exhausting."

"Happy, happy, joy, joy!!"

"Yeah, if I just complain about their complaining, I'm only multiplying the amount of irritating noise clogging the air. I'll tell you, though, what I have found helpful. At the conclusion of their quarterly covered dish lunch, or when I drop them off after an outing like today, I take a slow walk around the church property, paying special attention to the marvelous stonework. Stone stacked upon stone, rising up to support those glorious beams, which in turn support that classic slate roof.

"I look at those stones and I am reminded that we stand upon and are supported by the lifelong witness of these living saints. Today, George Winston insisted that we turn onto his shortcut, which turned out to be a dead end; but George Winston was one of the first to wade onto the beach at Normandy, somehow surviving that torrential downpour of bullets, only to lose the lower half of his left leg following a shrapnel wound outside of Bastogne. Jeanne Pitts may have whined about the food being cold, but at the age of seventeen, when her father was killed by a drunk driver, she took over the family hardware store and has kept it humming for sixty years. We had to make four bathroom stops for Tommy Lambert, but let's not forget that he had no opportunity to use anything but an outhouse until he was nineteen. And though he is always peppering me with questions about the next trip before the van pulls into the parking lot from the last trip, did you know he didn't leave his wife's bedside a single day for 2 ½ years prior to her death? No wonder he is always itching to go on a trip! Lord knows, we all have our idiosyncrasies. It's a shame we can be so infuriated by the quirks of others and clueless about our own."

With the furrowed brow of curiosity, Xani asked, "Daddy, what's an idiot-casy?"

"Congress. No, Xani, I'm kidding. An idiosyncrasy is a feature or a habit that is unique or special to someone, something that can leave people curious, confused, or frustrated."

"You mean like you and peanut butter?"

"Peanut butter?"

"Uh huh. When mom sends us to the store for peanut butter or something else, you stare at all the peanut butters for a long time like you don't know what you're supposed to get."

Howling, Hannah exulted, "You are sooo right, Xani! Priceless and precious. E, you . . . are . . . so busted."

Cowed and contrite, Elijah confessed, "Yes, I am. Yes, I am. You are a wise little girl, Xani."

Once the children were tucked in for the night, Elijah sampled some pumpkin chili while Hannah reviewed her lesson plans. Tess, arrived a little later, having dissected every conceivable topic, from the Tea Party's dismantling of the state of North Carolina to the location for the best Pad Thai in Charlotte, with Momma McKee and Company. For the festivities, Tess had dressed as a Sixties flower child.

"Hey T!" Elijah hugged his mom and snickered while asking, "Memories of Woodstock?"

Her face blushing, and with a voice of panic, Tess interrogated, "How did you know about that."

"Grandpa told me years ago. So, how do you carry on a conversation with Joan Baez when you're stoned?"

"This is humiliating. But to answer your question, there wasn't much conversation, because I was just trying to keep from throwing up on her dashboard. Longest ten miles of my life. Well, maybe not. The longest ten miles would be the first ten miles after the Rev. picked me up."

Looking at the costumed women of his life, Elijah observed, "You two make quite a pair. Pebbles and flower power, from the Stone Age to the Stoned Age. So, how was the conclave tonight? What ghoulish incantations were gathered up?"

Rolling her eyes, Hannah said, "Sorry, those discussions are above your pay grade."

"No doubt. But I do wish the room had been bugged. All Hallow's Eve. What's all the fuss about anyway? So much emphasis on the eve and none on the hallows."

Hannah shot Elijah that *I think I married an idiot*, look. "What in the world are you talking about?"

"Look, who among the costumed ninjas, jedis, and Ariels roaming the neighborhood next week in search of a sugar fix will have any idea that Halloween is to be just a prelude to the following day's celebration of the saints of the Church?"

Tess broke in, "Watch out Hannah, he is about to start channeling my father or he's morphing into one of those nut job, turn or burn preachers who run those Hell Houses that try to scare the kids into heaven."

"No, hear me out. Why do the kids grow up knowing so much more about Freddie Kruger than they do about, say, Teresa of Avila or Reinhold Niebuhr?"

"The Right Reverend McPheeters it is!"

"Well, now think about it. We have folks in the church who have so many Halloween decorations that they can't fit them in their house. They have to rent a storage unit year 'round and stuff it full of coffins, goblins, zombies, and jack-o-lantern lights so that they can spend two weekends putting it all up to scare the neighbors' kids on Halloween. Yet, not a one of them could tell you a single thing about John Witherspoon or Dorothy Day or Francis Makemie."

Baiting him with sarcasm, Hannah inquired, "So, does this mean we have to dress up Xani as John Calvin next year?"

"No, but she could pull it off, though."

"The way I see it," Tess opined, "Let Halloween be Halloween and God bless the Skittles. And then let us be intentional about teaching the children and their parents about the people of faith who paved the way for us through their enduring witness."

"You're absolutely right. Now you are the one sounding like Rev. Jordan."

Stretching the stretch of exhaustion after a long day, Hannah yawned, "Well, saints, the alarm goes off early and Nathan's alarm will probably go off earlier than that, so why don't we call it a night?"

"I'll second that motion."

"It's unanimous."

Elijah and Hannah went down to the study, helped Tess pull down the Murphy bed, and wrapped it with clean sheets.

"Luv ya, T!"

"I love you, too."

Climbing into bed is a vastly under-appreciated luxury. The unburdening of the day's weight and a word of gratitude for God and each other induce such a sense of relief and peace. Sometimes, Hannah would actually squeal with delight at how good it felt, and that was before any intramural exercise.

The next morning, when Elijah opened the pantry to grab a cereal box, he noticed that the bag of Ruffles on the bottom shelf had a sizeable hole ripped in the side of it, and the shrapnel of it contents were strewn across the floor like the crumbles you put on the top of a tuna noodle casserole.

"Hannah, did you get a little hungry during the night?"

"No. Why?" Elijah handed her the bag and she examined the evidence.

"Hmmm. Teeth marks."

"Well, it wasn't me!"

"Very small teeth."

"A mouse?"

"Could be." She dared not freak him out with the other possibility. "I'll put out a mouse trap and we'll see what happens."

That night in a fit of paranoia, Elijah took the box from his newly purchased weed whacker and laid it across the hallway leading from the kitchen to the bedrooms, supposedly to protect his family from the home invaders. Hannah just smiled at the naivete of the boy bred in suburbia. The rodent had managed to infiltrate a brick wall, subflooring, hardwood, and a cabinet door. Why would he think that a piece of quarter inch cardboard would repel a hungry lab drone?

The next morning Elijah jumped out of bed and ran to the kitchen only to find that the trap had not sprung, though the cheese was gone along with an entire granola bar. He lamented, "If this keeps up, at least he'll get so fat, even I will be able to take him down."

That night, another trap was set and the useless barricade was set in place. Just as Elijah was drifting off to sleep, he heard a bag rustling in the kitchen. His eyes shot open and he shouted, "Not the Cheetos!" He grabbed a tennis racket from the closet, ran down the hall, tripped over the barricade, somersaulted, and bounced up as Hannah flipped the light switch.

"Holy shit! It's a rat." There staring Elijah in the face was a bulked up linebacker of a rat on steroids, the man-eating kind you imagine ruling the deepest, darkest subway tunnels in New York. Elijah froze. If this had been *High Noon*, Gary Cooper would be dead.

Seizing the moment, in one movement Hannah hurdled the box as if it were the Big 12 Finals, snatched the racket from Elijah's hand and slapped the retreating rat into the wall with a big thud. The rat, now seeing stars, lay stunned by the baseboard. Hannah quickly grabbed it by the tail, whacked it on the floor for good measure, grabbed a hammer from the kitchen drawer, and quickly exited the back door, whereupon, she crushed its head on the concrete of the carport.

After throwing the deceased into a trash bag and depositing it in the trash can, she re-entered the back door, nonchalantly brushing her hands and walking over to the sink to wash them. In shock, Elijah had not moved.

"That . . . was . . . amazing! How in the world did you do that?"

"I grew up on a farm. We had a barn. Connect the dots."

"I don't know that I've ever loved you more." And with a sly smile, "Do you still have that Pebbles costume?"

"Why yes, Bam Bam, I believe I do."

The next day Hannah confirmed her suspicion. The Orkin man told her that the vanquished was most likely the momma rat and that they could expect six to eight visits from her litter. This had been the third house in the neighborhood to get hit. Apparently, the recently sold house down the street had been owned by a hoarder. The new owners had just torn down the structure to build a new home, and so the furry residents had fled like refugees looking for asylum, but Hannah and Elijah had no intention of granting visas, and so a trip to Jeanne Pitts' hardware store allowed the rat warriors to load up on traps and chemicals to combat their foes.

On Friday night, Tom, Spencer, and Madison Smythe were coming over for a dinner of grilled pork loin, mashed potato casserole, and caesar salad. If they were put off by the menu or the simple setting, they would never offer a hint of it. It is always a bit intimidating to host someone of great wealth, but part of the McArthur legacy, with the exception of Sean IV, is their unpretentious manner. Madison felt as comfortable here as she did at McArthur Manor up on Highland Street. In truth, she relished this refuge where she would never be looked at as if she had a dollar sign halo.

Joab managed to slip through an opening between chairs and made himself comfortable on the floor beneath the table, ever hopeful, often disappointed. Would there be any scraps tonight, because that pork smelled sooo goood? Joab, the chocolate lab, had great eyes for begging. The last couple of days he had been a bit nervous, though. The invasion of Ratzilla had spooked him. Joab may have been named after the great Jewish general, but with his tender heart, he was kind of a wuss. Elijah was only half-facetiously praying that the meal would not be interrupted by the spawn of Ratzilla. The Orkin man had taken care of four of them with appropriately placed dinner greetings in the crawl space and Elijah had snared two in the traps inside. They hoped they were close to eradicating the problem. At three occasions during dinner, the rat artillery accomplished its mission, signaled by a profound *SNAP!* Ever graceful, Hannah carried on as though nothing had happened, while everyone else flinched. *SNAP!* "Don't you just love, love, love this bread! Elijah picked it up at that new bakery on the square." . . . *SNAP!* "Haven't the leaves been glorious this fall? Have some more potatoes." . . . *SNAP!* "E, is that old crow tapping on the kitchen window again? More tea, anyone?" An artist at work. If anyone suspected what was happening, they were good sports and didn't mention it, though as they were saying their goodbyes, Madison leaned into Hannah and whispered, "Was that what you were telling me a . . . "

"Yes, the guillotines were busy this evening."

"I'll bet that takes care of it."

"I hope so."

Friends departed, the kids put to bed, and the dishes cleaned, Elijah and Hannah were ready to collapse when the phone rang. Elijah looked at his watch. It was 10:30. He sighed knowing that no one calls the preacher's house after ten with good news. Periodically, the phone would wake him from sleep with news of a death, an accident, or the impending demise of a church member. On many occasions, he'd get dressed, make his way to the Emergency Room or the Intensive Care Unit, knowing he possessed no magic words, but hoping his presence would somehow offer some succor to those frightened or paralyzed by the precarious nature of life. However, this phone call was different. It was Tamara and she was upset, bordering on hysterical.

"Elijah, they've got my boy! Stephen's been arrested in Charlotte."

"Wait. What? Arrested? What's Stephen doing in Charlotte?"

"He was taking his girlfriend to visit her parents for the weekend. They had driven down from Raleigh, eaten supper at the Cheesecake Factory, gone to a movie at Park Road Cinemas and were headed back to her parents' house when they were pulled over. Stephen was dragged out of the car, forced to lay face down on the ground, and was arrested on suspicion for armed robbery at an ABC store. He wasn't even there. He was at the movie with Sharon. But they were looking for a black man in a gray Honda with a missing hubcap, and the car I passed on to him was missing a hubcap. But Stephen was at the movie. What am I going to do?"

"I'll be right over. I'll call my dad and see if he can help us out."

Elijah didn't know whether to be panicked or angry. There was no way Stephen was involved in an armed robbery. Stephen is a second-year Park Scholar at NC State, one of the most illustrious honors a high school senior can be awarded in North Carolina. He is going to be an aerospace engineer and had spent the previous summer as an intern at NASA's Marshall Space Flight Center in Huntsville, Alabama. Sharon, his girlfriend, is a year older than Stephen, studying biomedical engineering, and had recently been elected to the university's homecoming court.

On the drive over to Tamara's along Edinburgh's silent streetscapes, Elijah marveled at the strange marriage of serenity and anguish that mingle at midnight in a small town. Elijah turned off the radio and opened the window welcoming the cool wave of crisp fall air. The only discernable activity was the ballet of leaves falling from the trees, their terpsichorean flirtation with the breeze bathed in the pinkish sodium vapor light of the streetlamps. Sirens were rare to infrequent. It was so quiet, the sound of a voice would disturb more than engage the ear. Houses were darkened and even the fluorescents of the convenience mart were taking a break. Somewhere siblings were fast asleep under the cover of a bedroom fort crafted with blankets, bedposts, and broom handles. Down the street a grandfather's snores were muffled by the mask of the CPAP machine, while down in the den his wife huddles in the corner of the couch under the reading lamp, unable to extract her attention from the newest Dan Silva spy novel. A nurse looks in on a patient in the telemetry unit. Newlyweds make love in the darkness. An exhausted lineman collapses onto a sagging mattress after the football game. Lullabies have been sung. Prayers have been said. Gracie's said goodnight.

However, the seeming slumber of the community is betrayed by the quiet angst, the alcohol inflamed emotions, and the rising fears that will forbid sleep behind many darkened doors this night. A nervous father peeks through the living room curtains for the thirtieth time, hoping to see the headlights of his daughter's Beetle pulling safely into the driveway. Police officers responding to a domestic disturbance wade through an amalgam of fact, fiction, blame, and denial. A husband is paralyzed by the decision of whether to call 911 or acquiesce to his wife's refusal to go to the hospital as her condition worsens. A mother's panic intensifies as her impotent quest for reason and information finds no succor, her son a scholar, a leader, a disciple, a heart for service . . . a suspect?

A word not found in the Bible but surely descriptive of a common experience in ministry is surreal and Tamara's phone call beckoned Elijah once again to join someone's journey into a Salvador Dali painting.

"This just can't be real," Tamara despaired as she climbed into Elijah's Jeep for the trip to Charlotte.

"I called my father and he is on his way over to the magistrate's office at the intake center. He has a lot of experience in working through these matters. He said not to panic, he'll find a way through this."

Tamara nodded but she may well not have heard a word of it. While there are times that shock paralyzes, very often shock slows your mind and dulls your motor skills just enough to make your world appear as a slow-motion instant replay from the NFL. Somewhere, John Madden is diagramming your sluggish deliberate movements on a telestrator. You are moving, functioning, buttoning your shirt, pouring coffee, driving to the dry cleaners, parallel parking, speaking to acquaintances, mowing the lawn, checking the mail, and making dinner, but at the same time, your senses are dulled to the noises, voices, and movements around you. Midway into conversations, you realize you haven't been listening, and even if you have heard the words, your mind cannot process them. You don't notice the bruise forming above your knee and cannot remember injuring it in the first place. You suddenly can't remember street names and struggle to organize your thoughts.

Through the years, Elijah has learned that when you accompany someone in shock, you must measure your words. Platitudes, theological pearls of wisdom, insights from your vast store of knowledge and experience—these are not helpful. Instead of telling them what you think they need to hear, listen. Even if there are no words or if the person in shock raises no questions, grace has a way of breathing into the silent spaces and the embrace of God's presence is felt. Sometimes the pastor's most important task is to not get in the way of the Spirit's work when the bottom falls out of someone's life. The pastor, after all, is not there to orchestrate God's Spirit, but is there at the service of God's Spirit, listening and looking for signs of the Spirit's work, offering gentle hints and light nudges to those whose lives have blown off course, helping them to rejoin the flow of the Spirit's movement.

There is rarely a moment when Elijah feels equipped to encounter the distraught, the dying, or the bereaved; and there is rarely a moment when Elijah leaves such encounters brushing off his hands and congratulating himself—"Well done, good and faithful pastor!" However, there are many occasions when such encounters leave him humbled by an awareness of God's presence and the privilege of having stepped on holy ground.

The ground below Tamara's feet at this point seemed far from sacred, and the sense of God's presence was tenuous at best. "I do not understand. I just do not understand. I worked so hard . . . so hard to help my children see the world not as a threat but as a blessing. I worked so hard for them to believe that if they pursued excellence, approached others with kindness, and didn't allow their peers to drag them down, that there was enough goodness in the world that the prejudice of some would not define their experience, nor obstruct their opportunities. And . . . it can all be shaken, it can all collapse, like a building being razed, oh so quickly. I worked so hard . . . "

"Yes you have Tamara. Yes you have." There is no denying it. Tamara Perry had insisted that her two children pursue excellence and promote goodness not for themselves but for the glory of God and the well-being of God's creation. Recent controversies surrounding the *tiger mom* phenomenon failed to consider the impact of being raised in the home of a strong and faithful African American single mom, and Tamara Perry was a fortress of strength and an archetype of faithfulness.

Paula Perry was ten and Stephen was six when their father Alfred died of pancreatic cancer. Tamara loved that man, respected that man, clung to that man, but on the day of his burial she made a vow before God that she would not allow her spirit to descend into the darkness of the grave, no not yet. There was too much to do. There were children to be raised, and by God, she was the one to do it. That very night, after family and friends had cleaned up following a feast of everything that's good about the South and returned to their homes and their lives, Tamara and the kids began a nightly ritual of reading for two uninterrupted hours. Winter, summer, spring, and fall; before bed; after ballgames; on vacation; even during finals week.

Though at times the kids resisted, they knew the futility of complaining about it and eventually began to look forward to it and depend upon it as a refuge from the chaos of the world around them. Paula and Stephen were the first siblings at the high school to be selected as valedictorian for their respective classes. Paula won admission to the Coast Guard Academy and is now a search and rescue helicopter pilot flying out of the Elizabeth City Air Station. In addition to being a Park Scholar, Stephen plays piano and Hammond B3 organ for the historic St. Paul A.M.E. Church in Raleigh.

"Elijah, this is 2013, not 1953. Why is a black man still more likely to be looked upon as a suspect than as a citizen? Why, in this day and age would politicians, elected to pursue the common good, be up there in Raleigh changing laws and gerrymandering districts so that my vote doesn't count, or even worse, that I don't have a vote at all? How can someone smile in a commercial like he has my interests in his heart, like he wants to be my best friend, and then pursue an agenda that eviscerates the public schools and strips programs that will help some of the folk in my neighborhood escape the grip of poverty? Why would my niece, a public school teacher studying for her masters, have two kids who qualify for Medicaid? Her husband, who has cobbled together three part-time jobs after being laid off from Broughton State Hospital, is uninsured! I don't get it, Elijah, I just don't get it, especially when people are buying $20 million homes and $500 million dollar yachts while lobbying for lower taxes."

Elijah had learned long ago that it was best to let the distraught or seething get it out without cutting in as if they had any inclinations for dialogue. Interrupting the seething or panicked individual mid-rant is akin to the carpenter who attempts to stop a buzz saw with his hand. Mid-rant is not the time to offer commentary, inject reason; and it is certainly not the time to contradict, or protest. Let them get it out, howl at the moon, fulminate against their foes, test-drive a tirade. In fact, Elijah had learned the wisdom of remaining silent for a minimum of sixty seconds once the diatribe fizzles out. Allow the breaths of bitterness to dissipate in the air.

Permit the silence to do its work, for just as fresh air helps in the healing of an open wound, so too does the air, uncluttered by words, provide the space necessary before healing can begin.

Tamara was livid. Though Elijah agreed with most of what she had said, he also knew that the complexities of life in community, the fact that unfamiliarity breeds distrust, and a whole host of contributing factors including personality, weather, biorhythms, cultural imprinting and even what you ate for lunch can influence whether our encounters with others go north or south. Elijah understood that the drama of this night was not, literally or figuratively, a matter of black and white. Rather, it was more of the gray hue of human brokenness that characterizes the vast majority of breakdowns in human relations.

At one level, it could be said that Stephen's arrest was a clear case of DWB. He was stopped when his only "crime" was Driving While Black. Yet, one could also say that the police were only acting on the information that was available to them: a gray Japanese sedan with a missing hubcap driven by a young African-American male in the vicinity of the ABC Store in Park Road Shopping Center. Were the officers influenced by their cultural assumptions and prejudices in their conclusion that they had their man? Probably. Was the encounter further influenced by Stephen's panic, having never been stopped and having heard the horror stories of young African-American men being swallowed up by the justice system, not to mention the humiliation of being frisked and handcuffed immediately? Probably. In a broken world, race relations have been, are, and will continue to be fraught with emotion, miscommunication, and a laziness that clings to parochial attitudes, refusing to take the risks and make the efforts that love demands. A fundamental failure of the church through the ages has been the tendency to tag people with terms like good, bad, more than, or less than. To be blunt, nobody farts orchids and everybody's heart could use a ride through a purifier. Self-righteousness in an oxymoron.

All those thoughts were bouncing around in Elijah's mind like ping pong balls in a bingo blower. But this was not the time for those conversations, though he felt comfortable that he could and probably would have those conversations with Tamara and Stephen. Yet, not now. A young man was frightened, humiliated, wounded, and angry. A mother was terrified, broken-hearted, and furious. Now was the time for listening, now was the time for assisting, now was the time to pursue a reunion for a mother and her son.

Just as they approached the exit off the interstate for uptown Charlotte, Taylor called and said that Stephen and Sharon were with him and that the reunion would take place at the home of Sharon's parents off Old Providence Road in south Charlotte.

The waterworks ensued as soon as Tamara entered the door. Mother and son embraced, their tears wetting each other's shoulders. The poignancy of the moment was not lost on the circle of family and friends around them as they honored the embrace with silence.

Elijah stepped over to his father and shook his hand, placing his other hand on his shoulder and speaking softly. "Thanks Dad. This means a lot."

"No problem, son. It was a privilege to meet Stephen and to help Tamara. In the end, it was more traumatic than complicated. They can't hold you for a crime when the actual thief is out robbing another liquor store. After the first robbery, the police paid particular attention to the other ABC stores, and sure enough, the dude tried to hold up the one over on Colony. A patrol officer walking out of the Harris Teeter saw the gray sedan in front of the liquor store, called for backup, and they took down the guy as he walked out of the store with a bag of money and a bottle of Jose Cuervo. Turns out, the gray car wasn't a Honda, it was a Mitsubishi; and it wasn't missing one hubcap, it was missing all four. When I arrived at the station, they were about to let Stephen and Sharon go anyway because the ticket stubs from the movie and the verification of the friends they sat with showed they were watching *The Heat* when the liquor store was hit. The only thing I did was expedite the process.

"You know, Elijah, the officers were just doing their jobs and Stephen will tell you that they treated him with respect. We have made a lot of progress in the 35 plus years I've been practicing law. Still, if you are a young African-American male brought into the justice system, and you don't have an advocate or a support system or resources? I wouldn't say you're screwed, but you're in for a rough ride for an indeterminate time and there aren't many statistics in your favor. We have come a long way from 1964 and Philadelphia, Mississippi, but we still have a long way to go before a black man can enter a store or walk the sidewalk of an affluent neighborhood without being looked at as a suspect."

"Well, thank you for what you do. I respect you more than you'll ever know."

As Stephen approached Taylor and Elijah to offer thanks, Elijah offered a roguish grin and a question. "Soooo, Stevie, apart from that, how was the movie?"

They snickered and shared the embrace of an adult mentor and young man, enjoying the evolution of a relationship from tutor/pupil to peers. Taylor convinced Elijah, Tamara, and Stephen to come and get some sleep at their place so that Tamara could catch up with Tess while Taylor took Elijah and Stephen out for a round of golf. Thus, a story that began in the surreal concludes in the surreal. One night a Park Scholar is mistaken for an armed robber and the next morning the handcuffs are gone and this same African American youth is stepping onto the first tee of the Charlotte Country Club.

Sunday morning dawned chilly and wet, a fact seemingly lost on Joab who was thrilled when Elijah donned his hat and raincoat and hooked him up for their morning saunter around the neighborhood. Joab looked up at a half-asleep Elijah, offering a single bark as if to say, "Come on, you old fart. So what if you get wet? Myself? I was made for this."

Elijah loves that dog, and though he'll occasionally grumble about it, he looks forward to these walks and has experienced them as a sacred time for centering and devotion. "All creatures of our God and King, lift up your voice and with us sing, Alleluia . . . Thou rising morn in praise rejoice . . . " As they crest the hill near the entrance to the park, Elijah looked back upon a slumbering Edinburgh as the brisk wet wind chills his cheekbones and he was struck with the notion that this dawn of a fall Sabbath could easily be just another summer Sabbath for the pastor of St. Giles, the *mother church* in the other Edinburgh across the pond.

It was hard to say what the day's weather would mean for attendance in worship. Cancelled outdoor plans would redirect some souls to church, but the chance to laze in bed on a rainy day could tip the balance in one's opinion of whether the Sabbath was set aside for rest or for the Lord. Augustine famously said, "You have made us for yourself, O Lord, and our hearts are restless until they rest in Thee." Well, at least for this day, the Spirit managed to ruffle enough hearts that the pews were well populated for worship at St. Martin. A traditional hymn of fall transformed disparate voices into one voice.

> We gather together to ask the Lord's blessing;
> He chastens and hastens His will to make known;
> The wicked oppressing now cease from distressing;
> Sing praises to His Name; He forgets not His own.

Turning on the pulpit light as he rose for the reading and proclamation of the Word, Elijah was struck by the contrast between the shalom of worship and the brokenness of the world he encountered on Friday night. As he offered the prayer of illumination and introduced the reading from Matthew 9, Elijah felt what he truly believed was true in the words of the Psalmist, "The Lord is our refuge and strength."

The Company You Keep

Reading from the Gospels: Matthew 9: 9-13

*As Jesus was walking along, he saw a man called Matthew sitting
at the tax booth; and he said to him, "Follow me." And he got up
and followed him. And as he sat at dinner in the house, many
tax collectors and sinners came and were sitting with him and his
disciples. When the Pharisees saw this, they said to his disciples,
"Why does your teacher eat with tax collectors and sinners?" But
when he heard this, he said, "Those who are well have no need
of a physician, but those who are sick. Go and learn what this
means, 'I desire mercy, not sacrifice.' For I have come to call not
the righteous but sinners."*

One: This is the Word of the Lord.

Many: Thanks be to God.

In villages, towns, and cities throughout Mexico and Guatemala, on December nights you will find families processing down the street, some with lighted candles in hand and others carrying on their shoulders statues of Mary and Joseph. They are sharing in the tradition of Las Posadas in which they reenact the exhausting effort of the carpenter and his pregnant fiance to get to Bethlehem and find shelter. As part of the ritual, the group approaches a home and knocks on the door singing, "I ask you for shelter, for my beloved wife can go no further." From inside the door, voices sing, "This is not an inn, go away. I cannot open the door to you, for you may be a rogue."

"I cannot open the door to you, for you may be a rogue." How easily those words become the creed of our lives as the alarms are triggered in our personal homeland security systems. Grace is imprisoned under the tyrannical rule of fear and suspicion.

Beware of strangers! It is an important lesson that we learn as children while our parents try so hard to protect us against all in this world that would threaten us. The news stories, of course, reinforce this lesson, showing us how the threats and the fears of strangers can be frighteningly real. And so we erect the walls and lock the doors. However, there are many times when we allow our fears to become the rationalization for excluding people from our lives who are really no threat at all. "Move on - I cannot open my life, my world, my heart to you lest you be a rogue." We judge. We degrade. We blame. We ignore. We legislate. We segregate. We criticize and proclaim as gospel these astounding over-generalized assumptions about the motivations and character and abundant sins of whole groups of people we have never met, and whose life circumstances we refuse to even attempt to understand. "I cannot open the door to you, for you may be a rogue."

There is a dangerous rising tide in North Carolina and across the land, threatening the well-being of the very people Christ so emphatically called us to serve. The common good is being drowned by a sea of self-interest and political gamesmanship. "I cannot open the door to you, for you may be a rogue."

We often associate the word "stranger" with someone we do not know. Yet in our daily walk we continually treat as strangers so many who cross our paths, some of whom we know quite well. We find all sorts of reasons, some confessed, some unconfessed, to separate ourselves, to arm ourselves, to insulate ourselves from the people who populate our world: Socio-economics; skin color; lifestyle differences; rumor and innuendo. By the time we enter adolescence we have learned well the lessons of separating and insulating ourselves from those who are different from us. In school we perfect the art of reducing people to categories: geeks, jocks, nerds, freaks, blacks, Hmongs, Hispanics, the rich, the welfare junkies, rednecks, girls with reputations, boys who walk or speak differently, etc.

Occasionally, the high school gym teacher manages to tear us from our cocoon, forcing us to join in a square dance with those to whom we would never speak in the school hallways. There aren't many things more objectionable to a high school senior than to be required to dress in gym clothes for a gym class on square dancing. Yet, at least we were forced to interact with those we would never come into contact with otherwise. However, for the most part we form our little circles and do not venture beyond the perimeter. "I cannot open the door to you, for you may be a rogue."

As we grow older that perimeter becomes more subtle but no less secure as we use everything from Myers-Briggs results to Biblical interpretation to zip code to preferred news channels, to the length of a school bus ride in order to justify separating ourselves from those who are different from us.

And then, someone like Jesus comes along, yes the child of Mary (that girl with the reputation). Yes, along comes someone like Jesus, the child Mary was carrying when she was excluded and denied shelter, and this Jesus proceeds to ignore every religious and social convention, sitting down to eat with the biggest variety of rogues you could put together in one room. Sinners and tax collectors, for gosh sakes! Oh the people he would hang out with: Prostitutes, paupers, Samaritans, and thieves. Sounds like an old song by Cher.

It is important to note that in the setting, time and context of Jesus' public teaching, when you sat down to eat with someone there was an implied social contract/covenant being made. To eat with someone, a most significant and intimate act, was to covenant or commit to being that person's friend for the rest of your lives. In other words, you had better think before you make reservations. To eat with him or her meant that you were open to the possibility that he or she would, in some way, be a part of your life for the rest of your life.

Do you realize the significance of what is happening here? Jesus, a teacher of the faith, was eating and making a life-long commitment to those who were considered ritually unclean; and to have contact with the ritually unclean was to render yourself ritually unclean, meaning, among other things that you would be barred from worship in the temple. And so we can understand the shock felt by the Pharisees, a group dedicated to keeping themselves unstained by the ritually unclean so that they would not miss any of the rituals of the temple.

They remembered what the psalmist had said, "the sinners [will not stand] in the congregation of the righteous." "God loves righteousness and hates wickedness." In shock and dismay because of the company Jesus was keeping, they turn to Jesus' disciples asking, "Why does your teacher eat with tax collectors and sinners?"

And hearing their consternation, Jesus censures their theology and our attitudes, "Those who are well have no need of a physician, but those who are sick. Go and learn what this means, 'I desire mercy, and not sacrifice.' For I came not to call the righteous, but sinners." In other words, our rituals don't mean much unless they flow from lives that are intentionally compassionate and habitually merciful. Jesus Christ is mercy personified, and so those who serve Christ will be those who are merciful.

Ignoring all of our social distinctions, class distinctions, lifestyle distinctions—nuking all the rationalizations we use to justify our prejudices—Jesus so easily makes himself comfortable in those places and among those people where we fear to tread.

I like the image of the physician here, because there is something about being in a doctor's office that acts as a great equalizer, shattering our distinctions and our pride and our prejudices. It's just hard to be too impressed with yourself in a waiting room when you have a specimen bottle in your hand or when you're sitting there half-naked in the examining room. Why does it remain so hard for us to learn that through the healing grace of the great Physician, those whose faults and failures we exaggerate and stereotype can become the friends we cherish? If we could just hear, truly hear and receive the lesson a rabbi of the Hasidic tradition offered a student's question about how to discern when the new day has begun. It isn't when the rooster crows or the light of the rising sun gives discernable shape to the tree. The rabbi said, "The surest way to know when the night is over and when a new day has come is when you can look into the face of a stranger, the one who is so different from you, and recognize him as your brother. See her as your sister. Until that day comes, it will always be night."[7]

Until we can understand that our well-being is tied to the well-being of the child in subsidized housing or the immigrant off of Nebo Road, it will always be night.

The savior's mother is turned away. "I cannot open the door to you, for you may be a rogue." Day after day we exclude people from our lives because in some way we consider them to be different, or inferior, or a threat. "I cannot open the door to you, for you may be a rogue."

How many times each day do we self-righteously exclude from our lives those who may be bearers of the grace of God?

I have shared with you before how my younger brother Zachary viewed the world through the eyes of autism. He was a beautiful boy and we found our way to be a family. Yet, now and then I could see the pain and strain in my parents' faces. It is so hard to not be able to connect with the child you love so dearly. Try as they might, we struggled to break through into Zachary's world.

My father came closer to finding a window than the rest of us. It began one morning when Dad set the sports page on the breakfast table while commenting on the reversal of fortune suffered by Mike Reid in the final round of the 1990 Greater Greensboro Open, dropping nine strokes to eventual winner Steve Elkington. Elkington shot 66 while Reid blew up with a 75. Something about the numbers clicked for Zachary. He looked up from his bowl of Lucky Charms, grabbed the sports page, and dove into the statistics. The numbers and the technical side of the game became his obsession. It was all so mysterious. He would memorize every statistic of the game for the rest of his days, right up until the accident that took his life.

One day Dad took Zachary out to the golf course to walk with him as he played nine holes as the evening sun faded from view and a new routine was firmly established. They walked those nine holes so many times and were often the only ones out on the course apart from the greenskeeper turning on the irrigation after they completed each hole. Cyrus Washington was his name and he had worked that course for forty years, his ebony face chalky and leathered from a life spent outdoors. He had this raspy voice that

---

7. As quoted in a sermon by Joanna Adams, Fourth Presbyterian Church, Chicago, April 21, 2002.

made him sound like an ancient jazz musician when he talked, and Cyrus talked often. The man was a walking archive of stories about the characters, crooks, movers, shakers, and saints whose Footjoys had clicked and clattered from cart paths to fairways, from the locker room to pro shop, from the 18th green to the 19th hole. Well, once Zachary started showing up with my father, Cyrus made it his mission to get through to him. Every time Cyrus saw Zachary, he'd go into this big dramatic greeting, calling him Professor Golf, the encyclopedia of the links. He gave Zachary one of the hats the caddies wore, and Zach wore that hat out. Cyrus would also sneak him the score cards of the club members once they'd been recorded. He said Zachary was the "official" statistician of the club. Of course, Zach memorized the numbers and Dad would duck his head in embarrassment when Zach would blurt out the handicaps of the golfers as they crossed paths in the parking lot or clubhouse. No context, just the numbers, so most of the golfers were none the wiser, assuming Zach was just this quirky kid. It was kind of funny, though. Dad and Zach would be ambling toward the pro shop and Zach would just blurt out "7" . . . "4" . . . "12." But his eyes would widen and his voice would crackle when the big handicaps walked past. "26!" "30!"

On one Thursday it was raining and Zachary was visibly upset because Dad cancelled his tee time. When Dad tried to console him, Zach spoke more clearly than he ever had. "But Cyrus needs me."

Do you know what it means to the parent of a child with autism, to hear that child verbalize a complete thought? It is a tremendous breakthrough, and when my father shared the story with Cyrus, why, you'd have thought he had won the lottery. Cyrus taped Zach's photo to the dash of the maintenance cart and cried harder than anyone at Zachary's funeral.

Typical parents of suburban affluence, a child with autism, and a 72-year-old son of sharecroppers who had once caddied for Bobby Jones. Very different life circumstances, circumstances usually marked by indifference to or prejudice against the one who will forever remain a stranger. "I cannot open the door to you, for you may be a rogue."

However, Cyrus, my father, and maybe even my brother, in his own way, would tell you that the well-being of one is dependent on the well-being of all.

After having been rejected at the doors of many residences, the weary travelers of Las Posadas approach one more door near the conclusion of the ritual. In celebration of the grace of God, this door is opened to them, the hosts welcoming them to a grand party, "Enter holy pilgrims, receive this corner, not my poor dwelling, but my heart."

Hundreds of years ago, no less a voice than John Calvin said, "There have always been those who, imbued with a false conviction of their own perfect sanctity . . . spurned association with all men in whom they discern any remnant of human nature . . . For where the Lord requires kindness, they neglect it and give themselves over completely to immoderate severity... "[8] Hundreds of years before that, the eminent Augustine wrote, "Unreasonable judgment becomes impious and proud; and it disturbs weak good men more than it corrects bold and bad ones."

And hundreds of years before that, when accused of partying with sinners, Jesus said, "Go and learn what this means, I desire mercy and not sacrifice." So when will we learn?

Isn't it interesting that in lowering *our* standards, *God* would increase our faith? Amen.

---

8. John Calvin, *Institutes of the Christian Religion*, IV, 1, 13.

4

Winter

WINTER SOLSTICE GARNERS SCANT attention in the life of the church because the Christmas Train is flying full speed through the station with no intention of stopping. For Elijah, December 21st serves only to remind him he'll be leaving for the gym in the darkness before dawn and returning from the church in the darkness after dusk. Like other parish shepherds across the land, by the first day of winter he has given up trying to make the distinction between Advent and Christmas for the people of his parish. By this point every effort to explain the separate sanctity of expectation and fulfillment, anticipation and incarnation, is met with ears that only hear, "Yada, yada, yada."

Though he won't admit it to his high-minded, liturgically sophisticated peers, Elijah is okay with that. Truth be told, each year he looks forward to the day after Thanksgiving so he can pull out his Nat King Cole Christmas collection and pop it in the CD player along with the Carpenters and the Vienna Boys' Choir. He loves Christmas and the whole glorious amalgam of the sacred, tacky, holy, and cheesy. One moment, he's lifting up the ancient prayerful hymn, "O Come, O Come, Emmanuel" and the next he's scouring the TV listings to find when the Charlie Brown Christmas special will be aired. One moment he is lighting an Advent wreath and the next he's covering the bushes with those newfangled nets of Christmas lights.

In life, I did not have the capacity to experience or understand the Christmas Spirit. In fact, I was more anxious and agitated, not because of over-scheduling and an infinite to-do list, but because of the frenzy of activity, the glare of blinking lights, and the unending assault of Christmas tunes.

T knew I would freak out when the Muzak at the mall offered yet again the voice of Mariah Carey chasing notes all over scale and proclaiming that youuuuuuu are the only item on her Christmas wish list. T would try to usher me out of the store before I started slapping my ears and shouting, "Make stop! Make stop!" But now, I see what they see and I hear what they hear and I experience what they hope for and it is all quite grand. But I still do wish that Mariah would find a different song for Christmas.

Hannah and Elijah have shared the spirit of Christmas together since kindergarten, two years before they made a pact not to reveal to their parents their doubts about the whole Santa enterprise.

T-minus 48 hours until what many see as the church's equivalent of the Super Bowl; opening night on Broadway; election night inside the Beltway; the Bubbas high holy days at Daytona. With the excitement of an eight-year-old Elijah reported, "Hannah! The paper says *A Charlie Brown Christmas* is on tonight! Ooooh rats! I have a stewardship meeting. Crap!"

Rolling her eyes, Hannah reminded him, "E, you do know we have the DVD, don't you?"

"Oh . . . right. You wanna watch it after the meeting?"

"I'll have the hot chocolate ready."

"I do love that show. When a distraught Charlie Brown pleads for someone to tell him the meaning of Christmas. And, ever so calm, Linus walks to the center of the stage, asks for the house lights to be turned down, and recites the King James Version of Luke's nativity . . . It gives me chills. That's gospel. That boy can preach, blanket and all."

"You have mentioned that before . . . (muttered) maybe a hundred times."

Unfazed, Elijah continues, "What ignites the Christmas spirit in you these days?"

"O, the usual, I guess. All the little things. The families lighting the Advent wreath in worship; the Muzak in the Hallmark store playing Amy Grant, James Taylor, Perry Como. I love all the music, really: everything from *Lo, How a Rose E'er Blooming* to the Drifters singing *I'm Dreaming of a White Christmas*."

"Don't forget Nat King Cole! Christmas isn't Christmas without Nat King Cole."

"What about Jesus?" Zing, preacher boy. Take that.

"Well yeah . . . that too."

"I love decorating the tree even though I don't get much help from you on that. I love Xani's excitement, your mom's Chex mix, Jimmy Stewart and Zuzu's petals . . . I love the brisk wind on my cheeks and snow under my feet, even though we don't see much of the white stuff around here. I love the memories of Christmas on the farm. Hot cider after evening chores in the barn. Lying awake and hearing my dad swear while putting together some toy on Christmas Eve. The man could take a tractor apart and put it back together but the Easy-Bake Oven and the slot car race track gave him fits."

"I remember you giving free Christmas carriage rides through Laddonia, riding by all the houses that had put up Christmas lights outside."

"Short ride."

"Except for that time you took me for a long ride out that gravel road behind the school."

"Yeah, I didn't think you'd ever figure out that it was the perfect place to make out."

"It wasn't so much that I was clueless and slow all the time. Truthfully . . . I was terrified."

"Terrified?"

"I don't know that I ever confessed to you how intimidating it was for me to transition from friend to boyfriend. Being your friend has always been easy, so natural. But, you are so beautiful, and the fact that you live so unaware of it makes you even more beautiful. I had a hard time coming to believe you could see me as more than a friend. Every guy in your high school stopped dead in his tracks when you walked by."

"Nooo."

"Yes. Your brother told me. There were a couple of guys who left football practice with broken noses because they were expressing their lust for you a little too graphically."

"Todd? He never told me that."

"He said that he once saw the principal let his eyes linger on you a little too long in the cafeteria. Said it creeped him out, but he wasn't going to slug the principal, because the prospect of a diploma for him was still on the board in Vegas."

"No way."

"Yes way. And do you remember the conference finals in the hurdles your junior year?"

"Yes. I won by at least ten meters, but my time was only .2 seconds faster than second place."

"Uh huh . . . You know why your time was only two tenths faster?"

"No. I mean hand timing isn't exact . . ."

"Yes. It is particularly inexact when the timer forgets to stop his watch because he's staring at your booty. You're lucky you didn't trip over Ol' Coach Brown's tongue when you crossed the finish line. He didn't have a clue about what your time was. He just made something up!"

"Who told you that?"

"You may have forgotten that my Uncle Billy was acting as the head timer that day. He said that when Coach Brown reported your time, it was a half second slower than third place, so he knew something was up. When Billy pressed him about it, the old coach said, 'Aw hell, Billy, how can you expect me not to get distracted. If your eyes are choosing between that ass and a stopwatch, what do you think is going to get your attention?' So, Billy changed the time to ensure that first place was at least faster than second place. Who knows, you could have set a record."

"I knew something was weird about that time."

"Anyway, Hannah, you are bewitchingly beautiful. You are irresistibly enchanting. Heck, even my gay sister says you are bodacious. I know there are a whole lot of people in this world in disbelief that you settled for some no name kid from Charlotte."

"You are crazy, Elijah Parish. I'm just your average redneck girl from Nowheresville, USA, smack dab in the middle of flyover country. I was always afraid I'd embarrass you. You were probably worried that I'd burp, fart, or cuss in front of your debutante friends, or even worse, the ladies of Circle #6. Truth is, at some point I probably accomplished all three. E, Lord only knows how intimidating it is to be your wife. A couple of the blue-hairs in the widows' pew look at you like you're a Chippendale dancer."

"Well, if I ever lose you, it's good to know I'll have a shot at wooing the geriatric set."

"Watch out for Widow Wilson. If you try to make a move on her, I'll haunt you from the grave. E, if anyone is intimidated in this relationship, it has to be me. You seem to be forgetting that I'm Eliza Doolittle and you're Professor Higgins in this story."

"Now wait a minute, Henry Higgins was an officious jerk as I recall."

"Okay, bad example, but you know what I mean. When you would come out to see me during high school with your rumpled Ralph Lauren shirts and your sophisticated city boy haircut and your smooth as sweet tea way with words, I felt like I was dating a celebrity. Everybody thought you were so exotic, so cool."

"They were sadly mistaken. And don't even try to pull that whole Charlene-Darlin-I-was-just-a-lump-of-coal-until-you-found-me act. You were the salutatorian of your class and had a mailbox full of love letters from Washington University's admissions office."

"I still think those were form letters."

"Well, let's just say they loved your form. I know I do. I do love Christmas and I do love you."

"You've always been my love and you are so stuck with this redneck."

"Be still my heart."

With that, Elijah planted a big sloppy on Hannah's lips and headed out while Hannah washed out her cereal bowl and walked down the hall to roust the children from bed to join in the liturgy of Christmas break. Madison was coming over to take Xani to the library while Hannah loaded Nathan and a sandwich bag full of Cheerios into his car seat for the mad dash of errands that needed to be completed on this first day out of school. A teacher with young children had better carb up and carry a bottle of Gatorade, because for him or her, there is no break during the break. For teachers, the break means plowing through all the to-dos not done since the start of school in August. Hannah had on her game face and was girded for the day's battle. She taped her list to the dashboard, slipped *How the Grinch Stole Christmas* into the DVD player for Nathan, and navigated the Pilot out into the maelstrom of panicking Christmas consumers. Ever organized, Hannah had completed most of her Christmas shopping during a trip to Charlotte's Southpark Mall with T a few Saturdays ago. So, today's tour of Edinburgh was all about baking supplies, perishable foods, Christmas cards, and an oil change.

It promised to be a long day for Elijah. He had bribed Jimmy Suddreth with the promise of a round of golf at the Charlotte Country Club if Jimmy would join him on what he was calling his Incarnation/Incarceration Tour. Christmas, the celebration of Christ's incarnation, promised to be a hard and lonely day for Josie Ellerbe. He couldn't change that because his family would be headed out of town, but he could take this day to shepherd her to the various institutions holding her family members.

The first stop would be up in Lenoir, where her son Frank was sitting in the Caldwell Correctional Facility just a few miles from the security camera at the ABC Store that had filmed his latest conviction winning performance. The second stop would take them up into the mountains and Banner Elk where Trace and Dickie were on the roll of the Grandfather Home for Children, a Presbyterian-affiliated home for troubled and at-risk children. Here, Josie would be able to see the boys sing in the annual Christmas program.

After the last fa la la, they would get on Highway 221 and head down the mountain to the women's prison in Marion where Shania would be spending the next few years plotting how to reclaim the methamphetamine market in the foothills. St. Martin was hosting a Christmas party for the inmates, carrying coolers filled with the makings for banana splits through the locked gates and razor wire along with songbooks filled with Christmas hymns and quilted blankets made by Circle #3 for the prisoners. The occasion would provide Josie the chance to spend some time with Shania, who in a short time had established herself as the baroness of bartering and bribing.

Jimmy suggested they take one of the Cadillacs from the funeral home because it would be a challenge to hoist Josie into Elijah's Jeep.

"Wouldn't it be a riot to pull up to the prison in a hearse?" Jimmy asked.

"Well, I hear there are a couple of women in Marion still waiting to find out if they are getting a death sentence, so it might hit a little too close to home."

"I guess you're right. Of course, the last time Josie saw this sedan, she was riding in it to her son's funeral."

"I hadn't thought about that. Do you think she'll be willing to ride in it today?"

"Absolutely. Even after the S.W.A.T. team carried her daughter away, Josie was sitting tall and proud in the back seat of this car. You could tell it made her feel significant, like she was somebody. She kept rubbing her hands on the leather seat as though she had been given the privilege of riding in the Queen's limo. I put in a CD of classical music and you'd have thought I was chauffeuring Elizabeth Taylor."

When they wheeled Josie out of her federally subsidized apartment and she saw the Cadillac, her eyes brightened like a child greeting her new horse. She had Jimmy take a picture of her in front of the Cadillac, and Elijah thought he heard her giggle as they slid her into the back seat. He later told Hannah that he thought Josie enjoyed the ride as much as the visits.

As expected, the visits bordered on the bizarre. The deputy sheriff in charge of the Caldwell County Jail that day was Officer Irene Fesperman whose stupefyingly striking appearance rendered new acquaintances flabbergasted and flushed. As Josie presented her I.D. to the deputy, Jimmy leaned over to Elijah and murmured, "Are you thinking what I'm thinking?"

"*The Longest Yard* . . . the first one. Yes sir, we're looking at Bernadette Peters, the warden's secretary."

"What would you call that get up?"

"I don't know . . . boobaliscious and beehived?"

Jimmy doubled over in laughter, swiftly drawing the stink eye from Officer Irene.

"Cheese it, Jimmy, the cops!" Elijah alerted his undertaker friend with a forceful whisper.

Rising back up to attention like a chastened frat boy, Jimmy tried to speak quietly through a clenched fake smile, "Boobalicious and beehived . . . that's perfect. How much hairspray do you think she used this morning?"

"I don't know, but if she's missing a toaster, I know where she could find it."

Again, Jimmy doubled over giggling, and again, Officer Irene gave him the stink eye. "Is there a problem, boys?"

Danged if she didn't sound like a cross between Betty Boop and Paula Dean!

Straightening up yet again, Jimmy grasped for an excuse, "No ma'am, uh I mean Officer. The Reverend and I were just talking about that new Melissa McCarthy movie, *The Heat*. It's hilarious! Have you seen it?"

"Didn't care for it. Wasn't funny. The Reverend shouldn't be watching movies like that anyway."

"No ma'am . . . uh Officer. You are right. I made him go. He . . . wouldn't have gone on his own."

"An accessory to a crime is still guilty."

"Yes ma'am . . . uh Officer."

The buxom badged beehive returned her attention to processing Josie for her visit.

"She's gonna lock you up, Jimmy."

"You'd like that, wouldn't you? Anyway, it's your fault . . . making me laugh and all. You may wear a robe but you sure ain't innocent. However, she is a piece of work. How in the world do you think she got that blouse buttoned this morning?"

"I don't know, but if I were you, I'd stand to the side, because if she busts a button, somebody's going down."

That did it. Jimmy lost it and ran outside howling.

Josie now processed, Officer Irene Fesperman directed her gaze toward Elijah and asked, "You boys, wantin' to visit the prisoner also? If so, you'd better retrieve the laughing Hercules out there so I can process you, too."

"Oh, I think Mr. Suddreth will wait out here while Miss Ellerbe and I visit with her son. We shouldn't be long. Neither one of them talk that much."

Once processed, Elijah wheeled Josie through two secured and barred doors. In between the two doors, a second officer collected all the contents of their pockets and relieved Josie of her purse. After being cleared by the metal detector, they were allowed to enter a common area where families could commiserate with their incarcerated blood kin.

Josie opened the tap for the waterworks as soon as she saw Frank.

"My baby! My baby!"

"Shit, Mom, I ain't your baby. I'm forty-four years old."

"Are you well, son?"

"Drier than a turd in the sun. Ain't like they ever wheel a keg in here, you know."

"But, you're okay?"

"I'm thirsty, Mom, real thirsty."

"I've been a prayin' for ya, Frank."

"Well then, why don't you pray that one of those guards or Dolly Parton out there passes out long enough for me to get the hell out of here? I'll tell ya, Preacher, there is one thing you could do for me."

"Yes, Frank?"

"I could use a Bible, a thick one."

"I think they are all the same length, Frank."

"Yeah, but some of 'em are heftier, thicker, you know?"

Elijah sensed there was an angle here. There was always an angle with Frank. With a sideways glance, he asked. "Frank, you found God?"

"Oh yeah, sure, Preacher. Me and God is tight, but what I really need is one of those fat Bibles." Leaning in with a whisper, Frank continued, "Now, don't say anything or nuthin', course, you ain't supposed to 'cause of one of those preacher rules, but you see, I saw a movie once where a guy cut out a hole in the middle of his Bible because that would be the last place the guards looked. He hid a small rock hammer in the hole and used it to dig through the wall and escape. When those guards and the boob queen there ain't lookin', that's what I aim to do."

"Frank, you're talking about *The Shawshank Redemption*, and it took that guy nineteen years to dig his way out. If you behave, you can get out of here in a year."

"You let me worry about that. You just concentrate on getting me that Bible. I saw a little pick hammer in the workroom I can steal."

"Frank, Lord knows I hate refusing a man a Bible, but you'll have to get 'the fat edition' of the Holy Word on your own. Is there anything else you want to say to your mother who came all the way up here to see you?"

"Nah. Next time bring some cookies; and don't say nothin' about what I told you."

"Right. Clergy—Church member confidentiality." Elijah wasn't worried about Frank's prison break. Frank wasn't going anywhere.

Josie just sat there and took it, just as she'd been taking it from her kids for years. While Josie is no angel and is known to drain those from whom she can extract benevolence, nobody deserves what her kids do to her. Her parenting skills were lacking, but it was never malevolence or indifference. She loved her children, but she just didn't have the tools to parent them.

As Elijah wheeled Josie back through the series of security doors and picked up their belongings, he noticed that Miss Boobalicious Beehive was bent over with her head buried in a filing cabinet. As they moved through the lobby, she didn't move or show any awareness of their presence. Maybe Frank could bust out of this place. Seeing her all hunched over and oblivious

to their foot traffic, Elijah guessed that filing required laser focus or could it
be that gravity had taken its toll and she could no longer bear the weight of
her coiffure and cleavage.

It was then that Jimmy caught his eye. Elijah had never seen that look
on Jimmy's face before: face drained of blood, saucer-sized eyes staring
a hole through Elijah. Sheer panic, as if a corpse suddenly sat up in one
his caskets; as if the dearly departed had asked for a glass of wine during
embalming.

"Are you okay, Jimmy?"

Jimmy abruptly shook his head no, took over command of the wheelchair and whizzed Josie out to the Cadillac like a paramedic bolting toward
the ambulance with a stretcher. He literally picked Josie up and sat her up in
the backseat with the ease of a parent negotiating a carseat. He then closed
the door, turned, took hold of a confused Elijah by the shoulders, pulled his
face up close, and in a voice both freaked out and frightened, squealed, "She
. . . she came on to me!"

"What? Who? What?"

"Beehive! She came on to me."

"Now, Jimmy, you've had women flirt with you before."

"No. This wasn't flirting. She came on to me, and I mean literally. She
asked me to come behind the counter to help her move the desk and as soon
as I entered, she backed me into a filing cabinet and jumped on me. Said she
was from Honea Path, South Carolina and her daddy used to take her to all
the Clemson football games. She said she had my picture on her wall as a
teen and wanted my notch in her bedpost now!"

"Sooo . . . what did you do?"

"What did I do? I got the hell out of there. Told her I had a heart condition and needed to go take a nitro pill because my ticker was showing its
temper."

"Quick thinking."

"Thank God, because she had a gun. I must have walked around the
block twenty times waiting for y'all. She scares me."

"Oh, the spells you cast over women."

"Hey, look at me. I stopped casting spells about twenty pounds ago."

"Are you kidding? You're an Adonis. Look at you. I can't wait to see the
reaction you get down at the women's prison."

"Oh crap!"

"Well, lover boy, we had better head up the mountain and hope we
don't get behind a truck on 321 so that we can make it to Grandfather Home
in time for the program. One question, though . . . "

"What?"

"Were they real?"

"Shut up, Reverend!"

The drive up to Banner Elk was smooth and quiet as Josie meditated on the mess of the Ellerbe clan and Jimmy sat in the state of stunned silence characteristic of someone suffering from post-traumatic-freak-out syndrome.

The setting of Grandfather Home for Children belies the life experiences of its residents. Wrapped in lush postcard mountains that beckon Floridians and the 1% in summer and skiers and church youth groups in winter, there aren't many people who wouldn't covet a condo, cabin, or chalet in this corner of the Carolinas. People of means who are within driving distance have played its golf courses, hiked its trails, skied its slopes, and dined in its restaurants. They have purchased Smarties, Tootsie Rolls, Pendleton blankets, Vasque boots, and Woolrich sweaters at the quaint Mast General Store in Valle Crucis; they have walked across the swinging bridge atop Grandfather Mountain; they have tailgated before football games at Appalachian State; taken ski lessons at Sugar and Beech mountains; sliced a drive in Linville while the kids hiked around the Falls; they have supped at Twigs or Timberlake's; and sipped Scotch at Headwaters before finding sleep at Chetola.

While one would assume ubiquitous Tarheel familiarity with the landmarks of the Blue Ridge, a conversation about them would leave the residents of Grandfather Home with vacant stares. Their world held no such delights. Prior to their arrival, their days had been spent falling further behind in school, suffering the stigma of special ed and free lunch, and finding trouble around each corner. Nights had been occupied with the futile attempt to evade a blow to the head, a cigarette burn to the chest, a front row seat for the interactive theater of their parents' drunken rage.

A casual observer would label Trace and Dickie as profane, incorrigible, out of control, and destined for prison time. However, the teachers, house parents, chaplains, and social workers at Grandfather Home possess the unique capacity to see the hidden and tarnished nugget of grace within even the hardest cases. While the boys intimidated the hell out of Elijah, the chaplain at Grandfather, a classmate of Elijah's in seminary, had gone spelunking in the cave of their life experience and mined a glimmer of light in their deep darkness.

The Rev. Amy O'Connor is an authentic Southie, which ironically is the opposite of a southerner. She was raised in that notoriously tough blue collar, economically challenged enclave on the south side of Boston where beer is mother's milk and profanity is the patois. Amy is tough, streetwise, regularly crude, and the antithesis of a Southern lady. Her roommate throughout seminary was Mary Margaret Davidson, a graduate of Sweet Briar, making them the oddest couple in the history of Union Seminary. Amy was abandoned by her birth mother, sexually abused as a child by an alcoholic uncle, and generally ignored by her father. Having raised herself, she ran away from home at the age of seventeen and didn't look back, working her way through college as a waitress and seminary as a bartender. Rough-edged, but with a malleable heart and a keen eye for justice, Amy couldn't find a fit in parish ministry but discovered her calling at Grandfather, approaching the students, not with sympathy but solidarity.

"Hey asshole, thanks for nothing. What were you thinking when you sent me Dillinger and Capone? The little felons are driving me bat-shit crazy!" Said simultaneously with cheesy grin, Amy grabbed Elijah with an exaggerated bear hug. Noticing Jimmy, she bellowed, "Damn! Who's the saucy Porterhouse steak? Can I touch his chest . . . for starters?"

"Whoa there, Amy, he's already been deflowered by one fully grown woman today. He's a little shaken."

"I can't wait to hear about that!"

Jimmy deadpanned, "You have no idea."

"Well, if you can dump the preacher, I get off at 4:00."

"Sorry, he's my ride. Amy, let me introduce you to my friend Jimmy Suddreth. If you're nice to him, he may give you a discount on a casket."

"Oh, I can be real nice . . . Hey, I did a funeral for a student's grandmother at Suddreth's last summer, but I didn't see you. I'd have remembered that!"

"I'm sure we both would have enjoyed meeting."

"Not to interrupt your witty banter," Elijah interjected, "but what are we dealing with here?"

"Well, in their first week here, they managed to steal the director's iPad, take a joy ride in the groundskeeper's Gator, and escape one night, only returning the next morning because they were cold, hungry, and unsuccessful at thumbing for a ride."

"Yikes."

"But they started getting the hang of things once they figured out we weren't going to slug them; or maybe it would be more accurate to say, once we figured out how to hack into their software. It's amazing to uncover what's underneath all the shit they've been submerged in from the day they were born—alcoholism, drugs, meth labs, verbal and physical abuse. Anyone looking at their file will tell you that if they weren't here, they'd soon be on their way to the High Rise in Morganton. They may still wind up there, but there's something underneath that's worth exploring as long as we can keep them here.

"Trace? Yes, he's crass and incredibly rude. Makes me look like Mary Poppins, but, you know, he's smart. He has a natural aptitude for the sciences. There's a physics professor from Appalachian State that volunteers here, helping the kids prepare for the Science Olympiad. He's been working with Trace on this event called the flying bird. Using balsa wood, rubber bands, and crepe paper, you engineer an actual flying bird. This is waaay beyond the balsa wood air disasters we made as kids. These damn things have actual flapping wings. When they launch the bird, it doesn't just coast to the ground; it elevates. And not only that, it follows a circular flight pattern as it gains altitude. Here's the kicker, they design it to gain altitude but not too much altitude because they don't want it to hit the roof trusses of the gym. Of course, the goal is to keep the bird airborne the longest. The professor told me that Trace's bird is already flying longer than the winner of the regional high school division last year. In just a few months, he's gone from flipping everybody the bird to amazing everyone with his bird."

Picking his jaw up off the ground, Elijah exclaimed, "That's amazing! Maybe I should have picked up a model airplane kit instead of a football for Josie to give him."

"Hell no! He'd be sniffing the glue. You stick with the football and we'll stick with the balsa wood."

"You know, I'm not totally surprised. Even though his daddy looks, acts, talks, and walks like an empty-headed doofus, a lot of that is an act. He's sneaky smart. You don't manufacture all that meth without blowing your house up, or develop the drug network he developed without a brain; a twisted, abusive brain, maybe, but a brain nonetheless. I hate to think what those kids watched from day to day. You wouldn't think they have a chance in this world, but for the grace they find here."

Shifting to the other Ellerbe, Amy said, "Like Trace, Dickie is as refined as a sewage treatment plant, but a lot of his vulgarity is a strange combination of a defense mechanism against Trace and an emulation of Trace. There is a very delicate compassionate soul lurking in there. We have a couple of therapy dogs here and he has taken to the golden retriever like a gearhead to a Ferrari. We have another volunteer here who rescues and places abused and abandoned dogs from all over the country. She even had a few of Michael Vick's dogs a few years back. You won't find a more wonderful, gentle woman, and she has taken Dickie under her wing and every day after school, she takes him over to her place and he works with those dogs with the same care that he receives from his therapist here . . . Don't get me wrong, we still have problems, but they are a witness to John's promise: 'The light shines in the darkness and the darkness did not overcome it.'"

Jimmy observed, "I hate to say it, but I know we're all thinking it; the best thing that could happen to those boys would be that they not return to their parents."

Amy answered, "Well, we'll work with them as long as we have them, but Elijah and I took the same theology class in seminary, and in the Presbyterian/Reformed view of the world, there's this thing we call total depravity. The folks we call white trash are no less righteous than the folks we call saints. Everybody shits sin. So our hope for those boys, no less than for ourselves, is that God does for us what we could not do for ourselves in Christ. So, I can't say what's ahead for any of these kids, but there is always grace."

Jimmy queried, "The saints are sinners and the sinners are saints?"

Elijah offered, "Well, maybe something more like, the saints are sinners and all sinners have the potential of saints, not because of our virtue but because of God's grace at work in us."

Jimmy replied, "Well, it's nice to know I have potential."

Elijah smirked, "Potential may be too big a word for you."

"Shut up, preacher."

"Luv ya, Jimmy."

"Ah, your love is like a hemorrhoid. It flames hot and irritates."

"Ever the poet. Let's get grandma. Thanks for all you do, Amy."

Amy waved them off saying, "It's like watching Beavis and Butthead walking into the sunlight."

When they found Josie, she was being hugged by Trace and Dickie, a poignant sentence in an otherwise grim novel. The Grandfather Home Christmas program had proceeded without incident, though at the conclusion of *We Wish You a Merry Christmas*, Dickie shouted out his imitation of Porky Pig, "ba-dee, ba-dee, ba-dee, that's all folks!" Yes, indeed, everybody is a hot mess.

They said their goodbyes and put Josie on her throne in the back of the Cadillac, pointing the car down the mountain toward the women's prison in Marion. Up to this point, Josie had remained mostly silent and pensive, but her reunion with the boys seemed to lift her spirits. Elijah took advantage of the opening to probe into the complex narrative of Josie's journey. "Josie, you grew up in Caldwell County, didn't you?"

"Yeah, lived in a two-bedroom shotgun house on the edge of Lenoir."

"Did you have any siblings?"

"There was eight of us. Three boys. Five girls."

"Wow! I had no idea . . . I don't remember meeting any of them at the funeral."

"Four of 'em is dead. One's in jail. Two of 'em were at the funeral home after you left, but neither made it to the graveside."

"Where did you fall in the line?"

"I'm the baby, number eight. My sister Eunice got the cancer and died when she was seventeen. My sister Mary was shot and kilt by her boyfriend when he found out she was pregnant. My brother Tom shot hisself after he got back from Viet Nam. My brother Sonny died of cirrhosis of the liver. My brother Bull is up at the Central Prison in Raleigh after beating a man to death in a bar fight in Granite Falls."

"A lot of heartache."

"Life ain't been no picnic, that's for sure."

"I'm so sorry."

"Tain't nothin' to fret about, 'cause it just is what it is."

"Josie, I know you are not feeling it now, but you are a mighty strong woman."

"Had to be. Had to grow up early. Mama did upholstery work at Broyhill and Daddy was always drunk or gone or both. I liked it best when he was gone."

"Was he an angry drunk?"

"Yep, and I have the X-rays to prove it. There was the broken arm when I was three; a broken orbital bone when I was ten; a couple of broken ribs the next year; and finally, a broken collarbone and nose when he found out about me bein' pregnant with Sam. He took off after that incident and never came back. Yeah, it was a lot better when he was gone, at least for a while."

"How did he not get taken away for child abuse?"

"Things was a little different back then. A lot of the bad stuff was just swept under the carpet. Anyway, Mama covered for him a lot, even though she was taking a worse beating than me."

"Why did she cover for him?"

"Well, it sure weren't love, I can tell you that. She was afraid. She knew he'd kill her and the rest of us before he went to jail."

"What a painful story!"

"Yeah. But it's the only story I got. It is what it is. I'm still payin' for it, though. I swear, this arthritis and my back problems gotta be connected to the beatings I took from Daddy, and of course, my husband Dickie took over where my father left off. Three broken vertebrae, a broken wrist, two more broken ribs, and a busted eardrum."

Jimmy chimed in, "And a partridge in a pear tree?"

"Something, like that. But the worst one was when Daddy found out about Sam."

"What happened?"

"I never mentioned to you that Sam wasn't Dickie's. When I was fifteen and tired of being hungry all the time, I took on a job sweepin' floors at the high school. My Uncle Hubert was one of the janitors there and got me the job. I'd work three to four hours after school, sweepin' classrooms, halls, the cafeteria and the gym. Sometimes it took five hours, but they only paid me for four, so I worked those brooms as fast as I could. One day, I was jes' dog tired, so it was taking me longer than normal. I thought I was the last one in the building, but wasn't scared or nothin'. It wasn't the first time I had to turn the lights out as I left. I jes' kept on sweepin' until I finished and went to put my brooms up in the storage closet. I was jes' whistlin' a happy tune. I enjoyed that quiet time to myself, no one yellin', no one fightin'. There was always so much noise in our house. Bein' in the school all by myself felt so peaceful; no one to tell me what I was doin' wrong; no one to tell me I was a loser.

"You know, daydreamin' can be a great escape, but it wasn't enough of an escape that night. It was December, around this time, and so it was dark outside, and it was dark in that windowless closet, too. I remember not searchin' for the light switch because there was enough light from the hallway to step over to where the brooms were kept. Except, as soon as I stepped in, the door suddenly closed behind me. It was pitch black and I froze in my tracks. Before my mind could catch up, I felt a knife at my throat and heavy breathin' in my ear. Somethin' pulled my arms back and forced me against the wall. I heard the light switch flip and was blinded by the sudden light as the guy turned me around . . . but I already knowed who it was. It was Uncle Hubert. He threw me down and raped me. Only took him about 20 seconds, but it seemed like forever. Before he got off me, he let the knife scrape against my neck enough to draw blood and he put his mouth next to my ear. I'll never forget this. He said, 'Let's just call that scratch a hickie, but if you say anything to anyone, I'll take this knife to your pretty little neck and slice it all the way through.'

"That was the last time I set foot in that school. After layin' out over three weeks, one of the teachers saw my daddy downtown and asked if I had been sick. He ran straight home working up a good head of steam by the time he found me behind the shed out back of the house. I think he was swingin' before he even got close to me. 'Course, by then I jes' knowed I was pregnant, and so I curled up in a ball to protect my stomach.

"He called me a no account waste of oxygen and demanded to know why I was playin' hooky. So, I told him and that's when he really got mad. Called me a whore and claimed it was all my fault. He said I probably had seduced Hubert, and was probably lying about it being him anyway. Said Hubert wouldn't have taken it if I hadn't given it. That's when he gave me a roundhouse to the nose and I blacked out. Sam was born 8 months later."

A pall of silence, almost reverence, pervaded the interior of the Cadillac, Elijah and Jimmy were both stunned and sensed this story deserved the same mute honor called for when touring a battlefield like Gettysburg or Normandy or a site like the 9/11 Memorial or Arlington Cemetery.

When Presbyterians affirm their faith and recite that puzzling description of Christ, *He descended into hell*, they are saying there is no place we can go, no place we can plunge that Christ would not go with us. Josie's faith was not the product of some fundamentalist threat of damnation. Why would Josie be afraid of hell when so much of her life had been lived there already? No, it was clear to Elijah in that moment that Josie's deep faith was based on knowledge of Christ's presence deep inside the gates of Hell. Josie had participated in every Bible study Elijah had taught at St. Martin, not because of Elijah's pedagogical mastery, but because the scriptures are the buoyancy that kept her from drowning. Her continuing presence in the community of faith is a contemporary template of Job's declaration: "For I know that my Redeemer lives, and that at the last he will stand upon the earth." Her perseverance and survival are a true product of the pilgrim's psalm: "I lift up my eyes to the hills; from where will my help come? My help comes from the Lord, who made heaven and earth."

Elijah was equally stunned by the dispassionate and detached manner in which Josie could relate such a horrific story. It was as though she was speaking of a recipe for biscuits or the weather forecast for the weekend. No rise in emotions. Calm. Matter-of-fact. Was she just numb to it all, anesthetized by time, her wounds having become calloused and impenetrable? Or was detaching herself from the narrative, as though she was speaking of someone else, the only way she could maintain the will to draw a breath? Yet, there was a peace about her that, while unsettling to others, seemed to detoxify such poisonous memories. Was it her conviction that what Christ said is true? "I will not leave you desolate, even to the end of the age."

It would be Jimmy who broke the silence before it became awkward. "Josie, I played football at the highest level of collegiate sports and I never came across anyone as tough as you, taking all those hits and still waking up each morning to face the day. Amazing. Now, I may not look it, but I can still bring it if called upon. I want you to know that if I were ever to come across Hubert or Dickie #1, I'd beat the living shit out of them, and you can rest assured that I know how to bury a body."

"Well, that's right nice of ya, but you're too late. They both died some years ago. But I'll tell you what, you pick me up in this Cadillac one day and we'll go over to Lenoir and you and me can spit on their graves."

"Sure thing! . . . I have to ask you, though, did you go to their funerals?"

"Hell yeah! Free food! I sure wasn't going to inherit anything from those bastards, so I figured I should at least get a couple of chicken legs and some tater salad!"

Elijah laughed out loud and the other two joined in. "Josie, you are a character!" Softening the edges of the conversation, Elijah said, "I knew your story was tough, but I had no idea about the depths of your suffering. From this moment on, I can't imagine seeing you in the congregation without thinking of the words of the great old hymn or sing the hymn without thinking of you. "Thou wast their rock, their fortress, and their might; thou Lord, their captain in the well-fought fight; thou in the darkness drear, their one true light."

"Thank you, preacher, that's one of my favorites. You mind if we stop for a bathroom break?"

Jimmy saw a halfway promising convenience mart up ahead and pulled in. Elijah said, "Josie, I'll run in to see if they have adequate facilities for you and come back out to get you." Josie could still stand and walk a few steps as long as there was a grab bar or something to hold onto. The clerk at the convenience mart was most gracious in making sure that the bathroom was clean enough for Josie to negotiate.

While they waited for Josie, Elijah and Jimmy purchased Cokes and Nabs, pondering all they had just heard. Jimmy said, "Wow, that was some story! Sounds like she's been to hell and forgot the way back. I can't believe she does as well as she does."

"You know, Jimmy, periodically, a church member requests a word with me about Josie, and I know they are not coming to compliment her shoes. You see, when members meet Josie for the first time, they see a woman in a wheelchair and their heartstrings are tugged, particularly when they learn she lives alone in subsidized housing with no family members up to the task of taking care of her. They resolve that they are going to find some way to help her and they come back with beaming faces and glowing reports of how good it made them feel to clean her apartment, take her a meal, pay her utility bill, or take her to the doctor.

"These happy reports continue . . . for a time. Sooner or later, though, I will be pulled aside at a covered dish supper or someone will just happen to 'drop by.' With solemn faces and conflicted voices they lean close to me and say something like, 'I think you need to know that Josie is becoming a problem for me . . .' Then, the concern expressed follows one of the various available tracks:

- 'I took her to the doctor three times and she called me again yesterday. I can't keep doing this.'

- 'I fixed the leak in her bathroom and replaced a few linoleum tiles in the kitchen, and fixed the toaster. Paid for the materials myself . . . and so yesterday she calls me again, not to say thanks, mind you, but to ask if I could fix the wobble in the dinette table. I mean, preacher, I've got a day job. I can't keep doing this.'"

Elijah continued, "I don't have any problem with the idea that helping others makes someone feel good, but compassion based solely on return on investment is inevitably bankrupt. Ministry in the community of faith is not sustainable if everyone just wants to make a cameo appearance. They want to take a turn at compassion with the idea that the need will go away. I don't fault them for limited energy. Lord knows, we all "flag in zeal," but when we start resenting people for being in need, we're entering into dangerous territory because if heaven's economy was based on whether God gets that 'feel good' sensation from our response to his gifts, God would have burned out and given up long ago. Josie's needs are not going to go away. She is not going to get better or become more independent. So, if we're going to be the community of faith, reflective of God's grace, burning out is not an option. We have to figure out what we can do on a sustainable level and practice it without being able to see an end point."

"No arguments here, Preacher man," Jimmy responded with a wry smile and a wink just as Josie exited the restroom. Elijah handed her a Diet Coke because Josie drinks Diet Coke like a drunk drinks Thunderbird. As soon as the Goodyears of the Cadillac hit the pavement of the highway, Elijah's phone rang.

"Hey, Mark. What's up?" The informal greeting was followed by several "uh-huhs," and finally, "I think you're right. That's what we'll plan to do. Thank you for your generous gift to those folks tonight. That is most gracious. Take care."

Following a ponderous sigh, Elijah screwed on the most empathic smile he could muster and turned toward the back seat. "Josie, that was Mark McArthur. You know he's coordinating the hot fudge Christmas party at the prison tonight." Yes, Mark McArthur, the retired but certainly not retiring furniture magnate, sponsored the yearly event at the women's prison, providing the ice cream, fudge, and all the fixin's along with spiced tea. Church members would supply brownies, chocolate chip cookies, and volunteer as servers. Typically, upon serving the sundaes, the McArthur Family Bluegrass Ensemble would play a set followed by Elijah's recitation of the Christmas story along with a prayer for the imprisoned. After this, they would sing Christmas hymns and carols, culminating with a rousing rendition of *The Twelve Days of Christmas* with the prisoners always shouting at the top of their lungs—"Five golden rings!!!"

"Soooo, Mark and the crew are there at the prison, and Josie, I hate to tell you but Shania is not going to be at the party. It seems that she broke the jaw of another inmate at lunch today in a fight over Jell-O. An inmate at their table said she wasn't going to eat her Jello, and as the soon-to-be-victim reached for it, Shania stood up and cold-cocked her right in the face.

The woman went down like a sack of flour at the loading dock of the bakery. Crazy thing is, Mark told me the woman fell face first into the Jell-O, so in the end she wound up wearing what she couldn't eat, and Shania checked into solitary confinement once again . . . still hungry. I'm really sorry that you won't get to see Shania, Josie. Mark said it might be best for us to take you on home, seeing as how you've already had a long day."

"That's all right. I was fixin' to work up the courage to ask ya if you could take me on home, anyway. I was afraid of lookin' like a bad mother who didn't want to see her kid at Christmas. You know I love that girl, but she and me have always been oil and water. I'm about give out, and would probably fall to sleep during the singing anyway. I am going to miss that sundae though."

Jimmy pounced on the mention of ice cream like a dog on a dead cicada. "Well, we can surely take care of that. We'll stop at the Dairy Queen on the way into Edinburgh." And so, the Incarnation Incarceration tour took a detour and Jimmy (banana split), Josie (peanut butter parfait), and Elijah (hot fudge milkshake) spent half an hour on the front porch of the DQ, laughing about everything from Christmas memories to coquettish sheriff's deputies at the county lock-up. It was so good to see Josie smile.

Church geeks like Elijah wake on the morning of Christmas Eve with all the energy and zeal of Vince Lombardi on the day of Super Bowl One. "LBJ (*Little Baby Jesus*) isn't everything; he's the only thing!!!" Somehow that doesn't carry the same adrenaline launching injection as the iconic coach's quote, so Elijah runs down toward the kitchen and sweeps Hannah up into his cradled arms singing—"And he shall purify–i-i-i-i-i-i-i-i-i-i-i-i-i-i-i-i!!!"

"E, I love you dearly, and you have a nice voice, but I think Handel just turned over in his grave."

"I know. I've never been able to get the hang of that warbling 'y.'"

"Oh, I'd say you're warbling. Just maybe not what Handel's score called for. Maybe you should stick with *Hark, the Herald Angels Sing*. So, are you ready for the big day?"

"Oh, it's a great day! I still have some polishing to do on my meditation, but I'm pumped for the services tonight."

The day dawned bright, brisk, and clear. The *Weather Channel* guy said the mercury could approach sixty. One of the perks of living in North Carolina is that winter takes what the sportscasters call TV timeouts. Gray skies become Tar Heel blue, accented with nature's cotton ball blimps. Temperatures reach the tipping point that draws hearts, spirits, bodies, and daydreams outside. Seldom do Carolinians relish a white Christmas, but this will do just fine.

St. Martin on Christmas Eve is a holiday photographer's dream. The grand live Chrismon tree; the hanging Advent wreath, suspended from the beautiful wooden truss, its candles accented with the greens and reds of the holly; and poinsettias aplenty. Hannah once warned Elijah not to stand still in the sanctuary for too long because someone would put a potted poinsettia on his head. The greens draped around the sanctuary like bunting at a political convention draw attention to the perpetually pleasing aesthetic of stacked stone walls framing the rich hues of the Willet stained glass windows, basking in the brightness of the spotlights strategically placed outside.

As usual the pews were full at five o'clock when the McArthur Family Bluegrass Ensemble would play pre-service music for thirty minutes. Mark McArthur was playing the mandolin long before he was running a furniture company and his lifelong love affair with the instrument was made obvious with the lush, rich, and clear tones of his cherished 1924 Gibson F2. He has long been known in the bluegrass community and since his retirement has actually toured with a few of the native Carolina bands. Mark's sister, Spencer, classically trained but bluegrass enlightened, plays cello, bringing to the group the great vibe of the various Yo-Yo Ma crossover duets with the masters of bluegrass. Spencer's daughter and Xani's hero, Madison, also classically trained but with great bluegrass chops, plays fiddle and sings, and has placed well at the legendary Galax fiddlers' convention. Her cousin, Seamus, loves Eric Clapton and Stevie Ray Vaughn but also is drawn to the artistry of Doc Watson and Tony Rice, using them as his inspiration on guitar. And finally, ever since returning to Edinburgh, Megan MacIntosh, a second cousin and Celtic music veteran, sings and plays guitar, fiddle, mandolin, and even an Irish Squeezebox when called upon.

Together, in that warm, welcoming sacred candlelit setting all dressed up for Christmas, they draw people to the place of awe before the miracle of the manger. Throughout the service, the interspersing of artful acoustic arrangements and triumphant organ infused carols frame the Proclamation of the grace filled good news announcing the enfleshing of God's sacred Word. "And the Word became flesh and dwelt among us, full of grace and truth; we have beheld his glory, glory as of the only Son from the Father." On this night, members, friends, family, and visitors do, indeed, behold the glory of God.

As Elijah rises to read Luke's Bethlehem narrative once again, he feels the peace promised by the angel chorus.

"On this sacred night, we read Luke's narrative of Christ's birth. Let us listen for the Word of our Lord."

Luke 2: 1-20

1 *In those days a decree went out from Caesar Augustus that all the world should be enrolled.* **2** *This was the first enrollment, when Quirin'i-us was governor of Syria.* **3** *And all went to be enrolled, each to his own city.* **4** *And Joseph also went up from Galilee, from the city of Nazareth, to Judea, to the city of David, which is called Bethlehem, because he was of the house and lineage of David,* **5** *to be enrolled with Mary, his betrothed, who was with child.* **6** *And while they were there, the time came for her to be delivered.* **7** *And she gave birth to her first-born son and wrapped him in swaddling cloths, and laid him in a manger, because there was no place for them in the inn.* **8** *And in that region there were shepherds out in the field, keeping watch over their flock by night.* **9** *And an angel of the Lord appeared to them, and the glory of the Lord shone around them, and they were filled with fear.* **10** *And the angel said to them, "Be not afraid; for behold, I bring you good news of a great joy which will come to all the people;* **11** *for to you is born this day in the city of David a Savior, who is Christ the Lord.* **12** *And this will be a sign for you: you will find a babe wrapped in swaddling cloths and lying in a manger."* **13** *And suddenly there was with the angel a multitude of the heavenly host praising God and saying,* **14** *"Glory to God in the highest, and on earth peace among men with whom he is pleased!"* **15** *When the angels went away from them into heaven, the shepherds said to one another, "Let us go over to Bethlehem and see this thing that has happened, which the Lord has made known to us."* **16** *And they went with haste, and found Mary and Joseph, and the babe lying in a manger.* **17** *And when they saw it they made known the saying which had been told them concerning this child;* **18** *and all who heard it wondered at what the shepherds told them.* **19** *But Mary kept all these things, pondering them in her heart.* **20** *And the shepherds returned, glorifying and praising God for all they had heard and seen, as it had been told them.*

One: This is the Word of the Lord.

Many: Thanks be to God.

"This will be a sign for you." It sounds like it could be an encounter in one of those old spy movies. You know, two guys in long khaki trench coats, belts cinched tight, fedoras pulled low over their eyes, each walking toward one another on the wet stone pavement near the center of an ancient bridge on a night of heavy fog and mist.

Warily, one of the mysterious figures scans his perimeter before leaning in and saying, "you will find a child wrapped in bands of cloth and lying in a manger." The other shadowy figure hesitates and scans his perimeter before similarly leaning in to say, "The cattle are lowing."

It seems that even God likes a good suspense movie. As a matter of fact, the readings of this season are often introduced with the words: The mystery of Christ revealed.

"This will be a sign for you." When I was a child I received a James Bond briefcase as a gift. Plastic Walther PPK, rubber dagger that popped out with the touch of a button, and a decoding tool to get to the bottom of any mystery. "This will be a sign for you." Even God likes a good mystery and for over 2000 years scholars, preachers, prophets, and the women of the circle #6 Bible study have been trying to decode the mystery in order to understand the significance of these strange events in a Judean wilderness.

It is a mystery. Imagine you are a visitor from a different culture and a different faith, being invited to a typical American Christmas pageant. What strange practices are these? Little boys in bathrobes carrying big sticks, a roaming amoeba of fidgeting angels bumping into one another on a crowded chancel floor; and is that little girl supposed to be a donkey or a beagle? And why all the drama around the plastic baby? It looks like a Betsy Wetsy. What a strange, mysterious ritual! What could it possibly mean?

"This will be a sign for you: you will find a child wrapped in bands of cloth and lying in a manger." Why would God be revealed in this way?

Tonight is not only the night before Christmas; it is also the eve of the end of all those annual Christmas social obligations in the neighborhood, at the office, at your cousin's farm, in the hotel ballroom. Only a few more sausage balls, Swedish meatballs, nut-encrusted cheese logs, and Rolaids to consume before your life improves from crazy to chaotic. You have seen beautifully decorated homes, catalogue-ready holiday wardrobes rich with satin, artfully wrapped presents, and the caterer of the month. Tomorrow you will sit down to color-coordinated place settings; maybe those golden plates that don't hold any food but serve as the base for another plate. Or maybe it's the wedding china and the sterling; reserved for high holy days and the night your boss and her husband come over for dinner. Napkins folded like origami and crystal glasses that you can't put into the dishwasher.

It is all so ironic when you think about it. You see, the original guest list of the Nativity would feel mighty uncomfortable around pastry-covered brie, fondue, holiday plates, cashmere, satin, velvet, and Swarovski nativity scenes. No, this crowd is more like folks I know who put a little bacon and barbeque sauce in the pork and beans for special occasions. No microbrewery beer for these shepherds. All they need is a cooler, some ice, and Pabst Blue Ribbon. You can put away the color-coordinated place settings and the silver carafes, because they'll be putting squeeze bottles of butter and Cheez Whiz on the folding table; and they'll drink out of cans, leaving the red Solo cups for the fancy folks.

Our nativities are always so sanitized, somber, and elegant, but God's advent on earth was anything but sophisticated and chic. It was probably a little more Nashville honky tonk than Vienna Opera House. "We didn't have no wedding by the sea, but the baby shower was one helluva paaarteeee!" That may be a more authentic Christmas carol than *Silent Night*. Maybe, that's why we keep dragging the three wise men into Luke's nativity even though Luke doesn't put them there at all. We make them kings without much scriptural support, possibly out of a desire to class up this crèche a bit.

It is probably fitting that the setting for the nativity is a barn, because Mary wouldn't have wanted a bunch of overripe shepherds slogging through her parents' home, and you can be sure they never would have made it past the concierge in the lobby of the Bethlehem Inn.

Many of you know my wife is the farmer's daughter and one of her brothers is a dairy farmer. He was telling me recently about an acquaintance that wanted to come see his dairy operation. When the guy showed up, he wasn't wearing the tall rubber boots that are the norm for that sort of work. No, he was wearing his nice boots. Well, when he returned home and entered the back door, there was nearly a riot as the stench of cow manure filled the room. Children scrambling to get out of there; his wife demanding that he go to the garage and strip to his boxers. Like the parent of a fast food worker, she was probably tempted to burn the whole outfit. Well, say hello to the VIP guests at the manger.

I love the great variety of nativity scenes—lovely nativities carved from exotic wood; ceramic figurines painted with intricate detail; children's nativities with pillow stuffed characters, plastic waist-high nativity characters with light bulb-abdomens calling attention to Christ's birth for all who drive through the neighborhood. One of my favorites is the Inuit themed nativity that Ernest and Helen Hunter brought back from their time as Volunteers in Mission in Sitka, Alaska. A polar bear and seal are there to adore the newborn king. And believe it or not, I saw this week that there actually is a Swarovski crystal nativity that costs more than Jesus probably spent in his entire life. I love them all, but that first nativity was anything but clean, silent, and refined.

One of my favorite Christmas treasures is a creatively funky children's book that depicts the nativity in a wonderfully original way. The angel Gabriel appears as a wild-haired adolescent in worn out work boots who flies a little out of control, like a skier who skipped the ski lesson. He careens into a tree as he offers his message to Mary.

In the following pages Mary is struggling with lower back pains, swollen ankles and fingers. In an imaginative way, the artist reveals an unpretentious, down-to-earth nativity that mocks our attempts to sanitize both the nativity and our lives. Did you know that you can now buy a fake wedding ring specifically made for pregnant women with swollen fingers, so that no one will give them disapproving glances when they go out in public? However, as hard as we try to airbrush the nativity and Photoshop our lives, the original nativity unapologetically proclaims that Christ appears not where we wish our lives could be, but where we are.

During my last year of college at Westminster way out in Missouri, I was living in an apartment with rented furniture, dirty dishes, and the Saturday paper strewn across the floor, and my phone rang. It was a couple from my home church in Charlotte who were passing through, of all places, Fulton, MO. He was a big Winston Churchill buff and Westminster not only played host to Churchill's *Iron Curtain* speech, but they also have a great Churchill museum and even a Wren Chapel brought over stone by stone from England. Well, the couple was calling me from the apartment's parking lot.

He was an executive, buttoned down and always immaculately dressed. They had a lovely home on the most prized real estate in Myers Park. You know them—all country club, Burberry coats, Lincoln Continental sedan, 12-year-old Scotch, expensive wine. I can't imagine ever seeing them playing volleyball out on their lawn. In fact, I couldn't imagine ever seeing them out on their lawn at all. Someone was hired for that work. You could say they were flirting with uptight.

Well, it was Saturday morning. I was wearing gym shorts and a wrinkled T-shirt. My hair was unwashed, my face unshaven, and I hadn't yet brushed my teeth, and so I had the kind of breath that makes you want to cover your mouth if you get within five feet of someone.

There wasn't anything to do but open the door when they rang the doorbell two minutes later. The apartment was a mess. I was a mess. I was mortified. They were kind and made no comment about the state of my affairs, at least until they climbed back into the Lincoln. It was one of those welcome to my life moments when all you can do is smile hard, swallow big, and pray for a hole to crawl into.

But, you know what? The original nativity tells us this is where Christ appears, amidst the messiness, embarrassment, and unpolished days of our lives. Christ did not come to inspect whether our lives are in order. Our Lord knows our lives are a mess, and Jesus jumps right in to help us shovel our way out.

Love is born this day right where we live, amidst the pain of a nation reeling from that needs-to-be-cancelled-but-never-ending-miniseries *School Shooting of the Month*. Love is born this day amidst the cracked porcelain of our relationships; amidst the dark corners into which we have backed ourselves; amidst the failure of will to forgive or be forgiven; amidst the hungry and the homeless and even the prideful who callously neglect them. Tonight, love takes its place beside us, not in the airbrushed portraits of our lives that we want every one to see, but amidst the pain, insecurity, clutter, doubts, splintered images, broken family portraits, and do-overs of our real lives. So let us open the door and welcome him. He can find his way around the clutter. He has seen it all before. Christ appears not where we wish our lives could be, but where we are. So let us welcome him. I hear he does his best work amidst the mess. Amen.

The moment before the benediction on Christmas Eve affords the pastor that rarefied encounter with awe known to delivery room parents, ascendant mountain climbers, whirling dervishes, stargazers, and monks in prayer. Elijah looks out upon a living candelabra of three hundred flames illuminating the beatified faces of worshippers who for this moment do not fret over some ephemeral Christmas *spirit*, but rather bask in the Christ child, made present by the *Spirit* of God. "Lift up your heads, O ye gates; and be ye lifted up, ye everlasting doors; and the King of glory shall come in." Even the cynical are sanctified on this night.

Squeezed into the third pew on the left, Elijah spies Jordan, Adele, Taylor, Tess, Hannah, Xani, and Nathan. He can't help but chuckle at the thought that eleven hours from this moment they will be similarly squeezed, along with Elijah, into Taylor's Suburban for the twelve-hour drive to the farm in Laddonia, Missouri. Convincing Xani that Santa was coming to the

Parish house during the Christmas Eve service wasn't as onerous a con job as he thought it would be. Of course, Santa didn't have much of a publicist in Elijah's home, anyway. Explaining his rationale, Elijah once said, "Hey, I'm not going to throw the fat guy under the bus, but if our intent is to help the kid grow into an understanding of the gravitas of the Incarnation, I'm not going to give St. Round Mound of Red all the credit, either." And so it is, that T and Papa, Beau, Mommy and Daddy received due credit and Santa was a second-tier gift giver. The stockings were hung by the Suburban headrests with care in hopes that miniature car passengers would ride without despair.

A tsunami of a cold front was rolling in from Canada and shirt-sleeved revelers of Christmas Eve would be rummaging for parkas, especially those headed to the windswept farms of Missouri's flatland.

"You know, Dad, every time I ride in this big black vehicle, I feel like I'm being ferried by the Secret Service. It is a smooth ride, though."

"We've got your back, son. You're safe with us, though I couldn't afford the bulletproof glass or the heavy steel doors, or the high-tech satellite communication equipment, or the LED light, armor, or the armed agents for that matter, but that fiberglass blanket surrounding us will withstand . . . not much."

"Thanks, I never felt safer. You know, it's a good thing we like each other, or this would be a mighty long Christmas day." Truth is, Christmas day is a long day for many. An elderly man sits alone in the discomfiting quiet of his urban apartment. Memories, once joyful, now torture him. These walls once played tennis with the sound waves of laughter and conversation each Christmas day as friends gathered for the annual party, so marvelously hosted by his wife. She died last summer and at times he forgets, leaning over to kiss her goodnight, but finding only her pillow. His only son is at his in-laws this year. A long day.

Like sour milk poured on cereal and the promise of a good day spoiled, a Christmas breakfast casserole of angst, resentment, and hostility mars the morning of a fracturing family before the coffee gets hot. Father, mother, sister, brother can't even open a present without opening family wounds they refuse to let heal. A long day.

Daydreaming as the lane markers are swallowed by the Suburban, Elijah muses on the number of homes where the annual angry yuletide liturgy is recited by the time the cinnamon rolls are ready: "Can't we just get through the day without fighting? It's Christmas!" A long day.

Elijah lightly laughs, and to no one in particular, says, "Yes, it is good we like each other." Elijah actually enjoys these biennial Christmas Day motoring marathons, well, at least until he loses all feeling in his tush as they cross into Illinois. The highways are empty except for preacher types who couldn't leave town on Christmas Eve. The contained space and slow-motion clock afforded plenty of time for Elijah to catch up with his parents and grandparents. He was always thirsty for their insights, their wisdom, and their humor. A question, one question, would ignite a rich rhapsody of conversation taking them around the globe, through the seasons of life, and into the depths of theological wisdom. It was like riding an all-terrain vehicle on wheels of literature, film, relationship, and faith.

Elijah decided it was his turn to fire the starter's gun. "So, what have you been reading?" It was Xani who caught a flyer, leaping forward with a title before the question mark ended Elijah's sentence. "*Oh, The Places You'll Go!*"

Simultaneously voices echoed through the Suburban with praise, not the praise of adults overindulging in cuteness, mind you, but the praise of those who share a great love for a classic text. Jordan exclaimed, "A masterful treatise on the human experience. Dr. Seuss crammed more of what we encounter in life into those few lyrical pages than you will find in most novels. Amazing."

"You are so right, Jordan," Taylor reflected. "There is ambition with all those high fliers. Yet, where there is ambition you can always count on a few prickly perches to offer discouragement.

Elijah, connecting life to the church as he is wont to do, said, "Don't forget the wisdom of stepping carefully around all those strange birds you come across along the way. There should be a hall of fame for all the pastors who were chewed up and spit out by a congregation because they didn't figure that out."

The Seussological conversation continued on through Tennessee and into Kentucky as they motored on through the weird and the wild. Eventually, Adele said, "What I can't believe is that it seems everyone in the vehicle has the book memorized."

Elijah shot back, "Why would you be amazed by our mastery of this semi-sacred text? Didn't you know that on January 1, Xani declared she wanted to read this book every day for the whole year? It would be amazing if we hadn't memorized it! So far, this year alone, we've read the book 360 days, and that doesn't take into account the number of times our little Seuss scholar conned more than one of us to read it in a day. It would truly be sad if we hadn't memorized it."

Taylor said, "Did it ever occur to you to have the audio downloaded onto her iPod?"

"... Uh ... well ... hadn't thought of that." The Suburban rocked with laughter as it lumbered on toward one of the places this gang would go.

Well, they were certainly on their way, but they weren't there yet. By the time they passed the exit for Santa Claus, Indiana, the snoring offered dissonant accompaniment to the choir of King's College Cambridge on the radio leading their traditional program of Lessons and Carols. Elijah was at the wheel and therefore in control of the tunes. So, like the typical TV slug with a remote, he kept switching back and forth between stations, from *In the Bleak Midwinter* to Dean Martin crooning *Baby, It's Cold Outside*. And indeed, it was cold outside, signified by the gathering frost at the edges of the windows. A front of frigid air was blasting down from Canada, reminding the populace of the plains that the Canucks and Habs are a hardy people. In the rearview mirror, he could see Nathan was getting a short break from the confines of his carseat, resting his head on Hannah's shoulder. Catching Hannah's eyes, they exchanged that smile that declares all is right with the world, or at least inside the Suburban.

The lights of St. Louis reported the news that the sun had clocked out for the day and also that it had begun to snow. For a Missourian traveling back from the East, the sight of the Arch whelms the soul with a sense of home, just as the voice of Jack Buck or Mike Shannon broadcasting a Cards game in summer could tug the hearts of Show-me state exiles to the banks of the Mississippi when life's chaos won't permit them to go there. Xani made sure everyone was awake to see the lighted Arch as they crossed the river. Most passengers returned to their naps, but while Elijah pointed out landmarks to Xani like Busch Stadium, Union Station, the Planetarium and the Zoo, he couldn't help but notice that T was wide awake, looking out the window in deep thought. She had been unusually quiet on this trip and it was obvious she was anxious. Her last encounter with Beau Swenson, Hannah's father and Taylor's best friend growing up, had not ended well. Elijah could sense that she was replaying the scene in her mind.

It was last summer when Beau had come out to see Hannah and Elijah after they lost the baby. They were all sitting around the table, pushed back from plates emptied of barbecue Taylor had brought on his way in from a deposition in Lexington. Beau had been disarmingly quiet and borderline sullen. The pause in table conversation was long enough that Tess was about to move to start the cleanup when she was buzzed by a stray thought like a fly on reconnaissance. "Beau, please tell me that the screwy legislature in Missouri isn't actually considering the nullification of federal gun laws."

Suddenly, everyone else at the table was mesmerized by some invisible object on the floor, the universal code for: "You're on your own, girl."

Beau shot Tess a glare that was direct and unsettling. "They sure are, and I'm all for it!"

"What?"

"You heard me, I'm all for it. It's about time to reject the consuming overreach of that Communist Muslim president. This legislation just recognizes the reality that we may have to defend ourselves against the assault of big government on our freedom!"

"Rush Limbaugh?"

"Yeah, I listen to him. What of it?"

"Why all the venom, Beau?" Tess was nonplussed by the sudden spike in Beau's blood pressure. Everyone else saw that Tess was unwittingly stepping into the teeth of a trap, but felt helpless to protect her. Of course, they weren't getting anywhere near that trap, and so maintained their laser focus on that invisible item on the floor, wishing it was a hole to hide in.

Tess continued, "Do you actually believe your President is plotting an invasion of the critical strategic target of Laddonia?"

The volume rises. "Wake up, Tess! He's already listening to our telephones. And by the way, he's not my President."

"Well, Beau, you may not like him, but unless you've changed your citizenship, he is your President. And as far as the phone goes, I wouldn't worry about the phone. You barely use it anyway, and unless you're manipulating the price of soybean futures, I don't think you're in danger."

"Don't patronize me, Tess. You and your liberal elite like to think you are so much smarter than everyone. When it comes to the essential work of the American farmer and your dependence on him; or when it comes to issues of security, and how to really prevent another Newtown, you don't know shit from Shinola!"

"Well, Beau, I do know that Shinola is a shoe polish that disappeared over fifty years ago, and believe it or not, I learned all about the other thing when I was potty trained, and I've been taking it from the Tea Party crowd for five years. But Beau, I'm no smarter than you, and you should be ashamed for trying to play the intellectual bigot card on me. You know I've always respected your mind and I've always held the family farmer in the highest regard. I know you are smart enough to know that guns, while useful for hunters, have seldom offered a lasting solution for humanity. And Beau, I also know you are smart enough to understand that the worst possible thing we could do to allay our fears of another tragedy like Newtown would be to put a Glock in the hands of Miss Bindergarten on her way to kindergarten."

"So maybe you oughta just put a gun to my head, because God took my wife, the bank wants to take my farm, you took my best friend, and you even took my daughter, which means you've got my grandkids, too. Hell, Tess, what else do you want? I ain't got nothin' else to give. Shit, I've got nothin' else to live for!"

Beau pushed back from the table with his cartoonishly muscular forearms, the product of decades spent throwing hay bales around like cotton balls. His rushed rise knocked the chair over, slapping the floor with a dramatic CRACK! Turning, he stormed toward the stairs leading down to the study, slamming the door behind him, offering one more jolting CRACK!! to his stunned family still at the table. The ruckus was loud enough that both Xani and Nathan awoke and could be heard crying in fear.

Hannah and Elijah ran back to calm them as Tess and Taylor remained at the table, dazed and silent. As only Taylor could, he waited for the oxygen to flow back into the room before grinning slyly at Tess, saying, "Maybe you should have stuck to the milk."

He was referring to a revealing experience at a previous gathering of relatives. In some ways it was the classic Norman Rockwell portrait: turkey and dressing, mashed potatoes and gravy, pumpkin pie, and kids at the kitchen table with the adults in the adjoining dining room. There was a lot of laughter going on at the kids' table and of course, the assumption always is that either someone has passed gas or a cousin laughed so hard that milk sprayed out of his nostrils.

Yet, when later asked what was so funny, Taylor's niece informed him that the laughter was actually prompted by the discussion that was going on at the adults' table. They found it hilarious that the adults were having this serious discussion concerning, of all things, 2% milk. It is crazy when you think about it. The whole clan is gathered at the table for the first time in a year, and they are talking about 2% vs. skim! Some couldn't handle the thought of pouring the watery consistency of skim over their Cheerios while those accustomed to skim felt that drinking whole milk was like sucking down a milkshake. It was ridiculous, come to think of it. All those college degrees around that table of siblings and in-laws and the best discussion they could come up with was one step removed from celebrating the virtues of pasteurization.

But anyone who's been to a family gathering knows what was going on. Two percent milk was the *safe* topic. Wanted to stay away from politics. Couldn't afford for conversation to stray into religion. Wouldn't want the conservative Baptist and the liberal Presbyterian to start a food fight. Wouldn't want the Fox News folks to challenge the MSNBC folks to a smackdown. So, 2% milk seemed to be about as bold a topic as they could afford.

"Maybe you should have stuck to the milk." Taylor wasn't scolding just as he wasn't patronizing. It was the loving voice of a close friend reminding Tess that in a world rife with conflict, she was safe with him. Tess smiled briefly and bravely, but Taylor knew she was mortified. Tess and Beau had shared a long history of good natured political jousting, and would usually end their disagreements with one of them saying, "I guess Henry Ford was wrong; some folks don't want a black car."

But this skirmish was different. Beau had reacted viscerally, angrily, allowing the opinion to become more important than the relationship. Tess had seen the train wreck coming, but couldn't bring herself to jump off the tracks or reverse course.

When Hannah returned to the kitchen with Nathan sleeping on her shoulder, Tess, now in tears, rose to embrace her.

"Hannah, I am so sorry, so sorry that I have hurt your father. I am so sorry that I obviously insulted him. Sometimes, I get so caught up in a debate, I don't see the signs that it is time for Tess to sit down and shut up. And I am truly sorry for any way in which I have taken you away from your home."

"Oh, T, believe me, he's thrown that dart at Elijah a number of times and usually I get right in his face, forcefully and quickly pointing out that no one has taken me away from anybody. We are here because we feel called to this place and the same would be true if we were in North Dakota or Shanghai. Don't apologize. Dad is just being an ass. He knows better. Anyway, this wasn't about guns or the Tea Party twits, and it certainly wasn't about you."

Tess' humiliation changed to concern. "Hannah, what's going on?"

"I don't know. He told me recently that he wasn't drinking; that he's been going to meetings, but now, I'm having my doubts. I'm starting to think the dark clouds are approaching again. I think he's depressed. I went down to check on him or maybe put my shoe up his colon, but he was snoring like a Harley. Let's try to get some sleep. We'll see what the morning brings. I may have to audible an intervention, but we've been down this road before, so you will see it as well as I can."

That next morning when Tess walked into the kitchen, Hannah was standing at the counter waiting on the Keurig, her eyes reddened from tears, her faced panicked.

"He's gone."

"Beau?"

"Yes."

"Oh no, what have I done?"

"You didn't do anything. These . . . these are his demons."

Hannah continued, "I got up to go to the bathroom in the middle of the night and noticed the light to the carport was on. I looked out in the driveway and his truck was gone. I went to my phone and saw he had left me a cryptic text: 'No worries. Need some space. Tell Tess I'm sorry. Luv ya. I'll be in touch.'"

"You think he's still in town?"

"No. Elijah went out to the diner and the fast food joints to look for his truck, but there was no sign of him. I called Billy and Carla, and then my brothers. Nobody had heard from him and the general consensus was to sit tight and wait. In spite of his bluster last night, everybody knows he won't go Columbine on anyone. If he's headed home, which is what we expect, he's already well past Knoxville. Billy said he'd be praying for him and would open an oil tanker full of whupass on him when he saw the lights of his pickup."

"I am so sorry."

"No reason for sorry. Let's just pray there's some light for his darkness. I swear, though, he can be such a selfish pr . . . jerk. Here, we just lost this baby and he has to find a way to make it all about him. I love my dad and I pray he's safe, but what a turd!"

"Depression has a way of momentarily taking the best out of us to give the worst in us a turn at the microphone."

About nine hours later, Hannah got the call that allowed her lungs to receive oxygen again. It was Billy. "He's driving up the road to the farmhouse now. The boys and I have got it from here. We'll keep you posted. And Hannah, the old coot will call tonight. I guarantee it."

Before Beau could even turn off the engine, Billy jumped in the cab and said, "Okay, here's the deal. I can drive or you can drive, but we're leaving for Columbia, right now, even if I have to whip your ass and tie you up like a calf at a rodeo." Surprisingly, Beau offered little resistance and even let Billy take the wheel of his treasured truck. He knew. He knew he had fallen down into that dark hole and the rope Billy mentioned was actually the grace of something to hold onto, and thus, his only hope.

Back on the Christmas highway, Elijah looked in the rearview mirror and could see that Tess was torturing herself by playing that whole chapter on a loop that went from beginning to end to beginning again. She had not seen or spoken to Beau since that night when Beau had charged her with the crime of taking from him what was left of all that was important to him.

Elijah caught his mother's eye in the rearview mirror. "T, it's the same show every time you replay it. You just be Tess, and you'll do just fine."

"I hope, but in the meantime, I plan on sticking with the milk."

West of St. Louis, the snow was sticking to Interstate 70 and by the time they exited onto Highway 19, the Suburban was slogging through five inches of the white stuff, the wind already sculpting drifts against farm fences and spraying Wite-Out on the windshield. Sensing that their destination was drawing close, the crowd stirred from their long winter's nap. One doesn't experience many white Christmases in North Carolina unless you're skiing the man-made stuff at Sugar Mountain, so the sight of all that white parachuting to earth in the glow of the headlights was quite the novelty for Jordan and Adele. Something about snow reveals the surviving effervescence of a 7-year-old in the eyes of the octogenarian. Adele said she now knew that which she had only mused when looking at the just-shaken snowglobe on her vanity at home.

Though we may lose our hearing, eyesight, short-term memory, and hair, age doesn't take away the childlike wonder and anticipation that a snowfall kindles. The expectation of playing in the snow combined with the suspense of whether school will be cancelled is a reflex emotion that continues to show up decades after the sled has been mothballed and the textbooks are out of print. Elijah saw that irrepressible joy in Adele's eyes and didn't have the heart to tell her the shock her parchment skin would suffer when she stepped out into the frigid wind-amplified cold of a Missouri winter.

There is a ubiquitous ecumenical cold-weather prayer in the Midwest that is regularly offered when stepping out of a car or house into a frigid wind that bites to the bone. "Jesus!!!" When the thermometer dips below 10 degrees Fahrenheit, the Lord's name is abruptly called upon by Presbyterians, Lutherans, Baptists, and Methodists alike. "Jesus!!!" Even Jews and Muslims can be heard beckoning Nazareth's carpenter when the temperature nears zero. The large Catholic population prefers the extended version of supplication. "Jesus, Mary, and Joseph!!!" So, as the weary Southerners unfolded themselves one by one from the Suburban, you could hear a litany of petition circle the vehicle. "Jesus!"—"Jesus!"—"Jesus!" Even Adele joined the chorus and she had never uttered the Savior's name in that context.

All the relatives were gathering at the home of Taylor's father, the Honorable Judge Angus Parish. The stream of family farm estate squabbles he had mediated in his youth was eventually replaced by a circuit court judgeship and later, a seat on the Missouri Supreme Court. That appointment had come a year after his wife, June, died. He had officially retired at the age of 74 but continued to substitute at various levels until last year on his 83rd birthday. For the last twenty years, Angus has "dated" Angie Fugate, the widow of the founder of First Federal Bank up the road in Mexico. They play golf three times a week in the summer and spend January through March in Siesta Key, FL.

Hannah's brother Tom had been vigilant in keeping the sidewalk clear as family members made their way inside. Angie and Uncle Billy's wife Carla, had decorated the house with enough Yuletide trinkets, lights, trees, and ornaments that visitors could be forgiven for thinking they had entered one of those Christmas stores in Myrtle Beach.

Angie was endearingly referred to as Queen Bling. Bottle blonde and brightly hued year round, she reminds you of the makeup lady at Dillards, only most of her jewelry isn't costume, it is big and real: diamond tennis bracelet, a macadamia-sized emerald ringed by diamonds on one finger to balance the 2 carat marquis on the other side, four or five precious stones scattered across the other fingers and a carat diamond in each ear. Angie didn't eschew costume jewelry, though. All those bangle bracelets would prevent her from ever sneaking up on anyone. Her holly leaf brooch was almost hidden by her angel-adorned necklace layered on top of the fur-collared Christmas sweater that was festooned with sequins and glitter. Angie's long, manicured fingernails were painted alternately in glossy red and green and at the hem of her black suede slacks, this seventy-year-old party girl with an artificial hip was wearing candy apple red, patent leather, four-inch heels, at least until everyone saw them.

Saint Swag, as she is also known, has a personality as bright as all the bling. When she makes you laugh, which is regularly, it is never a chuckle, a tee-hee, a snigger, or a titter. No, when Angie makes you laugh it is a drink spewing, belly cramping, pants peeing, slapstick showcase. Legend has it that one of Angie's stories made a dinner companion laugh so hard he had a heart attack and ended up getting a double bypass. It was a story of the time Angie's makeup mirror fell off the wall, hitting her in the face and how she stuck a tampon up her nose to stop the bleeding.

Unfailingly buoyant and colorful, Angie was a healing balm for the Judge when they started seeing one another a couple of years after my grandmother's death. Yet, her humor and spirit are often overshadowed by her reputation in the kitchen. Give her a pantry and a chafing dish and she could even seduce Liberace. Angus and Angie have never married; never felt the need to. Plus, as Angie points out, "Lord, let's not complicate things and create an opening for my money-grubbin' shyster-son in-law. Her nickname for him was Silsob (son-in-law-son-of-a-bitch). Angie and Angus maintained separate residences, often rendezvousing at the Mexico Country Club and then flipping a coin to see whether they'd head toward the farm or South Street. Their friends at the Club told them they were taking up a collection to build them a garage out on the parking lot because outside of dinner, there was usually his Lincoln or her Cadillac but seldom both. Yet, wherever they are, you can bet there is laughter.

In from the cold and after the line for the bathroom dwindled, hugs were exchanged, conversations from the previous reunion were rekindled, and family news was updated. Uncharacteristically, Tess was hanging toward the back, anxious about coming face to face with Beau. However, it seemed that the whole room breathed a sigh of relief when he tapped Tess on her shoulder from behind and said with a laugh, "Tess, I guess some folks don't want a black car."

"Beau, just to see you drive it, I'd buy you a pink Cadillac. Now use those beefy Republican arms and give me a hug!"

"Tess, I'm so sorry. I wasn't myself."

"Oh Beau, I'm more to blame. I took the bait so easily I couldn't see you were hurting; and all I managed to do was pile on the misery. I'm so glad you're feeling better. You look good. Hannah told me you went out on a date recently."

"Yeah, sweet lady . . . she took pity on me. She teaches over at the high school. She was Hannah's American Literature teacher, so you'd have a lot in common."

"I'd love to meet her. She sounds wonderful."

"I think so. She may pop over here once her grandkids go to bed. She lives here in Laddonia."

The peace talks continued and they may have even talked about 2% milk. The tables were set and squeezed in between the Santa napkin holders, gold plate chargers, the greenery, candles, red ornaments, and green goblets, were Christmas tree pitchers filled with spiced tea. And over against the wall was an antique sideboard along with a folding table with every square inch covered with casseroles, salads, and sweets. To a hungry traveler it was a vision of the eschatological feast in heaven. And if as on cue, Uncle Billy came bursting through the back door carrying a huge platter of the annual smoked brisket that Taylor, only half-jokingly, said was the real reason they had driven close to 900 miles through a blizzard.

"Whoa! Nobody told me the prodigal and his progeny had arrived. Let me take a look at you!" Approaching each new arrival with the two-handed politician's handshake, his strong calloused hands pressing palms and massaging shoulders, Billy glanced the way of Hannah and howled, "Damn, Hannah! You could melt butter while laying naked on a glacier."

"Oh, Uncle Billy, you do know how to woo a girl."

"Who's wooing? I'm just making a purely scientific observation. I don't woo, 'cause you can be damn sure Carla would cut my business end off with a hatchet."

In another context and from another person, Hannah might be offended, but this is just Uncle Billy. He may raise an eyebrow or two now and then, but if your life descended to hell, he'd gladly drive his pickup down there and help pull you out. Billy had done just that for Beau that summer, and Hannah would be eternally grateful.

Just as Elijah was trying to shake the image of Billy's business end out of his head, Angie called out his name with the request for a blessing. The minister's curse. A minister could be out walking the dog through the neighborhood and some stranger hosting a dinner party wouldn't hesitate to step out on the porch and ask the parson to come in to offer the blessing. Half the time, Elijah didn't know whether the request came as the desperate plea from a host mortified by the thought of having to pray in public or as an accommodation to the holy man. He had concluded that it was usually a combination of both, but he often wondered if there even was a blessing if there was no preacher . . . in da house!

> For the safety of passage,
> The reunion of family,
> A table filled with goodness,
> And the blessing of a Savior born this day,
> We give you thanks, O Lord. Amen.

Such a blessed night was this. At one end of the table, Elijah and Hannah were planning a summer bike trip through Iowa and into Minnesota with Billy's daughters and on the other end Billy was blustering about possibly leaving the Presbyterian Church to join Angie at the Catholic Church because the mass was shorter and he had never been there when they didn't have a keg flowing in the fellowship hall. Hannah's brothers were competing to see who could be the first to make Nathan laugh so hard that milk came out of his nose.

Elijah sat back and smiled. In that moment there were no meetings to attend, no crises to manage, no worship services to plan, and no visits demanded. He drew in that curative breath of relief, allowing himself to soak his spirit in a wellspring of gratitude, an emotion fundamental to our well-being, but an emotion mostly neglected because we're always on to the next big thing. Gratitude requires a pause button and we seem to be always confusing it with the fast-forward button. And yet, as Meister Eckhart suggested, "If the only prayer you ever say in your entire life is thank you, it will be enough."

Gratitude is too often viewed as an obligation, the voice of your parents ringing in your ear—"Did you write those thank you notes? Did you write those thank you notes? Did you write . . . ?" What most folks fail to realize is that gratitude is incredibly medicinal. When Elijah is walking with a family through the valley of the shadow of death, he is continually surprised by the way the presence of gratitude transforms the experience of dying for the patient and those who love her. There is profound sorrow, yes, but there is also laughter and immense joy made possible because of a prevailing wind of gratitude.

Of course, he has also witnessed the effects of gratitude's absence. Where there is no gratitude, there is no peace, and bitterness is given the space to fester and grow. As Mark Twain observed, "If you pick up a starving dog and make him prosperous, he will not bite you. This is the principal difference between a dog and a man."[9]

The next morning, ignoring the Arctic conditions outside, Hannah and Beau headed down to the barn to saddle up the horses and go for a ride. Hannah relished those rare opportunities to ride in fresh fallen snow. Elijah relished the fact that she did not ask him to go with her. He huddled up with Xani and Nathan in front of a warm fire and a flat screen to watch *The Polar Express*. As soon as the boy on the train pulls the emergency brake to allow a child of poverty to board, Elijah noticed Angie motioning for him to join a conversation at the dining room table. The kids were so engrossed in the story they didn't even seem to notice him stepping away.

Taylor was also located and asked to join the conversation along with Billy. It was rare to see such doleful expressions on the faces of God's jesters, Angie and Billy. Angie called the meeting to order by looking to Taylor and uttering the inevitable phrase most families confront sooner or later, a phrase that portends tough decisions and tough days lie on the road ahead. "It's your father . . . " Before she even completed the sentence, ironic smiles emerged on the faces of both Taylor and Elijah. They knew what was coming because, professionally, they had each initiated that conversation with numerous families. "It's your father . . . " "It's your mother . . . " "It's your *(fill in the blank)*."

Billy completed the sentence for Angie, but Taylor and Elijah could have written the script for him, though few could phrase it quite like Billy. "The Judge is slipping." Elijah detected tears welling in Angie's eyes. Billy continued, "He can't remember things for shit . . . It started out with the small stuff: the name of a colleague, my phone number, the name of his favorite restaurant on the Hill in St. Louis."

"Pietro's?" Taylor wondered.

"Yep, and then the lapses escalated. He forgot a doctor's appointment. He couldn't remember the name of Zeb Jackson, his closest friend and fellow Supreme Court Justice. He lost his glasses, then his wallet, and then his keys in the span of five days."

"That's not good."

"Right. I mean you could blow it off if he was a mere mortal, but this is the Judge. When a lawyer asks the Judge about a legal precedent, he doesn't just point them in the right direction, he'll most likely spout off the page and paragraph in *Westlaw* where it's located. Dude has the gray matter of a pachyderm. He never forgets anything. Remember, we have often talked about seeing a flicker of the Judge's light burning in Zachary. You know he

---

9. Twain, Mark, *The Tragedy of Pudd'nhead Wilson*, originally published in 1894.

could have memorized *Westlaw*, too, if it had ever captured his attention
the way golf did. And I don't have to tell you, Taylor, we could never sneak
anything by the Judge."

"Not that you didn't try."

"Well, we'll regale my misspent youth on another day, but this shit is
getting serious. Last week he drove up to Mexico for a haircut and he got lost."

"Lost?"

"Yeah, how does anyone get lost in Mexico, MO? Jerry Brown saw the
Judge circling aimlessly around the courthouse square six or seven times,
and so Jerry got in his car to follow him. He said something just didn't seem
right. The Judge then headed east and pulled over to the side of the road,
stopping right at the edge of a ditch down near the Military Academy. Jerry
pulled in behind him and just watched for a few minutes. He said the Judge
just sat there, staring straight ahead. It was 38 degrees outside and Jerry said
he had all the windows open, just sittin' there, not even looking around. So
Jerry got out to check on him. When he walked up beside the Judge's car,
the judge said, 'Is there a problem, officer?' Jerry said, 'Uh, Judge, this is
Jerry Brown.' And dad says, 'Of course, you are! Just pullin' your leg.' But
he wasn't. He didn't have a clue who Jerry was, and Jerry's been the Judge's
accountant for forty years. He even asked how Jerry's wife was doing, and
Jerry's wife ran off with the State Farm guy fifteen years ago."

"That was quite the scandal as I remember."

"No shit. Remember me tellin' you about Jerry cold cockin' the
guy out at the country club. Knocked him out. Broke his jaw and calmly
walked away singing, 'Like a good neighbor, State Farm is there.' Anyway,
Jerry asks the Judge if he was okay. Dad says, 'Sure. Absolutely.' So, Jerry
asks, 'Where you headed, Judge?' He said Dad tried to maintain a judge's
stoicism . . . but after an awkward silence, Dad's shoulders went limp and
with a warble of emotion in his voice, he confessed, 'I don't really know, sir.'
Jerry asked, 'Is there someone I can call for you?' Again, silence, and again,
'I don't really know, sir.'

"Jerry saw dad's phone in the cupholder and asked if he could borrow
it. He looked up the contacts and called me. When I got there, Dad feigned
humor and tried to pass it off as a result of a double dose of his heart medicine, but you could tell he was scared. But that isn't the most troubling thing.
Tell 'em, Angie."

"A few mornings ago, I woke him up and he looked at me; and his eyes
had the panic of someone waking up in a foreign country under the gaze of
a complete stranger. I leaned over to kiss him on his forehead and he winced
like a child getting a shot. Flustered, he fumbled for words, 'Uh . . . umm
. . . well . . . good morning.' I said, 'Angus, are you there?' And he paused for

a few seconds before saying unconvincingly, 'Uh . . . yes.' He was so pitiful. He didn't have a clue. He went into the bathroom and when he eventually came back out, you could tell the light had turned back on, but just like with Jerry, you could tell he was shaken. He put up a good front as if nothing had happened, and so I went with it. We actually had a nice day. Had lunch at the club and went to a matinee. The next day, I was riding with him and he ran a stop sign; came within a few inches of striking a young mom pushing a baby jogger. We skidded to a stop. He jumped out and was apologizing profusely. Lord, I thought he was about to promise to pay for the kid's college education. But suddenly, he just broke down and cried. By the time I got him back in the car, the mom was comforting him and apologizing for upsetting him. I'm scared, Taylor. I'm scared we're losing him."

Taylor observed, "He did seem awfully quiet and reserved last night."

Elijah said, "He sure did. Usually, the Judge and the good Rev. McPheeters are holed up in a corner using words like esoteric and historicity. They are always in deep conversation about such high-minded things, like realized eschatology or Niebuhr's perspective on war. I remember innocently wandering into one of their colloquies once and I felt like a second grader accidentally walking into the middle of a Major League baseball game. I was in way over my head. But last night there wasn't much interaction. The judge looked a little lost."

Billy said, "I think he knows the jig is up . . . and he's scared shitless."

Angie said, "He's been a lot more quiet lately. It's almost like he is afraid to say anything out of fear that he'll say something that will expose his confusion. He's always been so cerebral, reflective, and relatively quiet, but now he's trying just to appear reflective to hide the fear."

Elijah observed, "You know, I've seen some folks suffering from dementia withdraw, becoming passive and quiet; and I've seen others grow agitated, angry, and aggressive. They'll hit their caregivers, accuse everyone of stealing their hearing aids, and become obsessed with conspiracies. I kinda hope I go the passive route."

Billy laughed, "Not me! I'm gonna fight like a son of a bitch!"

"No doubt you will." Taylor said. "So, what's next?"

Angie said, "We went in for a couple of tests last week, and afterward I talked with Dr. Kelly, and he suggested that when you got into town, the four of us should meet with him and lay it all out on the table. He can meet with us tomorrow at 10:00."

Taylor nodded his head in agreement. "That sounds like a wise plan. Lord knows, this is not a case I relish arguing before the Supreme Court. Our dear jurist, even in the throes of senescence, could still pick my argument apart easier than a vagrant collecting cans."

Again Billy laughed, "What the hell did he just say? Somethin' 'bout throwing a séance?"

Taylor smiled, "Billy, allow me to put it in the patois of the farm. Even though he can't remember worth shit, if it comes down to a war of wits, he'll tear me a new one."

Billy chortled, "Well hell, why didn't you say so? Everybody here knows that's true, especially the little theologian there."

Elijah protested, "I plead the fifth. Anything I say will incriminate me. Anyway, that meeting tomorrow may be the hardest meeting any of us has ever attended. It certainly brings new meaning to the concept of speaking truth to power."

Taylor asked, "You think he'll be in denial? That he may react with anger?"

Elijah sighed, "No, I don't. I think, at least outwardly, he'll respond with dignity and grace. That's just who he is. But going into that meeting, we enter with established roles, established places and voices within the family's long-standing organizational structure, and we certainly know who is at the top of that chart, just slightly below the Lord. But that all changes tomorrow. There's going to be a tremor in the family structure. You've always looked to the Judge. You've always put your trust in the Judge. You've depended on the Judge. Tomorrow, the child becomes the parent. With each passing day, he'll depend more upon you. If he hands over his car keys tomorrow, and knowing the Judge, I think he will; when that happens I think we are all going to die a little on the inside. No, the Judge won't be in denial. I actually think we're more at risk for that. When we leave that meeting, the world is going to look a little different. Not too long from now, you'll be in a dilemma and you will instinctively pick up the phone to get the Judge's take on it. And you'll start talking before you realize you are asking for something that he can no longer give. I have heard it called the long goodbye, and it's hard, among the hardest things a person faces. Yet, it is part of the mystery and beauty of life. We just have to pray for the truth of Paul's observation—'Whether we live or whether we die, we are the Lord's.'

"Too often, I see families fighting the disease, constantly finishing sentences for a parent, correcting dad when he calls someone by the wrong name, getting frustrated with mom when she has slipped back in time, becoming bitter because mom can't provide the wisdom they desperately need . . . If they could just loosen their grip on the steering wheel a bit. Love him for who he is in that moment instead of being torn up by the angst of who he isn't. If he's lost in 1950, talking about getting a black angus ready to show at the state fair, just walk in the daydream with him. Let him enjoy it. Angie, if he calls you by Mimi's name, and he will, don't take it personally. You know he loves you with all his heart and that you have been a saving presence for him. When he calls you by Mimi's name, he knows he is looking at someone he loves deeply. He's had two great loves in his life, and he just knows he is looking at one of them. That's a high compliment. It's going to be hard, this long goodbye, but still, there is beauty and joy on the road ahead if you're open to it."

There was a silence at the table, signifying assent to the truth of Elijah's thoughts, allowing his words to soak in for a bit. But the silence only worked for so long with this crew. Billy broke it saying, "The little shit may make a preacher yet. Go figure." A welcome, healing eruption of laughter circled the table, enough so that it roused the Judge who was sleeping in his favorite chair across the way in the family room. Angie went over to help him up while Tess came walking up the hallway groaning, "I think I need a drink."

"What's up, T?" Elijah inquired.

"I swear, it's a good thing I love your sister to death because she is surely going to be the death of me."

"Dina Beth!!" A collective chorus.

"She was coming and then she wasn't coming and then she was coming but would be a couple of days late. Soooo . . . today she calls in a dither, freaking out about a *tingle* in her index finger."

"A tingle. Is that actually a medical term?" Elijah was rewarded with the stink eye for that.

"She said the tingle increased when she gripped her 7-iron. So, she decided she needed to go see this hand specialist up in Minneapolis. Has to go." Tess opens her hands like a conductor and everyone in the room joins the dramatic chorus: "It's a matter of life and death!"

Dina does have a flair for the dramatic and if she doesn't say, "It's a matter of life and death," at least twice a day, those closest to her would think there actually was something wrong.

"Sooooo, she's not coming to Laddonia?" Elijah knew the question was obvious in addition to knowing its answer, but he knew someone had to ask it in order to carry the conversation. There are certain established patterns and cues in family conversations and like a skier disqualified for missing a gate, a missed cue can kill a conversation. So, Elijah took the cue, allowing Tess to elaborate.

"Well, wouldn't you know it, Cara just happens to be playing a concert in Minneapolis on New Year's Eve." Cara, is Cara Jones, a rising star in the world of alternative music. She knows her way around a ballad and possesses what has become the industry standard, a voice that dances around a note without actually hitting it, an angst ridden tone that mimics a combination of an adolescent's whine and a constipated aunt's strain. The poetry pays no attention to the rhythm, its meaning about as straightforward as a Rorschach test. Like the Beat poets of old, she has found the intersection of faux nonconformity and commercial appeal. Dina and Cara have been dating for five months, but the family knows this relationship is headed for the crapper because a relationship cannot abide two high maintenance personalities. Somewhere, somehow, someone has to do some maintaining.

Life with Dina is full-throttle motocross, helmet required. One moment you are flying through the air, arms raised in the "look-ma-no-hands" position, and the next moment you are crashing into the hay bales; all tears, tantrums, and tribulations. At altitude, Dina is the uproariously entertaining, slapstick orchestrating, pranking, and punking life of the party. When she's in the zone, she can make the Venus de Milo laugh. There is no one you could enjoy being with more. Yet, you know the valley is coming and it is always a hard landing of self-doubt, self-loathing, and angst ridden eschatological torment. "It's a matter of life and death!!" Family members call it the after party, because there is always a mess to clean up, a head to hold over the toilet, a crisis to negotiate, and a shaken ego to massage. You cannot help but love Dina, pull for Dina, want to be around Dina. The most common thing said about Dina aside from her brilliance on the golf course is, "She makes me laugh." That will be her epitaph one day, but now and then, family members weary of being the janitor/counselor/cheerleader at the after party.

Cara, on the other hand, seems to prefer life in the valley. You just know she wore a lot of black T-shirts in middle school. Sullen, withdrawn, finicky, morose, and dark; and that's if you catch her on a good day. The family has seen her once, when Dina brought her to Charlotte for Thanksgiving. During the thirty-six hours of her stay, Cara emerged from Dina's room once, for the command performance of the Thanksgiving meal. When she demurred from the offer of a plate, Dina jumped in to explain. "Oh, it's just that she is on a fast."

Taylor, trying to be supportive, said, "Such discipline at a feast like this is a powerful witness of faith."

"Oh, I'm not a person of faith. The hunger sparks the creative spirit for my music."

"Oh . . . good for you."

"Besides, I lose my appetite at these faux family events and the feeble attempt of relatives to pretend they actually like one another."

Before Rev. McPheeters could offer her the refiner's fire, Tess interjected "Okaaaay . . . Dad, could you pass me the butter?" Believe it or not, Cara's mood grew darker when Tess confessed she had forgotten to purchase the particular blend of Darjeeling tea she had requested. Taylor later quipped that Tess was destined to be the target for one of Cara's brooding ballads. The next morning Adele reported that when she walked down the hallway, she could not help but hear the angry voices of Dina and Cara quarreling in Dina's room. They left in a huff before half the household was awake. Tess concluded, "This in not going to end well."

But it hasn't ended yet and Dina, laser focused on pursuing what she wanted, when she wanted it, would not be able to squeeze in an appearance at the Christmas gathering in Laddonia, where the cattle actually were lowing. They would miss her laugh and her energy. Elijah reasoned, "Well, look at it this way. Dina's going by what the scales are telling her—Minneapolis or Laddonia, Minneapolis . . . Laddonia . . ."

"Laddonia! Hands down." A human icicle had just burst through the back door. For Hannah, such a comparison is ludicrous. She looked like a fossil encased in a glacier, but there was an unmistakable gleam in her eyes. An hour on her horse and time spent grooming and feeding in the barn were more than recreation for Hannah. It had been a therapeutic time of re-creation. Elijah always felt a trace of guilt in these moments, recognizing how far they lived from the farm and how much she loved that place. And yet, Edinburgh had become an equally treasured place. He remembered what Hannah always said when he apologized for dragging her to the South. "No one dragged me anywhere. Home, by the grace of God, is where you make it and I wouldn't have it any other way. There are no regrets. You're stuck with me just as you have been your whole life."

The next morning in Dr. Kelly's private office, the Judge carried himself with the dignity and grace that Elijah had predicted. Before it was even suggested, he pulled out his driver's license and keys, handing them to Billy and quoting Ecclesiastes, "For everything there is a season, and a time for every matter under heaven." At that point, he was the only one in the room, including the doctor, with dry eyes. Faithful, fair, honorable, and strong. That is how everyone would remember the Judge even as his mind grew dim. Leaving the doctor's office, the Judge pulled Elijah to the side and whispered, "Before the cobwebs get too thick, I want to talk with you about . . . the service. I want you to lead it and enlist Billy to be the ego bouncer. I do not want my funeral to be a beauty pageant for preening politicians looking for a photo op. I hate it when those bastards elbow their way to the front pews like we shared some special bond, and I certainly don't want any of them getting access to a microphone. I want the service to be what it is supposed to be, a witness to the resurrection. I want you to preach a sermon. I want the congregation to sing *A Mighty Fortress* and *Lift High the Cross* and don't you dare let them sing *How Great Thou Art*. I don't care what they believe but they are going to leave knowing that I'm a Presbyterian. Can you do that for me, Elijah? I'm real proud of you."

"Judge, it would be a privilege; the greatest honor I can imagine."

"No, son. Your greatest honor was marrying my neighbor's daughter. I'm just an old farmer who was accidentally given a law degree and a judgeship."

"Love you, Judge."

"Love you, too, Preacher . . . and by the way, that was a mighty fine speech you gave yesterday at the dining room table. I liked that part about 'a tremor in the family structure.' That was good."

"You heard that?"

"Son, my mind's turning into oatmeal, but my hearing is just fine."

The exhaustion of the return trip to Edinburgh was mitigated by the inordinate grace of sleeping in your own bed. Time with extended family and the respite from church family had served as a healthy diversion for Elijah, allowing him to remember that he is more than a pastor; he is also a husband, father, son, nephew, grandchild, in-law, and friend. Time away also reminds the pastor that the church does not immediately collapse upon hearing the news of his or her absence. The classic hymn is based on truth. *The Church's One Foundation* is Jesus Christ her Lord—pastor not included.

Of course, this doesn't mean there isn't turbulence during re-entry: the parent's harsh words to the Sunday School teacher for her failure to ask Junior to read the daily Bible verse; the leak in the parlor; the committee chair furious about the reduction in his budget. Such issues are manageable in the ebb and flow of church life. A pastor is always navigating the hidden shoals of human discord, the inevitable unintended consequence of life together. *Blest Be the Tie that binds our hearts in Christian love*, but Lord, we sure could use some help the other 70% of the time.

In the church calendar, January is marked by the celebration of Epiphany. Ages ago, the Lord promised Abraham that through him "all the families of the earth shall be blessed." Christians understand that promise to be realized through Christ, the light of the world. Epiphany is the celebration of that light spreading forth across the globe. Though any number of sects through the centuries have sought to limit that light to those who pass the litmus test of their restrictive worldview, there are many disciples who perceive the light of Christ differently, understanding that it shines in surprising places as the Spirit of the living Christ works amidst people we do not know in ways we may not understand. To Elijah, Epiphany is the proclamation signifying that the light of Christ's love is far more expansive than we can imagine. In his heart, the church's mission is to be an instrument of God's grace and not the arbiter of God's judgment, for our mercy will always be found lacking when compared to that of our Lord.

In the dark of winter there is light and lightness as the church resumes its pre-Advent schedules and routines. There is a jolt of new energy as the well-intentioned earnestly try to make this the year that they will take their faith seriously. Yes, some of that energy will wane, but Elijah refuses to underestimate how the Spirit may be moving in their lives. One of the traditional readings for this time of year reports the building buzz surrounding this new teacher from Nazareth. Philip finds Nathaniel and says, "We have found him about whom Moses in the law and also the prophets wrote, Jesus son of Joseph from Nazareth." Nathaniel said to him, "Can anything good come out of Nazareth?" Philip said to him, "Come and see." Come and see. Elijah says this is to be the perpetual invitation of the church to both seeker and cynic. He does confess, though, to those days when he would personally like for a select few of those who have come and seen to rise and go.

From day to day as the light of Epiphany leads to the introspection of Lent, With Tamara doing such a wonderful job of preventing and extinguishing the typical church fires, Elijah is often freed to pursue his actual job description as a preacher, teacher, and pastor. But even Tamara couldn't protect Elijah from this one. The phone rang just after Xani had offered the blessing for supper. Elijah toyed with the thought of letting it go to voicemail but a misappropriation of priorities prodded him to answer it.

The voice on the line was blunt, truculent, and offered no identification.

"When are you going to learn how to preach?"

After a stunned pause, Elijah inquired, "Um . . . Bethany?" It dawned on Elijah that the unidentified voice on the other end of the line was Bethany McArthur, Sean's wife and the daughter of the Righteous Rev. Bishop Apostle Eddie Power, Senior Chief Executive Pastor of the Little Creek Apostolic Tabernacle.

"You didn't answer my question. Sean and I were there on Christmas Eve because we like the decorations and Daddy's service doesn't start 'til nine o'clock. You ruined the experience for us because you weren't preaching Gospel truth. On Christmas Eve, all those visitors and twice-a-year-members need to hear about the wages of sin, the consequences of not claiming Jesus as Lord, God's wrath, and the fires of hell."

"A Jonathan Edwards Christmas Story?"

"Who's he?"

"Oh, it's not important. What was your question?"

"When are you going to learn how to preach? Is there someplace we can send you, a conference or workshop? When my Daddy preaches or when I go up to the Baptist retreat center up at Ridgecrest, I am moved to take out paper and pen and write notes that I can use during the week. I hear clear black and white answers to moral issues and social issues. However, all I hear from you are theological dilemmas, stories, fancy words, and questions about scriptures that you evidently didn't figure out are straightforward. God said Creation took six days and he rested on the seventh. How can you mess that up? But you do. If you don't believe in the Bible, why would you even try to preach it?"

"Bethany, I am glad you have places and people that feed you spiritually and I'm sorry to be a disappointment to you; but you and I interpret God's Word differently."

"I don't interpret! It is what it is! The unvarnished literal truth."

"Well, that is your interpretation."

"My interpretation is that I believe in the Bible but you don't."

"Bethany, I believe in God. I believe in Jesus Christ. I don't stutter when I say the Apostles' Creed. But, it is our Lord that I worship. I don't worship the Bible. I believe the Scriptures of the Old and New Testaments to be the authoritative witness to the saving work of God. I believe that Christ is the Word made flesh and all Scripture points to Christ, because as John said this Word made flesh was with God from the beginning. I believe it is important to understand the historical and cultural settings behind the Scriptures to understand them more fully. I be . . . ."

Another voice jumps in. "Just shut up, you sanctimonious sumbitch!"

"Sean? I didn't realize this was a conference call."

"I oughta come over there and stomp that liberal apostate brain of yours with my size 11 Tony Lamas." Clearly, Sean was drinking again, heavily.

"Listen, I'm pretty sure this conversation is not taking us anywhere. So, let's just agree to disagree, say goodnight, and enjoy the evening."

Sean just wasn't going to let a good rant go to waste. "You and my cousins are ruining that church, your liberal co-conspirators killed the denomination, your Muslim-loving, socialist heroes are destroying the country, and if unchecked, they will go on to lay waste to the world."

"Wow! And to think it is all because I can't preach."

"Don't be such a smartass. Don't you know we'd be so better off without you . . . without all of you? We'd be wise to take a chapter out of the German playbook and corral you and all the other liberal, enlightened piss ants in one place and eliminate you with our own version of a Final Solution. Now that's a mission I'd sign up for."

In that brief moment of stunned silence, Elijah, thankfully, sensed the Spirit of God saying, "Say goodnight, Gracie . . . Say goodnight, Gracie."

Elijah swallowed hard and said, "This conversation needs to end. Sean, Bethany, the Lord be with you." Elijah could hear shouting on the other end of the line as he placed the handset in its cradle. He took a deep breath, turned to his family, smiled, and said, "I'll be just a moment. I need a walk around the block." Elijah headed out the back door with no coat to shield him from the cold, but Hannah figured his blood pressure had spiked to the point that he wouldn't even notice the temperature. She just hoped he would find his way back.

Morning dawned with the welcome songs of robins, finches, and cardinals beckoning spring to board the jet stream and come in for a landing. Their melodic songs masked their impatience. They hadn't flown all this way to wake up cold. By sunrise, Hannah was pulling into the school parking lot and Elijah was deep into negotiations with Xani and Nathan about the lagging pace of their morning routine. Ironically, the very words at the heart of his faith, the words that inspire hope for his congregation, are also the same words that generate fear in the preacher: It's Friday but Sunday's Coming. Yikes! So much to do but precious little time to do it. Sermon—Bulletin—Bible study class—Agenda for meeting after church. There is a reason you don't hear many clergy singing *Thank God It's Friday.*

St. Martin, by this time, was deep into Lent; the pancakes of Shrove Tuesday had long been digested and Holy Week was looming. The warm afternoons of early March had coaxed the blooming of the Bradford pears, and a topic of daily small talk was how long the trees would be enjoyed before the inevitable freeze would brown their blooms. Saturday morning there would be no sleeping in. As the elderly gathered for the sacred ritual of sausage biscuits and coffee at Hardee's, the Parishes were joining the other Type A parents at the fields of McArthur Park for Xani's first soccer practice. Yet, it would be a stretch to suggest that what transpired on the pitch could be called either soccer or practice. A more accurate description would be a biologist's performance art troupe depicting the random movements of an amoeba.

It was the weekend of the ACC Basketball Tournament, an annual religious festival in the Southeast that makes a significant dent in worship attendance. All the chatter around town was infused with the trash talk of the alumnae from the basketball factories along Tobacco Road.

As Elijah stepped forward to the pulpit on Sunday, he was both heartened by the presence of the faithful remnant and disheartened by the absence of those who deemed it too onerous a task to get from the pew to the barcalounger in time for the tip-off of the championship game. As worshippers prayed at St. Martin's, other worshippers pounded avocados into guacamole and donned vestments dyed in the colors of UNC, Duke, State, and Wake.

White Elephants, Stickers, Cristal, and a Father's Love

Reading from the Gospels: Luke 15:1-3, 11b-32

1 *Now all the tax collectors and sinners were coming near to listen to him.* **2** *And the Pharisees and the scribes were grumbling and saying, "This fellow welcomes sinners and eats with them."* **3** *So he told them this parable:*

"There was a man who had two sons. **12** *The younger of them said to his father, "Father, give me the share of the property that will belong to me.' So he divided his property between them.* **13** *A few days later the younger son gathered all he had and traveled to a distant country, and there he squandered his property in dissolute living.* **14** *When he had spent everything, a severe famine took place throughout that country, and he began to be in need.* **15** *So he went and hired himself out to one of the citizens of that country, who sent him to his fields to feed the pigs.* **16** *He would gladly have filled himself with the pods that the pigs were eating; and no one gave him anything.* **17** *But when he came to himself he said, "How many of my father's hired hands have bread enough and to spare, but here I am dying of hunger!* **18** *I will get up and go to my father, and I will say to him, "Father, I have sinned against heaven and before you;* **19** *I am no longer worthy to be called your son; treat me like one of your hired hands."'* **20** *So he set off and went to his father. But while he was still far off, his father saw him and was filled with compassion; he ran and put his arms around him and kissed him.* **21** *Then the son said to him, "Father, I have sinned against heaven and before you; I am no longer worthy to be called your son.'* **22** *But the father said to his slaves, "Quickly, bring out a robe—the best one—and put it on him; put a ring on his finger and sandals on his feet.* **23** *And get the fatted calf and kill it, and let us eat and celebrate;* **24** *for this son of mine was dead and is alive again; he was lost and is found!' And they began to celebrate.* **25** *"Now his elder son was in the field; and when he came and approached the house, he heard*

music and dancing. **26** *He called one of the slaves and asked what was going on.* **27** *He replied, "Your brother has come, and your father has killed the fatted calf, because he has got him back safe and sound.'* **28** *Then he became angry and refused to go in. His father came out and began to plead with him.* **29** *But he answered his father, "Listen! For all these years I have been working like a slave for you, and I have never disobeyed your command; yet you have never given me even a young goat so that I might celebrate with my friends.* **30** *But when this son of yours came back, who has devoured your property with prostitutes, you killed the fatted calf for him!'* **31** *Then the father said to him, "Son, you are always with me, and all that is mine is yours.* **32** *But we had to celebrate and rejoice, because this brother of yours was dead and has come to life; he was lost and has been found."'*

One: This is the Word of the Lord.

Many: Thanks be to God.

With chestnuts roasting on an open fire or at least being celebrated through the cheap stereo speakers on the bookshelf, the extended generations of a family gather in a circle around the tinseled tree at Christmas for the annual white elephant gift exchange. Have you ever played that game? I hate that game.

First of all, it long ago ceased being white elephant. The name white elephant derives from the storied practice of the kings of Siam who would give an albino elephant to particularly obnoxious courtiers, reasoning that the recipient would be financially ruined by the cost of trying to take care of the elephant. It was a gift no one would want. It was one of those gifts that screams, "So, what am I supposed to do with this?"

Thus, the theory behind the white elephant game is that you pull out the pink flamingos and the velvet Elvis paintings, wrap them up real pretty so that the room will erupt in laughter when your cousin, thinking she might be receiving a new purse, opens the package to find a Teenage Mutant Ninja Turtle lunchbox.

However, over time, people wearied of dragging home ceramic cats and paintings of dogs playing poker; and so, the gifts started becoming more desirable—Chic-fil-A gift certificates and jars stuffed with Snickers, Skittles, and Ghirardelli chocolates. You know this game? I hate this game.

Everyone takes a number, and in turn, each participant goes to the gift pile and pulls out a package, opening it for all the players to appraise. You see, each person with a higher number will have the opportunity to steal that gift from you, that is, until it has been stolen three times. "Do I want to take a chance on a wrapped package or steal Aunt Ginny's chicken sandwich and waffle fries? Just don't let me get stuck with something like a candle."

Granted, there are some folks who still get the joke, laughing with everyone else when they pull the well-traveled fruitcake from last year out of the gift bag, but more often than not you see a lot of measuring, coveting, camouflaging ("Don't want someone to steal my barrel of caramel corn"), and scheming ("She's crazy if she thinks she's going to walk out of here with that Cracker Barrel gift certificate").

Did you ever play that game? Not a fan. It's like a sociologist's petri dish, containing over half of the seven deadly sins (greed, envy, pride, gluttony). It's all there to observe in the family celebration of Christ's birth. Don't you find it unsettling to witness how easily the skin of civility is pulled back to reveal the avarice of the human heart?

The white elephant charade offers a preview of the circus that may ensue at the death of the family matriarch or patriarch. If it's this cutthroat over a pack of Milk Duds, Lord, help the peacemakers when it comes time to settle an estate.

Watching a war movie, we are offended when a soldier pillages a fallen enemy's belongings, and yet, isn't that what so often happens while they're still singing the last hymn at mom or dad's funeral?

I had a cousin who died a couple of years ago. The graveside service of his mother a few years before had been a sight to behold, complete with an out of tune solo accompanied by a boom box and a dog with sleep apnea who snored through the proceedings. My cousin's funeral, however, was a sad symbol of his loneliness in life. Hardly a living soul there. The congregation was made up mostly of tombstones.

Anyway, my cousin had a rather unhealthy obsession with guns. My aunt's house had become an armory—shotguns, pistols, and rifles everywhere. Yet, by late that afternoon, the place had been cleaned out by relatives who were a little vague on the details of why all the artillery had vanished. "You know Van had a habit of loaning those guns out." "Yeah, but they were here yesterday and he was already dead."

The apostle Paul said, "Oh death, where is thy sting? The sting of death is sin." It may not be what Paul was referring to, but it seems to me that the real sting, the most grievous sin connected to death is the way family members treat one another in the aftermath. Battle lines are drawn, wars are declared, lawsuits are filed, and relationships are irreparably harmed as heirs fight over heirlooms and assets. You probably have war stories some-where in your family tree, or maybe your family tree is covered with the frost of broken relationships and bitterness as a result of fights over stuff.

I read an article this week highlighting the top ten family feuds over an estate, including everything from a stripper to baseball legend Ted William's frozen head. The courts are clogged with family members waging war over momma's pearls and Uncle Jimmy's mutual funds. London's *Financial Times* reported that the number of family estate battles litigated has doubled over the last five years. Relationships utterly destroyed over stuff, over money. Is it really worth it?

Another article offered the practical wisdom of giving everybody a page of stickers when Uncle Buford dies. They would then take turns plac-ing stickers on the items they want to claim. It's practical, a worthy idea, but isn't it a sorry statement of what is important to us?

The children of Viacom chairman, Sumner Redstone, have been waged in court battles for years, and he's not even dead yet. Kids have been fighting over their fair share since Adam chose Abel's cheeseburger over Cain's fruit salad. Honestly, we are slow learners.

"There was a man who had two sons. The younger of them said to his father, 'Father, give me the share of the property that will belong to me.' So he divided his property between them. A few days later the younger son gathered all he had and traveled to a distant country, and there he squan-dered his property in dissolute living."

With understated language Jesus describes what is a most scandalous encounter. "Dad, you know that IRA account that's supposed to cover the cost of your care over at Plantation Estates? Yeah, how about cashing that in for me. You know, people are living so long these days, and if I wait until you die, I may be too old to enjoy it!"

How would you like your child to greet you with that one morning? Speechless! I'd just be speechless! Narcissism wouldn't begin to describe what would prompt such a request. Brazen and bold and heartless. And, in the first century a demand like this would be culturally abhorrent.

In that decidedly patriarchal society, fathers were to be revered, de-ferred to, their wishes respected (Ah, the good ol' days!). So, this son's re-quest would have been a bitter insult. Not only that, it would have also been a disturbing departure from the values that all Israelites hold so dear, even to this day. You see, the inheritance would have been a portion of the fam-ily's land and in that world, you don't give up the land. Do you remember God's promise to Abraham? "I am the Lord who brought you from Ur of the Chaldeans, to give you this land to possess." The promise of land was and is integral to Israel's identity. To sell the land, in addition to reducing his father's ability to earn an income, would invoke the scorn of the whole community toward the family. There are some things you just don't do. You don't tick off a waiter before he serves your food. You don't wear tube socks to the gym. You don't ask the Pope to pull your finger. And in Israel, you don't sell the land. You just don't.

But, the younger son did, and Jesus tells us that the boy lost it all in (you gotta love this phrase) "dissolute living." It's somewhat ironic that we read this text as college students drag themselves back to class after the spring break trip with their friend, Bud Light. "Dissolute living." Did you see the ESPN documentary on athletes and money? Chastened and broke former pros chronicling the millions of dollars they blew on Bentleys, jewelry, prostitutes, gambling, and nightclubs. Just one night out would cost five figures as the Cristal poured freely and they massaged their egos by taking a stack of hundred dollar bills and throwing them out over the crowd. It was called *making it rain.* (It's what we do in the church office every Monday morning, right?) Make it rain.

Well, for the younger son, the rainstorm came to an abrupt end, figuratively and literally. Money's gone, drought ensued, famine caught up with him, and all the boy had left was a beer mug from Hooters and an *I'm Big on the Pig* T-shirt from the farmer who hired him to feed the animals his ancestors declared unclean.

It is said that home is the place that when you go there, they have to let you in. Well, the hungover young destitute exile certainly couldn't count on that. You see, in that time and culture, his choices would have resulted in being disowned from the family. So, for the prodigal, going home was as wise as Fredo accepting Michael's invitation to return to the Corleone estate.

But, maybe, just maybe his father, if running low on compassion, would at least rather see him working than see him dead. Still smelling of pig manure, the son walks up the farm road practicing his confession when he sees his father awkwardly running toward him, looking like he could trip over his sandals at any moment. The boy just hopes he's not carrying a knife. But the father carries no weapon, just a bear hug and a big sloppy kiss.

Again, this was something you just didn't do. Parents didn't run to greet their children. Children ran to greet their parents. Yet, before junior can even grovel, dad is fitting him with a brand new Brooks Brothers blazer, his grandfather's ring, and a shiny pair of Allen Edmonds finest loafers. Fire up the grill, "for this son of mine was dead and is alive again; he was lost and is found!" And they began to celebrate. Well, most of them did. Number one son was busy outside nailing together a big ol' chip on his shoulder singing that annoying blues song that every parent grows so tired of hearing. "It's . . . not . . . fair!"

The older son may have been the responsible one, the dutiful one, the hard-working one, but he was no less calculating than his little beer-breathed brother. At some level, he too was working the system, positioning himself to take over the family business if and when the old man would ever die. The father knew that. If your child's motives are so often transparent to you, how much more does the Lord know the motivations of our hearts? "Lo, before a word is even on my tongue, thou knowest it altogether." The father knows what's going on. And yet, again, he defies social convention, leaving his guests to go outside and be with his boy. "All that is mine is yours."

In the end, this story isn't primarily about the soap operas we produce in the quest to seize what we think we deserve and even what we know we don't. This story is about a God who sees right through the scheming, the coveting, the manipulating, the extortion, the pandering, the suing, and the hostility that can be found circled around the Christmas tree, in the courtroom, or behind the tears and hugs at the funeral home; and yet, this God loves us anyway, clumsily running down the road to welcome us home.

This is a story about a love that ignores cultural taboos, cuts through religious dogma, and will not be deterred by the politics of family greed. It is a story that forces the question on us: If we are to reflect God's love, will we be exclusive or inclusive? Will we be ambassadors of extravagant hospitality or will we be gatekeepers checking IDs and zealously guarding our fair share?

You see, this story is about Jesus' response to the critics' complaints that he was too cozy with the tax collectors and sinners. This story is a rebuttal to the idea that we can ever deserve God's love. This is a story that proclaims that true love can never be deserved. It can only be given or received. And, in Christ, it has been given.

You are never so far from home that God can't run you down to welcome you home. That is the love we have been called to reflect.

Six years ago, I was a student minister in my first week at a little church on the south side of Charlotte. It was late in the day. I was the only one left in the office, and as most honest preachers will confess about their early days, I didn't have a clue. Well, suddenly a young man appeared with a story that I would hear periodically through the years. He was traveling home to eastern North Carolina, but his car broke down and he was stranded. He had managed to collect $36, but needed $20 more to pay for the repair. He needed the money quickly because the repair shop would close and then he'd really be stuck. I was a deer in the headlights, stuttering, mumbling, and stuttering some more. Well . . . uh . . . I don't have access to the emergency fund yet . . . I'm the only one here . . . Um, we don't give out cash . . . Uh . . .

He said, "I'll leave my driver's license with you, so that you'll know I'll return to pay you back." He handed me a piece of paper that was supposed to be some kind of temporary license. Uh, I don't know . . . I'm uh, new here. Deer in the headlights. I pulled out my wallet and reached for my change. "Uh, I have $14.32" . . . "Thanks. God bless you" and he was gone . . . He didn't come back.

Oh, I kicked myself, reciting P.T. Barnum's proverb. "There's a sucker born every minute." I wish I would have framed that *license*, not to remind me of my gullibility, but to remind me of all the times I have given Jesus a fake license, promising I'd be back to repay the debt. But I never would, never could. And yet, Jesus is always wearing out his Nikes as he runs down the road to find us, enveloping us with a love we can never repay.

The gatekeepers fume: "This fellow welcomes sinners and eats with them." And, in a short three-act play, Jesus basically answers, "Yep . . . So what's your point?" Amen.

5

Spring

IT IS SAID THAT March arrives like a lion and leaves like a lamb. However, this year March debuted as the Tasmanian Devil and departed like Daffy Duck. The early April flowers were certainly not short on irrigation, but Monday night the clouds broke and Tuesday morning the sun's spotlight allowed the tulips, azaleas, dogwoods and lilies to garner rave reviews from the most dour of critics. A late date for Easter this year meant the church grounds would make even Monet jealous. The garth of St. Martin was an explosion of color—pinks, whites, purples, and yellows covered nature's floral jewelry bordering grass so green it would stain the canvas shoes that ventured onto it. While the colors bedazzled the eyes, Southern noses began their annual revolt. Very soon the entire South would be blanketed with the yellow pollen paste that sends sneezing, snot-blowing sinuses in search of antihistamine.

Approaching the church door that morning, Elijah saw that it had been forced open, shards of glass scattered on the stone beneath his feet. Instinctively, if not wisely, he stepped inside, drawn in by the inexorable compulsion to see what's been damaged or stolen. Curiously, the hallway to the church office showed no signs of robbery or vandalism. The flat screens were still on the walls of the classrooms; the furniture in the reception area was undisturbed. The door to the church office was kicked in as was the inner door to Elijah's office, but Tamara's computer was still on her desk and it appeared the file cabinets and safe had not been touched. There was even an envelope

containing money from Sunday's sale of church cookbooks that Patsi McTav-
ish, the czarina of fundraisers, had forgotten to put in the drop box.

Peeking into his office, Elijah saw that everything on his desk was in its
place. His treasured baseball, signed by Stan Musial, was still on its perch.
Yet, once inside, he turned around, his heart rate doubled and his eyes became as wide as those of a Cavalier puppy facing a Great Dane. Someone
had taken a red marker and scrawled a message across the wall.

I MISSED YOU THIS TIME

BUT THE MISSION WILL BE COMPLETED

YOU'RE NEXT!

Surrounding the cryptic message, it appeared that the messenger had
circled his art with bullet holes. Suddenly, a rising chorus of sirens began
ringing out. It was far different from the normal emergency response in
Edinburgh where the sound of a single fire truck accompanied by the shriek
of a police cruiser might momentarily disrupt the laconic tranquility of
an Edinburgh evening. This was way outside the boundary of ordinary. It
sounded like every emergency vehicle in the county was wailing the lament
of crisis. Elijah was about to find that to be an understatement.

Lost in the fog of firing synapses scrambling to sort out the order of
what needed to be done, Elijah almost didn't hear his cell phone ringing.

"Where are you?" The voice was familiar, the panic within it was not. It
was Jimmy, and he was as freaked out as Elijah was confused.

"At the church."

"I'm coming up the block. Meet me outside."

"What's going on?" It took a second for Elijah to realize Jimmy had
hung up before he even asked the question. He ran outside and jumped in
the van the funeral home uses to transport bodies.

Jimmy mashed the gas, speed limits be damned. Of course, it didn't
matter. All the cops were preoccupied anyway.

"There's been a mass shooting at McArthur's Plant #1 and the corporate offices."

"What?"

"Some nut went through there with a Bushmaster. Multiple casualties. That's all I know."

"I think I may know who it was."

"The shooter?"

"Yeah."

"Who?"

"Sean IV"

"You shittin' me?"

"No, he called me a couple of weeks ago, or I should say Bethany called me to complain about my preaching and Sean jumped on the line, noticeably drunk, ranting about how his cousins, the liberals, and my preaching were destroying the world."

"Your preaching caused me to miss a tee time once, but destroying the world? That's a little over the top."

"He said they, whoever *they* are, should borrow a chapter from the Germans and come up with a *final solution* for us. He said he'd sign up for a mission like that."

"That sounds like Sean, but damn, mass murder?"

"Last Friday, the Superior Court threw out his lawsuit against Mark, Spencer, and McArthur Furniture Company. The attorney who filed the motion to dismiss was my father."

"No way!"

"Yes way. So, Mark tells me on Sunday that Sean had left him a voicemail that morning. All it said was 'Matthew 16:2-4.'"

"Okay, so I'm embarrassed to say I don't have that one memorized."

"Don't worry, neither did I. So, we took a Bible from the pew and looked it up. Jesus is being confronted by the Sadducees and the Pharisees and is asked for a sign from heaven. 'When it is evening, you say, 'It will be fair weather, for the sky is red.' And in the morning, 'It will be stormy today, for the sky is red and threatening.' You know how to interpret the appearance of the sky, but you cannot interpret the signs of the times. An evil and adulterous generation asks for a sign, but no sign will be given to it except the sign of Jonah.'"

Jimmy asked, "What is that supposed to mean?"

"Who knows what it means in Sean's mind, but given what's going down, it could be he saw himself as Jonah going to Ninevah/Edinburgh predicting its destruction because of their wickedness."

"But do you really think Sean is capable of something like this?"

"Yesterday morning, it was my turn to get a voicemail from Sean. All he said was, 'The storm is coming.' I called Mark and also K.C. at the police station. K.C. said he'd try to keep a couple of cars near the plant and tell his guys to do a few drive-bys at the church and our houses. Mark was going to hire a couple of off-duty officers to keep an eye on things. They even went out to his place, but Bethany didn't know where he was."

"Uh oh."

"That's not all. You called just after I arrived at the church. Someone had broken in. Nothing stolen. No signs of vandalism until I stepped into my office." Elijah reported the graffiti and the bullet holes.

Stunned, Jimmy was silent for a moment before stating the obvious. "You mean if we had not gone on that bike ride this morning . . . "

"Yes. Thank God Tamara had a doctor's appointment and the preschool was closed because of a teacher workshop in Hickory. If I had showed up with the kids at the usual time, I . . . " Elijah couldn't even complete the sentence.

"Don't even go there, Elijah. Let's focus on what is."

"Yeah, I'm afraid of what we're going to find there."

"Elijah, we're heading into a war zone. Nothing prepares a person for that."

Jimmy pulled the van up to the police barricade that had already been erected. Recognizing the van, the officer waved them through. Jimmy knew all the policemen by name, the small town partnership between the police and the funeral home being morbid but necessary. The police provided escort for each funeral cortege and Jimmy regularly met them at all hours of the night after every suicide, fatal heart attack or stroke, and the occasional murder. Yet the officer, like Jimmy and Elijah, had the dazed visage of those entering the ungodly and surreal.

Stepping out of the van they spotted K.C., Police Chief Ken Carpenter, at a makeshift command center and walked toward him.

Elijah asked, "How bad is it?"

K.C. said, "Bad. Real bad. Sixteen dead including the shooter and thirteen injured."

"The McArthurs?"

"Mark is dead. Spencer's okay, just rattled; and . . . " K.C. stopped midsentence knowing he needed to be careful about what he said.

"Sean IV?"

K.C. said nothing but his eyes said it all.

"K.C., there's something you need to know." Elijah stepped aside with the Chief and recounted the morning's discovery while Jimmy went with an officer to gather information about the transportation of the bodies. Of course, he couldn't walk through the crime scene until investigators had what they needed and that would be a while. When called upon he would beckon his workers to help him move the bodies to a central location for identification. Just the thought of standing in that temporary morgue with the coroner and officers as families entered individually to identify their next of kin made Jimmy sick to his stomach.

The wail of sirens continued unabated as ambulances transported the injured to the hospital where Jane and a score of other physicians were summoned in accordance with the Community Disaster Plan. Jimmy, Jane, and Elijah had gone through the Disaster Preparedness Training just a month ago, assuming as anybody would, that they would not have to put it into practice so quickly. They would later compare it to playing a Little League game one day and starting for the Yankees the next.

Given their conversation the previous day, K.C. was not surprised by Elijah's report. "In retrospect it all fits together. You know we had two officers stationed here, but somehow he slipped by them. I need to get back to the chaos, but stay here and I'll have an officer take down your statement."

"I'd like to see Spencer."

"Yeah, I know. There are a few other people you're going to want to see also, but that can't happen just yet. In the next fifteen minutes this place is going to be overrun with federal agencies; FBI, ATF, Homeland Security, and a bunch more I can't even remember the initials of, all of them fightin' for position, press, and power. It's going to be one helluva pissing contest. And look, the media vans are already pulling in. Listen to all those choppers. It's *Apocalypse Now* all over again. Elijah, the zoo has opened all the cages and the animals are coming to Edinburgh. You won't be able to spit without someone wanting to put it under a microscope or on a TV screen.

"I know the Feds would skewer me like a shrimp if I let you talk to Spencer before they took your statement. After that, we'll get you to her and the others. I'm also going to need you with Jimmy over at the temporary morgue. Wait here and call Hannah. Tell her you are okay and will be late for dinner, but nothing else."

A gaggle of federal helicopters was lining up for landing in the field behind the plant, soon followed by a caravan of black SUVs through the front barricade. This was going to make the crowd at the Ellerbe sting look like a lone grade school hall monitor. Elijah quickly called Hannah who uttered a cry of relief at the sound of his voice. Elijah also got in touch with Tamara who was just leaving the doctor's office over in Morganton, totally unaware of the maelstrom that had descended upon her hometown.

Elijah was grilled for about an hour by three different federal agencies, though it seemed interminable knowing that he could not be present with church members in distress. When the presiding agent, a real hard case, finally closed his notebook, Elijah resisted the urge to suggest the agent would have made a good proctologist. Rather, he simply sighed deeply. This certainly wasn't how Elijah had envisioned his day. One of the agents at the table with them motioned for Elijah to follow him. Channeling Major Clipton from *Bridge on the River Kwai*, the agent began, "Madness! Madness!"

"River Kwai?"

"Yeah."

"Fits, doesn't it?"

"Sadly. I'm Isaiah Mitchell, by the way."

"Isaiah and Elijah. Don't know about you, but I sure don't feel like a prophet today."

"Not hardly. I know you need to do your job, so let me help you find your folks. I'm a Presbyterian elder. New York Avenue in D.C."

"Lincoln's Church."

"I like that connection. It has long been a thoughtful church, willing to wrestle with difficult ideas. I'd imagine that's why Lincoln attended, though I doubt there were any black elders serving at the time."

"You know, Martin Luther King, Jr. preached there sometime in the late sixties."

"1968, I believe. Just a couple of months before his assassination . . . OK, I need to warn you, you are about to see some pretty gruesome stuff. Before we go in, this is a list of the victims we've identified. There are a couple of others we're still tracking down. How many names do you recognize on the list?"

Looking down the list, Elijah felt like what they used to call a "tomato can" boxer, being pummeled mercilessly and repeatedly by Mike Tyson. Punch drunk, Elijah stammered, "I know nine . . . no, ten of them. Seven are church members." Elijah felt a growing, painful throb moving from the back of his head to the front. "Isaiah, are you familiar with the Cry of Dereliction?"

"Hmmm. Is there some connection to Good Friday?"

"Yes. Jesus' lament from the cross, 'My God, my God, why have you forsaken me?' It is actually a direct quote from the 22nd Psalm. The Psalmist continues, 'Why are you so far from helping me, from the words of my groaning? O my God, I cry by day, but you do not answer; and by night, but find no rest.' That will be the elegy of far too many family members tonight."

"Madness."

"Indeed." The scene inside was as graphic and gruesome as Isaiah had warned. As with a tornado, it was easy to follow the path of destruction from the plant to the executive suite. Blood splattered across machinery, then doors, then desks, computers, copiers, whiteboards, and carpet; periodic pools of blood congealing beside cloth-covered bodies. Here and there a stray lifeless arm or leg would peek out from beneath the sheets exposing the truth that we cannot hide from death. As Isaiah lifted sheet after sheet, Elijah was nauseated not so much by the brutality of death, but by the bizarre reality that he had been laughing with these people, shaking their hands, inquiring about their work, their families, and their vacation plans just two days earlier. When they came to Mark McArthur's body, Elijah collapsed to his knees looking upon a dear friend's face, void of the breath of life. The shock had sufficiently infected Elijah that tears were not forthcoming and the only prayer he could muster was, "Into Thy hands."

Though retired, Mark kept an office in the executive suite. From there, he shepherded the planning for the foundation the family was establishing. If not traveling, he was there every day and had already been instrumental in the building of a transitional housing complex for homeless families. Today's shock was violent death. In years to come the shock would be the sudden loss of so much leadership in the community. Thankfully, his sons, Seamus and Ian, were out of the country visiting a supplier in India. Though they would not be spared the grief of death, they had been spared death itself, and their children would have fathers to read bedtime stories and recite familiar prayers.

Isaiah broke through Elijah's fog, suggesting they go see Spencer. She was in her office staring blankly out the window. Standing and sitting around the office were Tom, Madison, Spencer's assistant Dani, her VP of Design Kevin, and Agent Sarah Lambert who introduced herself as the agent in charge of the operation. The room was loud with silence. At the two extremes of human experience, we are left mute. There is the silence induced by awe and wonder, but there is also the silence prompted by catastrophe. And so, the Psalmist's description of praise is strangely germane to the apocalypse in Edinburgh. "There is no speech, nor are there words; their voice is not heard; yet their voice goes out through all the earth, and their words to the end of the world." Truly, the message of their silent grief would trouble spirits to the farthest reaches of the globe as news agencies started the marathon of minute-by-minute updates examining and speculating about each sub-atomic particle of new information that filtered through any crack in the police barricade. Within the hour a mother cooking dinner in Minsk and a business executive turning in for the night in Shanghai would hear in their own language a commentator parsing the blood-stained sage silk suit worn by Spencer in her first appearance before the cameras.

Upon seeing Elijah, Spencer and Madison rose to meet and embrace him. There was no wailing, no surge of sobbing, just the quiet dignity of a strong leader whose spirit has temporarily been broken. They stepped over to a small conference table and sat down. Any pastor who says he or she is equipped for such a moment is either lying or a fool. Though you want to

offer some profound thought that offers salve for the soul, some Shakespearean lament, or some Niebuhrian reflection on evil, or some Lincolnesque
observation of strength in weakness, the mind goes blank. Elijah had confessed to Hannah that occasionally in tragic situations, it is as though he is
the recipient of the mourner's compassion because she can see he has not a
clue about what to say. "There is no speech, nor are there words; their voice
is not heard; yet their voice goes out through all the earth, and their words
to the end of the world."

The best you can muster is just being there. When desolation holds the
spirit hostage, words intrude and words of hope cannot be heard.

It was Madison who finally broke the silence. "Would it be okay if I
stayed at your place tonight? I have a feeling our yard is going to be literally
crawling with TV cameras and reporters."

"Certainly."

"Mom just talked to Seamus and Ian. They are on a layover in Dubai
returning from Mumbai."

"That's a hard call."

Spencer spoke with the raspy voice that has just uttered the deep cry
of dereliction, "Second hardest thing I've ever done; only topped by the conversation I had before that."

"Millie?"

"Yes. Since we're being held here for now, I called her. I didn't want to
do it by phone, but it would have been worse for her to see it on TV. Her
sister from Charleston is with her, thank God." Millie was Mark's wife, hospitalized with stage-four breast cancer that like suburbia was busy annexing
unincorporated organs. It would not be long. She was scheduled for transfer
to the Hospice House in the afternoon.

"I will certainly go see her."

"I would say this will kill her, but I think the cancer will accomplish that
first. I don't know if that poor woman had a happy day in her whole life."

"Her wedding day?" Madison asked.

"Certainly not. Her father, who was really hungover, stepped on the
train of her dress before the ceremony, and it took a lot of sweet-talk to co-
erce her down the aisle. At the reception, she locked herself in the bathroom
because the caterer had overcooked the canapés."

"Surely, the days when her sons were born."

"Nope. Pregnant with Seamus, she was put on bed rest for six weeks
and in that time she fired eight nurse assistants. You did not want to get anywhere near her, which is good because once Seamus was born, she wouldn't
allow anyone but Mark and the maid in the house, and some nights, Mark

wasn't even welcome. I didn't even get to see Seamus until the day of his baptism when he was six months old."

"What about Ian?"

"Eighteen hours of labor and post partum depression."

"Ugggh."

"Madison, think about it. How many times in your life have you been in that house?"

Squinting her eyes and jogging her memory, "Twice?"

"And one of those times we were quickly ushered out because you forgot to take off your shoes. She was a hard, bitter woman. She lost that Miss Highland Games pageant to Momma McKee and she never got over it . . . I can't believe I'm saying this and I may burn in hell for it, but when she agreed for Hospice to get involved, I have to admit that, in a way, I was relieved, grateful even; just thinking that Mark would finally be able to live and be free of all that."

Elijah said, "Spencer, we all felt that way. Nouwen suggested that there is a choice between bitterness and joy. Some folks just live into bitterness, while others can actually experience joy even in times of profound sadness."

"Let's hope, but that's going to be a tall order today. You know, he took such good care of her and never let it all drag him down. Millie's a hard person to be around, always so negative, always finding a dark cloud attached to every silver lining. Yet, he never spoke poorly of her. I just wanted him to be able to enjoy a season of . . . life. When I first got to him, he was still conscious, and he just looked . . . so . . . scared."

"I'm so sorry, Spencer, this is all a horror movie come to life, images that will never be forgotten, but you can't let that image define Mark for you."

"I know. I know. That seems rational, but rational didn't show up for work today. Crazy came instead. It happened so fast, but the playback is only available in slow motion. I wasn't in my office; I was standing out by the cubicles with the logistics team talking about supply lines. We heard the rat-a-tat out in the plant. It was loud enough that all our heads turned in that direction, but actually, it sounded like a bad bearing in one of the lathes. Then the door burst open and Sean, all dressed up and painted in camouflage, was spraying the room with bullets. Marge . . ." Spencer's voice catches for a moment. "Marge was standing right in front of me and was hit along with Tina, who was standing by me. They fell into me and we all went down. Marge was dead instantly, but Tina was hit in the shoulder. She's in surgery now. I couldn't see anything, but I could hear Sean tearing through the room and into the executive suite of offices. Then, there was an eerie silence. I heard Mark's voice but I couldn't make out the words. Then came another clatter of gunshots.

"Sean ran back into the cubicle area shouting, 'Where's the bitch!!' Immediately three shots rang out and I heard a body fall to the ground. Then silence. I heard another voice saying, 'Gunner down.' It was one of the off-duty officers Mark had hired after the phone calls you two received. Of course, I didn't realize that until there were a couple of other voices and they started searching for anyone still alive. Surreal doesn't even begin to describe it. It's like . . . like looking into one of those old Viewmasters. I can see it. I'm standing there talking about a fabric shipment. You pull the lever on the side and I'm cowering under the dead body of a friend. How . . . how can that be?"

"Unfortunately, evil doesn't come with Cliffs Notes, and we can no more explain it away than you or I could put on a red cape and spin the world back to 8:00 a.m. this morning."

"I don't look good in red, so that's not happening . . . Elijah, I need your help. I've got to go out there in a few minutes and offer a press statement on behalf of the family and the company."

As Agent Lambert stepped up to the table to ask Spencer a few questions, Elijah grabbed a notepad and scribbled the following notes.

- Our hearts are heavy with the loss of family and friends. We grieve for wives and children, mothers and fathers, grandchildren and friends who will not be able to welcome their loved ones home tonight.

- Evil refuses easy explanation and so rather than asking why this happened, we will ponder other questions: How do we honor the lost and how will we choose to live into tomorrow? It is my prayer that we will choose joy rather than bitterness, hope rather than despair, reconciliation rather than revenge, love rather than hate. Heartache will have its day; but bitterness will not define us as individuals, as families, or as a company named McArthur.

- The Psalmist proclaims, "Weeping may tarry through the night, but joy cometh with the morning."

It appeared Agent Lambert was going to be with Spencer awhile, so Elijah slid the notepad across the table to Spencer, who silently mouthed a thank you. Elijah stood, hugged Madison and stepped over to a waiting Isaiah who would be escorting him over to the temporary morgue being hastily assembled at the fire station across the road from McArthur's. Like the prophets of old, Elijah and Isaiah would be offering news the recipients did not want to hear. People react to tragic news as if they were ordering coffee at Starbucks. "I'll have a wailing lament topped with hyperventilation."

"I'll have an angry denial mixed with body slaps for the messenger." "I'll have quiet sobs, no, make that stoic resolve."

The whiplash-inducing emotions ricocheting off the walls of the fire station threw Elijah into an out-of-body experience. He could see himself speaking to the bereaved. He could hear his voice uttering the time tested words and prayers of succor that had comforted Christians through centuries of plague, fire, earthquake, war, epidemic, and random violence. Elijah was striving to be as present to the victims' families as possible, yet emotionally, he felt somewhat detached from the scene. His mind had not transported him to an afternoon stroll at Wrightsville Beach; he was still in the firehouse. Engaged but detached. Is it possible? Pastoral but preoccupied. It seems incongruous. The odd blend of sensations puzzled Elijah. Had his mind initiated some sort of emergency emotional defense mechanism? Was he experiencing the onset of shock or the after effects? Was there a leak in his compassion tank? Had he entered that realm known by soldiers at the front and investigators in the Special Victims Unit, seeing a horror which human eyes are not equipped to assimilate? Was it because he was an interloper, trespassing into the space of another person's tragedy?

This disequilibrium was not debilitating. His eyes communicated what they needed to communicate, as did his voice. He would be the only one who would know about it, but it just felt odd.

Those who had not received any news from family members employed at McArthur Furniture Company had gathered outside the fire station, the anxiety of some evolving into anger as they peppered police with questions they could not answer. Others stood silently by, identified by glazed eyes and trembling hands. One by one, families were ushered into the dining room of the firehouse that had become a makeshift anteroom where the families would learn which of three lists contained the name of their loved one: Safe/Treated and Released; ER/hospitalized/surgery; Deceased. It seems strange to pray that a spouse, child, or parent be in surgery, but once word of the lists filtered out to those waiting their turn in the parking lot, that is exactly what they could be heard praying.

There were sixteen victims whose families would not win this lottery of lists.

- Tiffany Woodson—Shipping Department: She was a teen mom before it became a path to MTV celebrity. Life had been hard. A restraining order had just been lodged against her latest boyfriend after he had slapped her three-year-old.

- "Marty" Martinez—Off-Duty Police Officer working security for the company: He had just returned from his honeymoon.

- Mavis Nunnelly—Shipping Department: A grandmother scheduled to retire in two weeks. Was supposed to sing a solo at her church on Easter Sunday.

- Todd Deland—Shipping Director: A member of St. Martin. Was the star quarterback for the high school and played at Appalachian State. Organized the church softball team and served as a youth advisor.

- "Zamboni" Moten—Janitorial staff: A beloved member of the McArthur Furniture family. Born with Down Syndrome, Zamboni possessed a perpetual smile and was a meticulous wizard with a broom, which is an essential skill in a furniture plant. Wood shavings, dust, and fabric threads were an industry-wide nuisance that didn't stand a chance against the great Zamboni. His smooth, pirouetting motions around that industrial equipment, accompanied by whistled tunes, introduced the McArthur craftsmen to the ballet without having to buy a ticket. Every Sunday, Zamboni unlocked the doors of St. Martin, served as a greeter at the front entrance without regard to the weather, and then found his favorite spot on the front row.

- Terrence Jackson—Upholsterer: Little League Baseball coaching legend; took two teams to the Little League World Series; Before a line drive shattered his elbow, Terrence pitched for 2 years at UNC.

- Lanie Maguire—Upholsterer: Divorced mother of two, now in their twenties and unemployed, living at home; A thirty year smoker, she had just been diagnosed with lung cancer in the last week.

- Erin McArthur Ebbet—Receptionist: A member of St. Martin; sang in the choir; Retired teacher who went to work for the family business; cousin of the shooter; two girls at UNC.

- Heather Schonfeld—Designer: Graduate of the Savannah College of Art and Design. One of her designs is currently being featured in a furniture exhibit at the Metropolitan Museum of Art. Commuted regularly to services at Temple Beth El in Charlotte. Next door neighbor of the Parishes.

- Ted Sandoval—Designer: Graduate of the Pratt Institute; Flamboyant; Hilarious; Always in crisis; A member of St. Martin; Sang in the choir; Beloved.

- Tawny Fribourg—Decorator: A former supermodel who graced the catwalks of New York, Paris, and Milan. Originally from Germany. Always the life of the party. When Dina was in town, the two would get together at some point. The manager of the ABC store was guaranteed a good night.

- Marge Cannon—Operations Manager: Chair of St. Martin Worship Committee; organized the most efficient Communion team in Christendom; veteran marathoner; new grandmother.

- Jackson "Jumper" Jones—Maintenance: a handy-man who could fix anything. A local legend on the basketball court, Jumper had taken a self-destructive turn during his senior year. He was convicted of possession and distribution of crack. He served five years in Raleigh and by the grace of God and the strong spirit of his mother, Jumper had pulled his life together and was loved and respected throughout the community. He had two sons.

- Sidnor Lincoln—CFO: Treasurer at St. Martin; Chair of Thistle County United Way; widower; was planning his annual fishing expedition to Lake of the Woods, Ontario.

- Tammi Rogers—Administrative Assistant: Wife of the police officer who put Sean IV down; mother of two; leader of a Brownie Troop.

- Mark McArthur—Retired CEO: Clerk of Session at St. Martin; philanthropist; revered in the furniture community; humble; epitome of a servant leader; not just grounded in faith, but guided by faith.

The loss was staggering, not just in terms of the numbers, or the worldwide attention suddenly focused on Edinburgh, but also the impact upon the community. Leadership capital in small towns across the country is in short supply as plant managers disappear along with the plants they managed. The collective stamp the victims made upon Edinburgh was impressive as evidenced by the storm surge of obituaries that would overwhelm the Edinburgh paper on Wednesday and Thursday. The work of the County Planning Board, the United Way, the Samaritan Center and Clinic, the Hospital Board, the School Board, the Arts Commission, along with the councils of several churches would each be diminished by an empty seat at their meetings.

Of course, this impact was minor when compared to the loss of relationship and the shattering of the illusion of innocence. Small town residents like to brag about unlocked doors, idle police departments, children riding bicycles across town, and the absence of metal detectors, alarm systems, and violent crime. It is an illusion. There is no such thing as an idle police department. Even Barney Fife worked nights and weekends. Among the nefarious effects of random violence is the way it isolates us, weakening our capacity to trust, intensifying our propensity to suspect. Doors are locked. Security systems are installed. Blinds are drawn. Neighbors are scrutinized, and yet, anonymous. Parks are empty. Front porches disappear. Sidewalks carry less traffic.

How would this egregious assault at McArthur Furniture leave its mark upon the community? Already, news websites and network anchors were posting headlines and previewing stories stirring up suspicions, stoking fears, and merchandising blame. *Could the Mayhem at McArthur Have Been Avoided? What Clues Were Missed By the Authorities, the Company, and the Church? When Will We Learn To Take Mental Illness Seriously?* Already, the NRA had posted a statement saying that the massacre could have been avoided if only McArthur employees had been allowed to carry Glocks. Already, parents were telling their children they could not play outside at a friend's house.

As Elijah stepped out of the temporary morgue into the temporary notification room, he spied a wall-mounted flatscreen with CNN rebroadcasting Spencer's statement to the press. Her words did not stray noticeably from the notes Elijah had scribbled on the notepad in her office, and yet, she lent them a certain gravitas he knew he could never muster. Elegant strength would one day be Spencer's epitaph. Endearingly eminent was the paradox of her mien.

Once outside, the chill of an early April evening awakened senses dulled by shock along with the dramatic gloom and cyclic despondency of the rue morgue. Elijah noticed that the dull headache induced by the morning's message on his office wall had blossomed into a demi-migraine. His body ached from a day of tensed muscles. The roadway outside the fire station was humming with the sound of generators and the where-are-my-sunglasses glare of klieg lights. John, chapter one, says that the light shines in the darkness, but Elijah sensed this was not the light John was talking about.

Elijah knew better than to enter the gauntlet of reporters and he sure didn't want to go back into the fire station, so there he stood, paralyzed between the press and purgatory. Not, only that, his car was at the church and he couldn't call anyone to pick him up because the authorities still had possession of his phone as part of the investigation.

Just then, his new prophet pal, Isaiah, tapped him on the shoulder, saying, "Need a lift?"

"Here I am. Take me."

"A little twist on Isaiah 6?"

"It is said that a prophet speaks what the Lord knows the people need to hear. And I certainly needed to hear that I had a ride."

"I need a stiff drink. Care to join me?"

"That's tempting, but truthfully, I just want to get home to my wife and kids."

"Understood."

As Agent Isaiah pulled up to the church Elijah was surprised to see the place surrounded by crime scene tape.

Isaiah calmed his fear of the potential disruption to the church. "Don't worry, they should be cleared out by morning. The vast majority of our attention is going to be directed toward the plant along with Sean McArthur's home and property. Oh, I almost forgot, here is your phone."

"You went through it already?"

"Yeah, you're clean. But does your wife know you are shopping for a new bike?"

"Busted. No, those Treks are a bit much for our budget. Maybe some day."

Upon thanking Isaiah for the ride, Elijah climbed out of the car saying, "The Lord be with you."

"And also with you. If I'm still around Sunday, look for me in a pew."

"That would be great."

As Isaiah pulled off, Elijah glanced at his phone. Sixty-two messages. They'll have to wait for now. All he wanted in the world was to be home, Hannah in his arms, Xani, Nathan, and Joab at his side, and a tall glass of sweet tea to sip. The entrance to his driveway appeared as the light that near-death veterans recount drawing them in. Hannah met him at the back door. Solace, relief, thanksgiving, sorrow, and joy wrapped ribbons around them as they silently held one another under the light of the carport. "There is no speech, nor are there words . . ." Once again, these words of the Psalmist suit the polarities of human experience—terror and awe; despair and joy.

Xani and Nathan, trailed by Joab came running by them into the carport for the start of the Cozy Coupe 500. Hannah and Elijah sat on the back step and watched, engaged yet as silent as a golf gallery before the putt. After ten minutes, Elijah simply asked, "So, how was your day?" They both grinned and proceeded to wade through the play-by-play. Already, it seemed what they were describing couldn't be real. Elijah felt as if he was telling Hannah about a movie he had seen. When Hannah shared the highlights from the news coverage, and how her heart seized when it was reported that a pastor had been an additional target of the shooter, she wept, knowing how close the asteroid had brushed by her world. "What if the preschool had been in session today?"

"I know . . . but we just can't go there." Elijah was speaking as much to himself as to Hannah. "We are here, safe, and together. That is our reality and that is where we must live. We can only be grateful and hope to be strong for those who weep tonight."

After a long silence, Hannah nodded and said, "You know, you ought to think about becoming a pastor."

"Really? I was thinking more along the lines of truck driver."

"Truck driver? You? Cowboy boots, beer gut, hyped on caffeine, 'Breaker, breaker, 1-9, Good buddy.' You? I know truckers. I'm related to truckers. I've eaten in truck stops. And you, Elijah Lovejoy Parish, are not a trucker. Heck, I'd make a better trucker than you."

"There's no doubt about that. I was thinking more along the lines of UPS. I mean, everybody's heart sings when that big burly brown truck rolls into the cul de sac. Oh, ho, the big brown truck is a-comin' down the street, Oh please let it be for me! Everybody wants to see the UPS man come. He or she is bringing a package you ordered or a gift for your birthday, and the beauty of it is that he's not bringing you the bill! The UPS guys I've known always seem so pleasant, chipper, and light on their feet; and not only that, they get to wear shorts to work. I think about that sometimes when I'm bringing the folks a sermon they'd just as soon not hear. Think about it. 'Let's see, would I rather open that package with those new shoes or take up my cross? Hmmm.'"

"You'd get a sore back carrying all those packages."

"Hannah, today I feel like I'm carrying Jupiter on my back."

"That's ironic, Holst called Jupiter the bringer of Jollity."

"Well, today, Jupiter brought the fat and forgot the jolly."

They gathered the kids and the dog, telling them it was time for the Cozy Coupes to head for pit lane. Too tired to cook a meal and not wanting to eat out, knowing Elijah would be besieged by friends, church members, and reporters looking for details, they settled on pbjs and apples. After baths and bedtime prayers for the kids, they skipped the floss and collapsed into their bed, holding onto one another for dear life, the day impressing upon them that life indeed is dear and also precarious.

It was well after 1:00 a.m. when Hannah awoke, noticing Elijah was not there. She put on a robe and out in the hallway noticed the light coming from the stairs down to the study.

"E?"

"Hey."

Arriving at the bottom of the stairs, she saw Elijah at his desk looking through a scrapbook. She asked, "Couldn't sleep?"

"Did you know my brother had signed scorecards from Tom Watson and Phil Mickelson?"

"No."

"We had gone down to Hilton Head for a long weekend and Dad took Zach to the third round of the Heritage Classic at Harbour Town. Hale Irwin was lining up a putt on the 18th green when Zach made a random groan. Irwin stood up and gave the gallery the stink eye and a course marshall hustled over and told Dad and Zach they'd have to leave.

Watson and Mickelson were signing autographs over by the putting green and saw what happened. Watson motioned for Dad to come over as he was coaxing Zach toward the exit. Turns out they both had relatives with autism. Zach just stood there stone silent as Watson and Mickelson made a fuss over him. Zach's eyes betrayed what his voice could not say. Wide open with surprise. He was so nervous he started reciting the winners of every major tournament from the last hundred years. They were blown away. Payne Stewart ambled over in amazement and gave Zach a golf glove. The boy wore that glove every day. T had to wrestle it off of him before he took a shower."

"I remember being curious about the story behind that glove."

"I guess you could say it was his talisman. He wouldn't leave the house without it. And oh how Zach loved Lucky Charms. Mealtime could be a chore for T, because it wasn't like she could serve him Lucky Charms for every meal. I'll never forget his twelfth birthday. T and Dad took us to the *Beef 'n Bottle*, that grand old Charlotte steakhouse, and when the waiters brought out the entrees, T had arranged for them to bring Zach this big golden bowl filled with Lucky Charms. It was one of the rare moments I saw him smiling from ear to ear."

Though captivated by Elijah's fond remembrance of my life, Hannah thought it odd that they would be sitting in the study talking about Lucky Charms at 2:00 a.m. on the night following the massacre at the McArthur. "Given the events of the day, I would doubt that cereal is to blame for keeping you awake. What's up?"

"Yesterday was April 3rd."

It took a moment for that to sink in. Hannah's furrowed brow was the telltale sign she was sifting through all of her software to locate the significance of that date. Her eyes widened with discovery. "The accident."

"Sometimes I wake up at night with my mind racing, trying to figure out how I could have avoided that wreck. What would have happened if I didn't swerve and just let her car hit me? Could I have taken a different route to Dina's game? I had just stopped at a 7-Eleven to get Slurpees for Zach and me. What if I hadn't stopped or what if I had chosen a place further down the road to stop?"

"What-ifs only serve to rob you of life. Every moment you spend in that maze of what-ifs is a moment lost; a moment you can never get back."

"I get that. I know that. Yet, somehow I forget that when I'm asleep. And now, once again, on April 3rd, I escape while others perish. Don't get me wrong I'm grateful to be alive, but why am I the one living? Theologically, I know I can't attribute that to providence. I'm constantly pushing people away from the pop theology of assigning tragedy to the capriciousness of God. If you affirm that God is love, you can't say that God took Zach or that God needed Zach more than we do. That's ridiculous. When that car went over the embankment, God wasn't marking off an item on his to-do list. No, I firmly believe that when Zach died, Jesus was the first one to weep. I believe he wept for Zach, for me, for my parents, for Dina, and for the two girls whose lives are forever marked by the desperate need to hear The Backstreet Boys at that moment. It was an accident and accidents happen in a limited and finite world. I know that, but yet again, on April 3rd, I'm alive and others are dead."

"E, listen to what you just said. On April 3rd you are alive and others are dead. You could say the same thing on April 2nd, June 10th, October 3rd, and December 25th. People live and die every day. It's the nature of God's good creation, and yes, it is a maddening mystery that can eviscerate your spirit when you lose someone, but what is it you will say at every funeral you conduct over the next few days? 'Whether we live, or whether we die, we are the Lord's.' I don't know how or why, but regardless of which side of that equation you may be found, God is with you."

As the subject of that conversation, I, Zachary "For All the Saints" Parish, wanted to shout, "Amen, sister! Preach it!" Birth, life, joy, sorrow, death, resurrection—It's a package deal and the CEO of the whole operation present with you every step of the way whether you sense it or not. Jesus wasn't kidding when he said, "I will not leave you desolate." Elijah believes that and he will know that one day. He'll figure it out. It's like Paul said, "For now we see in a mirror, dimly, but then we will see face to face. Now I know only in part; then I will know fully, even as I have been fully known."

Now, about those Lucky Charms, I was endlessly fascinated by those shapes in the same way I was always tugging on my mom's charm bracelet. Well that, and those marshmallows tasted so damn good. I rejoice in the knowledge that one day Elijah will be forever freed of the guilt of being the one "left behind."

Hannah walked around the desk and pulled Elijah up to her. "Come to bed. You know, the Bible says the two shall become one flesh."

"I have always liked that verse."

Elijah woke at dawn to the sound of his Bach Fugue ringtone. It was Jimmy.

"Wake up, Tinker Bell. You and I have a busy day ahead of us. We have to organize a marathon of mourning. You up for this?"

"God didn't give Moses an excused absence, so I know I'm not getting one. Meet me at my office at 8:00."

"You know you have reporters camped out in your front yard?"

"No interviews today."

"Good luck with that."

Elijah turned over to Hannah, kissing her softly on the cheek. "Smile pretty for the camera."

"What?"

"Jimmy says there is a gaggle of reporters out front."

"What?"

"Good thing we closed those shutters when we came back up here last night. Otherwise, people on the other side of the world would be scoring our love life."

"Oh Lord, my Dad would lose his lunch, though as a performance, I'd give it a ten."

"I don't relish facing any cameras."

"Thank God the fridge is full and school is cancelled today. Time to hunker down. I can't imagine the chaos around Spencer's house. Madison was going to come over last night to get away from it all, but decided she didn't want to leave her mother. She may come over this morning if we figure out a way to sneak her in the back door."

Just as Hannah said this, they could hear the back door opening and Madison's soft voice calling their names. Hannah grabbed a robe and went out to meet her while Elijah showered and dressed.

Hugging her, Hannah said, "I am so sorry, Madison. I . . . I don't know what to say other than we love you and are here for you. I'm so glad you are safe."

Evoking wisdom far beyond her years, Madison said, "We'll be fine. I'm just heartsick for all the people who weep this morning. This is just awful. It reminds me of the Tour de France, you know, where they classify the different mountain climbs, and if the slope is absolutely insane, they label it Beyond Category. That's what this apocalypse feels like, Beyond Category."

"How's your mom?"

"She's a strong woman. She's employing a stiff upper lip and operating in full CEO mode: arranging visits to all the families of the victims and making sure everyone in the company gets a phone call from her or my cousins. She's already talked to Jimmy about arrangements, ordered flowers, and asked Momma McKee to coordinate catering. Last night was tough though. We went to the Hospice House to see Millie, and you know it's never been easy with Millie. It always has to be about her. She went on and on about how bad a time it was for this to happen, as if it would have been okay to happen after her funeral. It was like she was blaming Uncle Mark for taking the spotlight away from her. Then she started blasting Mom for not getting Sean under control, like Mom could have snapped her fingers and have Sean behave."

Elijah, entering the kitchen said, "When Spencer snaps her fingers, I know I behave."

"I have to say, though, Mom was awesome. She took it all, never getting defensive, maintaining a composure of calm and a spirit of empathy even when Aunt Millie said Sean never would have dared to do this if Mark was still running the company. She even blamed Mom for sending Seamus and Ian overseas and keeping them away from her in her hour of need.

"Later, when I told Mom that was the first time I ever wanted to open up a can of whupass on a Hospice patient, she just smiled and said, 'Well, let's cut her a break. She's suffering two deaths, Mark's and her own. She's hurting and she's lashing out. I just happen to be the easiest target.' I do love my Mom."

"So do we," said Elijah. "How did you get here without being detected by the paparrazi?'"

"I ran. The reporters don't know there is a tunnel that runs from the house to the carriage house, so I managed to slip out the back door of the carriage house and into the woods. Having lived my whole life at The Thistle Estate, I know about every square inch of the woods behind the house, so they didn't stand a chance."

Impressed, Hannah bestowed the highest props a 17-year-old could receive, "You're Katniss Everdeen from *The Hunger Games*!"

"Bring it on."

The phone rang and Elijah answered it to hear a wounded but familiar voice on the other end. He excused himself and walked down the hallway.

"Bethany?"

"I know I'm the last person you want to hear from, but you are the only person I felt I could talk to. Is there any way that I could meet with you?"

"Yes . . . could you meet me at the church at 10:00?"

"Yes."

"To avoid the reporters, park beside Highlands Florist, come up the back alley and enter the door at the end of the educational building."

"Thanks."

Elijah kissed Hannah and the kids, who were lined up for bowls of Cheerios, hugged Madison, and prayed he could match her stealth on the way to the church.

That would not be the case as the phalanx of reporters and cameras surrounded the Jeep before he could get out of the driveway.

"Rev. Parish, can you tell us how you feel about being a target of Sean McArthur?" Click, click, snap, snap.

"I'm sorry, I won't be offering any interviews. This is not about me. It is about all those who woke to grief this morning. Let us care for them."

"Isn't there any message you'd want the world to hear?"

"The light shines in the darkness and the darkness has not overcome it."

Half the reporters didn't know what that meant and the other half who did stepped back to let him go. Elijah raised his window and took a circuitous route to the church.

The day was a blur of phone calls, meetings, visits, and funeral planning. By the time Elijah walked into the foyer outside of his office, Tamara already had workers replacing drywall in Elijah's study and had set up a temporary office in the church parlor. Along with Jimmy, she had also put together a spreadsheet with time slots for the slew of memorial services, receptions, and graveside rites that would dominate the next three days. Elijah joined the fray and set up visits to the victims' families. All activity stopped cold when Bethany appeared in the foyer. Elijah had failed to mention that he was meeting with her. While Tamara and Jimmy picked their jaws up off the floor, Elijah welcomed Bethany and led her into the parlor.

"I know this seems really weird to you."

"Bethany, I think we'd both say that after yesterday, everything seems a bit bizarre. How are you faring?"

"I'm crushed, confused, hurt, humiliated, angry at him and angry at myself for getting sucked into his orbit. If only I would have known how far he had gone over the edge, believe me, I'd have put a stop to it. I would have shot his ass. It would have been worth the death penalty to keep him from destroying all those lives . . . I'm sorry, I know I shouldn't say that. Truth be told, I couldn't shoot anyone. I've never even held a gun. I'm . . . I'm just so pissed I couldn't see how deep he was into his little war against his cousins. Talk about freaky, you know what came in the mail yesterday? The bill for the Bushmaster rifle, the Glock, the ammunition, the camouflauge fatigues, and even for camouflage face paint. If only the bill had come a day earlier, maybe I could have . . ." Her voice trailed off into weeping and she grabbed a handful of Puffs from the box on the table beside the stately wingback chair that swallowed her petite frame. Bethany continued, "I'm sorry to be such a mess."

"Don't worry, it is certainly understandable considering the circumstances."

"Yeah, these circumstances sure do suck. Before I get into what brought me here, let me say how sorry I am for that phone call. That was totally uncalled for. You have never been anything but kind to me. Actually, I enjoy your preaching. It's real. It makes me think and it makes me wrestle with the fact that everything isn't black and white. There is a lot of gray in life. Everything sure seems gray today."

"I'm sorry for that phone call. You didn't deserve that. It's just that Daddy and Sean kept pounding me with the bullshit that you, and what they called 'your liberal ilk,' are Satan's emissaries of moral degradation, preachers for the perverse, architects of America's destruction."

"Sounds like I've been busy."

"It's all b.s. I know that now and I'm sorry I joined in painting you with it. That wasn't right. I know you are a good man doing good work. I know you to be compassionate, and I hope, merciful."

"Bethany, I'm not in charge of the mercy department, Christ is; and in Christ you were forgiven long before you came to me, long before you were born. So, who am I to deny what Christ has freely given?"

Bethany grabbed another handful of Puffs to stanch a second stream of tears. "I'm . . . grateful."

"So, what brings you here today?"

"I had nowhere else to go, and I'll completely understand if you want no part of this, but before I ask, let me give you a little background. Sean is, excuse me, *was* bipolar."

"I didn't know that. I can see it now that you say it, but I didn't know that about Sean."

"Well, life with him was always a roller coaster depending on whether he was manic or just plain mad. He was so much fun when he was up, so charming, so funny; but when he was mad, we had problems, bad problems."

"Was he abusive?"

"Now and then, he'd slap me around pretty good, especially when he was off his meds."

Elijah was amazed at how Bethany spoke of physical abuse with such nonchalance, as if Sean forgot to walk the dog "now and then." He had to ask the question. "Bethany, not to get in the way of your story, but I have to ask, were you abused as a child?"

"Physically by Daddy, you know, 'Spare the rod, spoil the child.' Sexually by a church deacon. That was the reason for my first abortion. Hell, it was Daddy who took me to the abortion clinic up in Asheville. Funny, it was the day after he had railed against the evil of abortionists in a sermon. Daddy couldn't take the humiliation of having a pregnant 14-year-old and he was not going to give up the contributions of his revered deacon."

"I am so sorry, Bethany. Didn't do much for your image of God, I suppose."

"It is what it is. To be honest, I don't know what I believe anymore, which I guess is one reason I'm here. Daddy and Sean were close, real close. They seemed to get off on trashing the gays, the liberals, Obama, the welfare addicts, the blacks, the immigrants, and the abortionists (that both of them had paid for the services of, by the way)."

"Doesn't sound much like Jesus, does it?"

"I guess not . . . but I need to do some studying on that. Anyway, Daddy gushed over Sean like a traveling salesman at a titty bar. Of course, he loved Sean's money even more. I think Daddy blames me for what happened yesterday."

"How in the world could he land on that idea?"

"You see, I kicked Sean out of the house 10 days ago. He had been real edgy, like he gets when he's off his meds. One night at supper, he was bitching about my cooking and actually said, in front of the kids, mind you, that he had never known a slut that could cook. I tell you, I was a hair's breath away from grabbing a frying pan to lay upside his head, but I held it together because of the kids and out of fear of what he would do. About that time, Sean V dropped his juice glass on the floor and the grape juice went flying. He started crying and Sean IV stood up with fire in his eyes and shouted, 'Men don't cry and they sure as hell don't drink grape juice!!' Then, he reached across the table and slapped him across the face. He knew he had done it then. He shrank away and stumbled back toward the bedroom. All the kids were bawling by that point. Tell you what I did. I walked calmly down that hallway, looked into the bedroom where he was sitting on the edge of the bed with his head in his hands. Still calm, not raising my voice, I told him he had ten minutes to get out of the house, and if he did anything to harm me or the children, I have cousins in this county who would hunt him down, castrate him, beat him to a pulp, and then kill him."

"You go, girl. What did he do?"

"He left. But that's where it really starts gettin' weird. He left by way of the porch outside our bedroom. I didn't even see him take off. When I went back to the room, the door to the outside was open and in the middle of the bed, he had piled all of his medicine along with a scribbled note saying, 'These pills are just the tools of Satan, an obstacle to prevent me from pursuing my destiny as a warrior of righteousness.' Below it, in big bold letters, he wrote, Joshua 8:7. Now, my Daddy beat the Bible into me, so I didn't even have to look it up. "You are to rise up from ambush and take the city. The Lord your God will give it into your hand.""

"After yesterday, those words send a chill up your spine, don't they?"

"No kidding."

"Did you tell anyone?"

"I e-mailed Mark and Chief Carpenter. K.C. said they'd do their best to keep an eye on him. One of his officers found him out at the lake. He said Sean had set up a campsite on our property there. Of course, you can't arrest a man for camping on his own property, so Sean chased him off."

"Mark and I had received the same kind of cryptic message from Sean. Mark had hired a couple of off-duty policemen to beef up security at the plant and K.C. assigned a couple of patrols to keep an eye on The Thistle Estate and the plant. I think we found out it is mighty hard to control madness, though."

"I couldn't figure out why he was camping out when we have a second beautiful home right here in town. I guess he had convinced himself that he was a commando for Jesus, out in the woods preparing for battle."

"Nobody would disagree with you about that now."

"Here's the thing, Elijah. My Daddy's bromance with Sean ended abruptly yesterday and now he's acting like a jilted lover. He was shouting at me over the phone last night, saying that Sean had either been possessed by or sold his soul to Satan. What is it with the people in my church and our love affair with Satan? There are plenty of Sundays when Daddy talks more about Satan than Jesus. I never told him, but it seems to me that we have more fear of Satan than we have faith in Jesus."

"That's a wise observation, Bethany."

"Anyway, he's shouting and screaming louder than the last night of revival and talking about Sean burning in Hell, but when I interrupted him long enough to ask about burying Sean, he went all Colonel Jessup on me, like 'I ought to reach through this phone line and rip out your eyeballs.'"

"So I guess compassion is not his strong suit?"

"You could say that. He said Sean didn't deserve to be buried, he deserved to hang on a tree so that the birds could eat his flesh."

"Joseph's dream?"

"So much for Daddy's claim that Presbyterians don't read the Bible. So, then he says, not only would he refuse to bury Sean, but if I pursued it, he'd disown me. He said I was unclean, having lain with Satan and all, so he wasn't sure he wanted anything to do with me. He said that the children obviously needed to be exorcised and that he had a mind to take custody of them. Let me say this for real: That . . . Ain't . . . Happening. Listen, Sean was crazier than Norman Bates and what he did was horrendous and evil, but he was my husband and there was a time when I really loved him, so I feel like I've got to follow through and bury him, so to speak. After that God can do what he wants with him. I just feel it wouldn't be right not doing my duty and bringing closure to this horror. Now I couldn't blame you if you refused and told me to get the hell out of here. You certainly have reason to, and I'm at fault for that; but, could you consider doing a private committal service for me and the kids? Jimmy has agreed to do the cremation and I'm donating his brain for research. Someone will have fun with that. So, I was thinking we'd spread his ashes out at the lake. We did at least have some good times there with the kids. It would just be a very simple brief service with scripture and prayer. Again, I understand if you can't. I mean, I don't want to get you in trouble with Spencer."

"Bethany, I'd be glad to do it. I think Jimmy can help us figure out a way to do this discreetly."

"I was sorta thinking about early Saturday morning. Hopefully, all the reporters will be getting drunk at The Ale House on Friday night, so maybe they'll be too hungover to chase us out there that early."

"I think we can make that work. I'll talk with Jimmy and we'll come up with an escape plan. I'll give you a call or better yet, I'll have Tamara drop by with the details."

"Probably a good idea. Anyone who calls me right now will be on a conference call with the FBI, NSA, Rupert Murdoch, and four or five countries listening in."

"I'm sorry for all the tribulation in your life right now. Tell me, though, what's next for Bethany?"

"Oh, I'm getting the hell out of Dodge. We need to lay low for a while. My sister lives in Tampa and so we're going to get a temporary place down there and I'm putting all the property here on the market. We need a new start in a place far away from here. It may be Tampa or somewhere else in Florida. I just don't want my kids to have this hanging over their heads every day they go to school. Confidentially, once we get settled, Mom's gonna leave Daddy to come and be with us. That poor woman has suffered so much."

"I have a good friend who pastors a church in Tampa. When the time comes, I can put you in touch with him."

"That may be helpful at some point. First, I need to shake loose of the church chains Daddy choked me with all those years. I am so grateful you will do the service for me. Are you sure? I don't want to get you in any trouble with your folks here and I certainly wouldn't want you to get fired over this. Emotions are high, right now."

"We'll be fine. Bethany, I can't choose a hymn without someone complaining about it. I've been fussed at before," he said with a grin.

"Touche."

Elijah walked Bethany out of the office as Jimmy and Tamara, busted and flustered, stumbled over one another trying to appear as though they were deep into funeral planning. Truth is, they were totally talking about Bethany, exhausting all the scenarios of why Bethany McArthur, the new widow of a mass murderer, would want to meet with her husband's prime intended victim.

The rest of the morning was spent scheduling visits, organizing receptions, plotting funeral times. It was all reminiscent of those old war movies where the generals are hidden deep in a bunker plotting strategy and troop movements as they stand around a large map-covered table. This was when Tamara was at her best, that is, organizing volunteer troop movements, handling egos, and nudging the sluggish. If she had been a WWII general, the war would have ended two years earlier. The string of services would commence on Thursday morning and continue through Saturday afternoon with a couple of memorial services delayed a week or two as families spread across the globe made their way to Edinburgh. One consequence of being a furniture town rolling with the changes in the furniture culture meant that people with blood or business connections to McArthur dwelt in places like Hanoi, Kuala Lumpur, Jaipur, Brasov, and Porto Velho.

That afternoon Elijah could be found in a succession of living rooms, sitting on a couch, balancing a notepad on one knee, nursing a cup of coffee with the opposite hand. While the purpose for each visit was the same, the emotional temperament and spiritual temperature Elijah found during this tour of woe were incredibly disparate.

The saddest settings are observed when meeting with families who possess no mast to hang onto during the storm. Bereft of faith they cannot comprehend the choreography of life and death. With no tether, they are thrust into the churning, murky waters of loss. Having failed at controlling life, they flounder all the more with death. The solace and hope of resurrection remain outside of their grasp because the vocabulary of faith is no more accessible than Sanskrit for them. Do you know why the 23rd Psalm is read and *How Great Thou Art* is sung at almost every funeral? Because when the pastor asks the family if there are any scriptures or hymns they would like to include in the service, these are the only ones that bear any mark of familiarity for them.

At the service, they are hidden behind oversized sunglasses and dark suits, perched on the pew like cats on a hot tin roof. A sanctuary is foreign turf for them, and so their whole experience of the ordeal is all awkwardness and discomfiture. The liturgy, music, prayers, and Bible readings bear little meaning for them. Like adolescents in an art appreciation lecture, it is all blah, blah, blah to them. It's not that they are being insolent, they just don't get it. The prayer they whisper to themselves is, "Just get me out of here and give me a drink." Their pastor is named *Johnny Walker*. It is so sad to see someone look so lost in the very place they were made to feel most at home.

The most disturbing setting is experienced in sitting with the family only held together by the glue of dysfunction. There, tension is more prominent than grief. A daughter cannot be located, having disappeared from the life of the deceased fifteen years earlier. Junior, recently out of rehab, is in a shouting match with mom over the question of whether the girl he met at a Marilyn Manson concert the previous week can sit with the family at the funeral. A sister and brother won't speak to one another because of a dispute over who inherits the beach house. Wrought with antipathy, there is no room for grief or gratitude or faith. In those beautifully appointed living rooms, the deceased's presence is defined by hostility.

The whiplash of emotions through the afternoon leaves Elijah exhausted as he climbs the brick stairs to Spencer and Tom's courtly Georgian manor. The intimidating brick edifice belied the warmth, hospitality, and grace one would experience inside. Tom greeted Elijah at the door, TV remote in one hand and a crying Cavalier King Charles Spaniel in the other that wanted nothing more in this world than to lick visitors to death. No callers, apart from a couple of prickly prudes, could resist Ellie's profound brown eyes, flopping ears, and need for love. She's the homecoming queen that didn't score well on her SAT, which seems to make her all the more lovable. I wouldn't say her morals are loose, but when you approach her she falls on her back and goes all spread eagle, an act of total submission and a plea for a belly rub. The only way she would provide security in the event of a break-in would be delaying the intruder's exit long enough for the police to arrive. I could see the officers descending on the intruder, who is down on his knees, gushing with baby talk and scratching Ellie's belly.

Tom greeted Elijah with a smile and welcomed him into the foyer. The floor was a glistening diagonal pattern of black and white marble tile; the walls, a pale yellow accented with heavy white molding—elegance. Tom walked Elijah back to the library while updating him on the status of the McArthur world.

"Spencer is on the phone with an executive search firm about the positions she'll be posting for hire. Seamus will take on the role of CFO and Ian will head up operations, so, primarily, she's looking for designers. Couldn't ask for a worse time to deal with personnel issues, but a lot of people and the town itself are depending on the company to remain vital."

"How is Spencer faring?"

"Oh, you know Spencer, she can compartmentalize things pretty well. Yet, I worry about her just like I worry about you. You guys are like that performer on the old Ed Sullivan show. You remember. This dude would spin a glass plate on top of a wooden dowel, which is a feat in itself. But, like you, he would keep adding more dowels and more plates, running back and forth to keep them all spinning while the audience held its breath waiting for one to crash."

"Tom, that's a little before my time, but I certainly can appreciate the image. I would imagine, though, that my plates are shattering more often than Spencer's. She's an amazing woman."

"I just wish you'd slow down a bit. I certainly hope you are not going to be leaving us anytime soon. I'm sure a number of larger churches would jump at the chance to call you."

"Oh, you're stuck with me as far as I can see. I'm just glad you haven't voted me off the island so far. And Tom, I certainly didn't enter the parish pastor parade with any illusions about it involving a corporate ladder. I do hope Spencer allows herself the space for rest and healing."

"You and me both. She should be off the phone in a minute. You are staying for dinner, by the way. Hannah and Madison called and they are bringing over some taco soup they whipped up today. Seamus and Ian will also come by when we're ready to talk about the services."

In the library, Spencer was standing behind her desk, phone to ear. "Yes. Yes. That's correct. Listen, I have to go now. My pastor is here."

My pastor is here. Church insiders know that is all they need to say to end a phone call quickly. It leaves people stammering with no idea how to respond. It takes a real hardass to say, "Well, God can just wait!" So, most of the time, the caller stumbles toward hanging up. "Uh . . . well . . . sure . . . uh . . . well . . . amen . . . I mean goodbye." Some pastors will tell you that is often the best thing they offer to the patient during a hospital visit, getting off the phone with some Aunt Iris who has never learned how to use a period. My pastor is here. With four simple words, a prayer has been answered before the preacher offers to pray.

"Elijah, your timing was perfect. That guy just wouldn't stop talking about the time his second cousin was shot during a drug deal gone bad, as though that will bring me solace right now. However, he is relentless in pursuing the right candidate for a position." Spencer embraced Elijah and asked if he would like something to drink, but was interrupted by Tom.

"Got it covered, Spencer, just the way the boy likes it; tea so sweet the spoon gets mired when you try to stir it."

"Thanks. It's been quite a day, just as I am sure it has been for you."

"I feel like a character in a Salvador Dali painting."

Spencer knows her art. The décor of the library was understated elegance—dark mahogany wood walls with raised paneling and fluted ornamentation framing the built-in bookshelves. Its beauty was revealed in the lack of ostentation. The room was comfy and the hosts made you feel right at home, as if at any moment everyone would toss off their shoes, kick up their feet, pop popcorn and watch a movie. Closer examination would reveal that the Smythe's library was far from your typical family room, for on opposite walls were original works of Edward Hopper and Andrew Wyeth, not to be confused with the panel of Ansel Adams photos behind the desk. Spencer had studied American Art at Brown. When asked, Spencer would say she prized these works more than she should. There was no intention to impress, no desire to display wealth, and she abhorred conspicuous consumption, but she was enamored by art in the way a Midwesterner is captivated by the coastline—beauty that should never be taken for granted and always cherished.

The three sank into the succor of overstuffed chairs and for a moment, just gazed at one another, their eyes conveying the unanswerable. What fury hath hell wrought? Spencer's preternatural calm could be disarming at times, but in this moment Elijah coveted such an ability to maintain this unruffled mien. You knew she had to be stressed, but she appeared so relaxed. She was dressed in jeans, not the price-gouged denim of the social climbers, but well-worn Levis that she had married with a Brooks Brothers pinpoint, a strand of pearls, and a pair of floral print Lilly Pulitzer ballet flats.

"I am utterly broken, Elijah. There are so many people hurting today. It's overwhelming."

"Is the anesthetic of adrenaline and shock wearing off?"

"I think so, though the darkness is being held at bay by the to-do list. Furniture Market begins in High Point the day after Easter and I'm missing a significant percentage of my leadership. I'm going to get cauliflower ear from talking on the phone to Seamus and Ian as we scramble to come up with a plan B. Tom has already been talking with your dad about preparing for the lawsuits, the first of which will be filed tomorrow according to our sources. I know how many people are depending on our capacity to weather this storm and I know how much this community is relying on us to thrive. But all of that is trifling when compared to the reality of those who awoke this morning next to an empty space that should be filled with a warm snoozing body and the sound of his or her breathing.

"I can't stop thinking of Mitzi Deland, beautiful girl. She will be walking across the stage down at Presbyterian College next month to receive her diploma and the month after that, as you know, she is supposed to walk down the aisle at St. Martin to hear you ask her 'Who brings this woman to be married to this man?' And her father will not be there to answer, just as he won't be at PC to take pictures. Todd was rapturous when he talked about the graduation and wedding plans, which, of course, was *all* the time.

He was even working up a surprise dance number with the best man and the maid of honor. The last line of the toast was going to be something like, 'And may this night be a *Thriller!*' The best man and maid of honor would then jump out on the floor with him, bring him a red leather jacket, and the three of them would proceed to do the *Thriller* dance along with about eight of the guys from the plant. I think Ian was even in on it. Before they went overseas, I saw Ian limping around with an ice pack taped to his thigh. He said he had strained a quad at practice.

"And, Elijah, this is confidential; I'm the only one who knows; but Tawny Fribourg had just found out she was pregnant. Her parents didn't even know and she was to drive down to Mooresville yesterday evening to share the news with the father. She's been dating Henri Legrande, the Formula One driver who is making a go of it on the NASCAR circuit. I'm not sure how I'm going to handle that little nugget of information. Part of me thinks the most caring thing to do would be to let the news die with her, but what if they were to read a medical report? Surely, the pregnancy would be mentioned."

"Spencer, every reporter from CNN to the Shanghai Daily has someone scouring every blade of Edinburgh grass in search of a scoop. I would guess they already have it and will be broadcasting photos of a pink lined pee strip in the next half-hour. So, before you even see the parents or Monsieur Horsepower, they may well know."

"You are right. I don't even have contact information for them. Nevertheless, I want to be in touch with them. So much sadness. Forgive me, Elijah, but it really sucks."

"That's about as elegant a word you can use in this tragedy. Theologians speak of redemptive suffering, but at this point it is tough to discern any redeeming value in the last thirty-six hours. What we cling to is the promise that there is nowhere suffering can take us that God won't go with us. 'I lift up my eyes to the hills' . . . "

" . . . From where does my help come? My help comes from the Lord who made heaven and earth." Catching the wind of that thought, Spencer reflected, "I loved my brother so much. He was such a good man. He was such a gentleman long before he put on the medal of an Eagle Scout. So thoughtful. I've never encountered anyone who could be called wise before puberty, and certainly no one who maintained that maturity during and after the pimples and the testosterone. But Mark was always the steady one. To be honest, he was the adult in our house growing up. You never met my parents or my uncle. That was a bit of a wild crowd, only a couple of degrees closer to sanity and sobriety than Sean. Were it not for Mark, I'm convinced I would have played the role of Daisy Buchanan quite well. But Mark took me under his wing and provided the parenting I wasn't going to get with our parents, who were usually off to a party.

"Mark had such common sense. You know, our father wanted to send Mark to Choate for high school, but Mark would have nothing of it. He stared father down and said, 'If I'm going to work in this business in this community, I want to go to school with these people. If you send me off, they'll never trust me. You can't put your trust in someone with whom you don't have a relationship.' How many 14-year-olds think like that?

"Of course, Mark was not immune to embarrassment. Did he ever tell you about his first date in high school? It was the Homecoming Dance and Mark was a freshman. He was so shy around girls, which meant he was a wreck whenever one of the school dances was approaching. It's crazy, because he was so good-looking that every girl in school, including the seniors, would have jumped at the chance to go with him. So, he didn't work up the courage to ask anyone until a week before the dance. His date lived out in a rural part of the county where her dad based his heating and air-conditioning business. Their house was in the middle of nowhere and there was no such thing as a GPS, so when Mother asked Mark if he had directions, he said he knew the general area of where they were going. Mother would come to understand later that his idea of 'the general area' meant the State of North Carolina. Mark was 14 at the time, which meant that Mom would be the chauffeur. Back then, she was driving a Porsche 911, which would be great if you were driving your date to the dance, but if you are larger than a toddler, somebody is going to crush a vertebrae climbing into that backseat.

"Well, by the time they made it to the general area, it was apparent that they were utterly lost and already a half-hour late. They wound up stopping at the Moose Lodge in Glen Alpine to call for explicit directions. Nerves were frayed by that point. Mother was supposed to be dining at the country club and Mark just wanted to bag it and go home. The family legend is that Mother said, 'Hell no! If I'm missing a shrimp cocktail for this, you are surely going to suffer through this dance or die trying.'

"Turns out, Mother was a prophet. Mark's date was already in a pissy mood because they were so late they would have to skip the barbeque at her best friend's house and head straight to the dance. She wouldn't even look at Mark and there wasn't a word spoken in that car all the way to the Knights of Columbus Hall. Mother dropped the frosty couple off, squealing her tires as she tore off in search of a martini and the moment Romeo and Juliet stepped into the foyer, they ran into Jackson Smythe, yes, Tom's older brother who had just dumped Mark's date a week earlier, having dated her for three months. Mark's date burst into tears and ran off into the corner of the dance hall with Mitzi Cooper. She sobbed through the whole dance, so Mark was standing there with nothing to do but sniff his boutonniere, drink Mountain Dew, and eat Doritos over at the snack table."

"Why didn't they just leave?"

"How? It's not like he could text Mother and even if he came up with a quarter for the payphone, he sure wasn't going to call the country club and have them drag Mother away from her martini. She was already pissed. So, Mark stood there for three hours watching his date sob into Mitzi's arms, and Mitzi's date spent three hours giving Mark the stink eye. To cap it all off, before they could drop her off at the end of the ordeal, Mother had a flat tire, so Mark had to change the tire while his date sat on the edge of the ditch with her head buried in her knees. Mark said that, like any guy on a first date, he was nervous about walking her to her door, but when they finally arrived at her house, she jumped out of the car and slammed the door in his face, so at least he didn't have to worry about what to say to her."

"Who was this girl?"

Spencer smiled, "Oh, didn't I tell you . . . ? Her name was Millie."

"Whaaaaat???"

"Yes. It never got a whole lot better, did it?" The room erupted with laughter. Almost choking, Spencer chortled, "The poor boy just couldn't take a hint."

With the arrival of Hannah, Madison, Xani, Nathan, and the families of Seamus and Ian, the rest of the evening was that curious cocktail shared by the faithful in the face of death: tears and laughter, memories and mourning, losses confronted and hopes affirmed. Driving home, Elijah was drained but whelmed by the grace of being allowed entry into the interior of his church members' lives. Beneath the patina of class, vocation, ethnicity, and education people are people. Shakespeare's Shylock unintentionally speaks not just for himself, but for all. We are not as distinct as we think. Each of us has eyes, hands, organs, dimensions, senses, affections, and passions. We are "fed with the same food, hurt with the same weapons, subject to the same diseases, healed by the same means, warmed and cooled by the same winter and summer."[10] If pricked, we bleed. If tickled, we laugh. If poisoned, we die. And if wronged, the impulse is revenge but the cure is mercy.

No matter our station in life, we are finite and limited, self-seeking and manipulative, vulnerable to injury and wired for relationship. The wiring may be faulty and hazardous, but we cannot deny the desire to be loved. Yes,

10. Shakespeare, William, *The Merchant of Venice*, 1556-1558.

beneath the patina, the mask, and the masquerade, people are people and Elijah considers it a privilege to have access to that interior space, for that is where relationship begins.

The next three days would be a marathon for the mournful and those who minister to them. Funerals, memorial services, graveside rites, columbarium inurnments, receptions stacked on top of one another; relatives arriving, relatives leaving, horrors revisited over and over as survivors have to repeat the story to well-meaning visitors, cousins, and neighbors. Even the local grocery stores would feel the impact and be hard pressed to keep up with the demand for baked goods and casserole ingredients as ovens churned out meals to deliver to the grieving.

Elijah, like all pastors, possesses that dark conservative outfit euphemistically referred to as the marrying and burying suit. Its fibers would certainly be tested for durability in the coming days.

In life, I could not comprehend the swirl of emotions that surround the sacred ritual of the funeral. Autism robbed me of the roller coaster ride that families jump on in Funeral Land. Your world has been turned upside down and you suddenly are called upon to manage family traffic, wade through estate matters, and organize rituals at a time when you cannot possibly think straight. You are bombarded with voices expressing opinions about what you should do, say, feel, sign, eat, pray, and wear when all you really want to do is crawl in bed, shrouded with a comforter. And yet, for a person of faith, there is meaning in the madness. On this side of the accident that took my life and the funeral that followed three days later, I can see how important the rituals were to my parents and my siblings. The church was the mast to which they could lash themselves in the storm. In fact, it was the ministry of the church that moved them to the eye of the storm where there was calm and the stars could be seen breaking through the clouds. The scriptures speak of it as the peace which passes all understanding.

Undoubtedly, for many, the funeral is a culturally mandated empty ritual to be endured, where platitudes of praise are heaped upon the departed that bear scant resemblance to the person known by the people in the pews. It would be odd for a eulogy to begin, "Let's face it, Harry was an ass, but he was our father and we loved him for that even though we rarely could say we liked him." In most movies, the funeral comes across as a superficial exercise for the marginally faithful where the scriptures are read but not heard, where the preacher's voice is the irritating buzz in the background that holds no meaning for a serious and sophisticated mind focused on more important things. It is to them that the prophet cries out, "Have you not known? Have you not heard? The Lord is the everlasting God, the Creator of the ends of the earth. He does not faint or grow weary; his understanding is unsearchable. He gives power to the faint, and strengthens the powerless."

At the memorial service held for me, I came to understand the truth of these words as I witnessed the palpable presence of God holding my parents and my siblings close. I came to understand why believers would sing about *leaning on the everlasting arms.* I came to understand how the German pastor Martin Rinkart, having conducted well over 4,000 funerals over the span of one year in a plague stricken Eilenburg, could still pen the words:

> Now thank we all our God
> With hearts and hands and voices;
> Who wondrous things hath done,
> In whom this world rejoices.

I came to understand how Horatio Spafford, having lost all four of his daughters in a shipwreck could write:

> When peace like a river, attendeth my way,
> When sorrows like sea billows roll;
> Whatever my lot, Thou hast taught me to *know*,
> It is well, it is well, with my soul.

I came to understand how a suffering Job could say, "For I know that my Redeemer lives, and that at the last he will stand upon the earth;" and Martin Luther proclaim, "The body they may kill; God's truth abideth still."

It was the embrace of God and the succor of the faith community that sustained my parents through those days when they had every reason to abandon hope. So, at the funeral, what remains nothing more than noise to many is life and hope for the disciple. My discovery of this truth made me the poster child for the scriptural promise, "For now we see in a mirror, dimly, but then we will see face to face. Now I know only in part; then I will know fully, even as I have been fully known."

As the multitude of funerals drew to a close on Saturday afternoon, Elijah would remark how the Spirit of God had set up camp at St. Martin through the week, poking through the darkness of death with warming rays of light and grace.

The morning had begun with a brief private service for none other than Sean McArthur at his lake property, where the squirrels scurrying through the pines outnumbered the worshippers. In attendance were Bethany and her children, Elijah, and in an extreme act of mercy, Spencer and Madison. Together they read from the Psalms and prayed, trusting God in his mercy to make some sense out of what they most certainly could not.

The awkwardness of the moment was mitigated by the words of Christ from the cross, "Father, forgive them, for they do not know what they do."

Following the service, Spencer and Madison rode with Elijah out to the Hospice House where Tom, Seamus, and Ian met them so that they could share an intimate memorial for Mark with Millie, who was now fading in and out of consciousness. She was cognizant enough to recognize everyone and understand why they had come and you could see the confluence of gratitude and grief when she opened her eyes.

After this was another funeral at Suddreth funeral home where Jimmy provided Elijah caffeine and crackers. Then it was back to the church and the frenzy of activity in preparation for Mark McArthur's memorial. The Governor, a college roommate; U.S. Senator Wilkes, a fraternity brother; and half the furniture industry would be in attendance.

Standing in the fellowship hall following the memorial service for Mark, Elijah spied Spencer across the room where she was busy clearing tables and folding tablecloths as the last of the visitors filed out toward the kind of normalcy Spencer could only covet at this point. He wasn't surprised by the sight of the mourner donning the apron of the hospitality committee. When the church is being the church at its best, which isn't always, there is an all-hands-on-deck mentality that refuses to stand by while others serve. The servant leader reflects the witness of Christ who came not to be served but to serve others.

Elijah joined the table and chair brigade as the room was readied for the Sabbath. The clack-clack of table-legs contracting and chairs stacking is a familiar percussive anthem in the life of the church and offers a sign to disciples of the grace they are privileged to share together in this sacred place. Wordlessly, members will pair up to flip tables, fold legs, and lug those ponderous slabs of fiberboard to the closet. Elijah knew not to question Spencer's participation in cleaning up at the reception for her own brother's funeral. He knew she would have it no other way, so as she approached the next table, Elijah grabbed the opposite end and they flipped the table on its side.

Spencer asked Elijah, "Could you unlock the church office for me? I need to get a copy of the third-graders curriculum for tomorrow." Spencer had been teaching the third-grade Sunday school class for twelve years. Elijah was praying she would still be teaching it when Xani and Nathan came through, because the kids in Spencer's class always seemed to come out knowing more about the people of the Bible than their own parents did.

Elijah, though sensing it was fruitless, offered Spencer an excused absence anyway. "Spencer, you don't need to teach tomorrow. We can get someone to cover the class for you."

"No, I need to teach the class."

"Spencer, Hannah said the third graders could join her in the second-grade classroom. Sleep in. Allow your body and your mind to rest. We've got your back."

"Elijah, you are not hearing me. I need to teach tomorrow. I have to be here with those children. To skip Sunday School this week of all weeks would render everything you said in that pulpit today superfluous. This has most certainly been a confusing and traumatic week for these children and they need to know that God will not abandon them in the face of tragedy; and I need to be the one to tell them that. And Elijah, I need them. I truly believe that when Jesus said, 'Let the children come to me,' he wasn't just talking about what his presence meant to the children. He was also expressing what the children's presence meant to him. Somehow, through these belching bundles of bedheaded energy, Christ is present to me. I need them, right now, Elijah. I need them."

"You've sold me. See ya Sunday."

6

Palm/Passion Sunday

As promised, Spencer could be found teaching in her classroom during the Sunday School hour. D.A. and Momma McKee were busy readying palm fronds to hand out to worshippers entering the sanctuary. As Elijah stepped forward to the pulpit, the gravity of Christ's journey to the cross weighed heavily upon him, knowing he was looking out upon believers yearning to make sense of all they have claimed to believe in light of the massacre at McArthur's.

"He did not hide his face"

Reading from the Old Testament: Psalm 22

Reading from the New Testament: Hebrews 5:7

Psalm 22:

1 *My God, my God, why have you forsaken me? Why are you so far from helping me, from the words of my groaning?* **2** *O my God, I cry by day, but you do not answer; and by night, but find* no rest. **3** Yet you are holy, enthroned on the praises of Israel. **4** In you our ancestors trusted; they trusted, and you delivered them. **5** To you they cried, and were saved; in you they trusted, and were not put to shame. **6** But I am a worm, and not human; scorned by others, and despised by the people. **7** All who see me mock at me; they make mouths at me, they shake their heads; **8** "Commit your cause to the Lord; let him deliver— let him rescue the one in whom he delights!" **9** Yet it was you who took me from the womb; you kept me safe on my mother's breast. **10** On you I was cast from my birth, and since my mother bore me you have been my God. **11** Do not be far from me, for trouble is near and there is no one to help. **12** Many bulls encircle me, strong bulls of Bashan surround me; **13** they open wide their mouths at me, like a ravening and roaring lion. **14** I am poured out like water, and all my bones are out of joint; my heart is like wax; it is melted within my breast; **15** my mouth is dried up like a potsherd, and my tongue sticks to my jaws; you lay me in the dust of death. **16** For dogs are all around me; a company of evildoers encircles me. My hands and feet have shriveled; **17** I can count all my bones. They stare and gloat over me; **18** they divide my clothes among themselves, and for my clothing they cast lots. **19** But you, O Lord, do not be far away! O my help, come quickly to my aid! **20** Deliver my soul from the sword, my life from the power of the dog! **21** Save me from the mouth of the lion! From the horns of the wild oxen you have rescued me. **22** I will tell of your name to my brothers and sisters; in the midst of the congregation I will praise you: **23** You who fear the Lord, praise him! All you offspring of Jacob, glorify him; stand in awe of him, all you offspring of Israel! **24** For he did not despise or abhor the affliction of the afflicted; he did not hide his face from me, but heard when I cried to him. **25** From you comes my praise in the great congregation; my vows I will pay before those who fear him. **26** The poor shall eat and be satisfied; those who seek him shall praise the Lord. May your hearts live forever! **27** All the ends of the earth shall remember and turn to the Lord; and all the families of the nations shall worship before him. **28** For dominion belongs to the Lord, and he rules over the nations. **29** To him, indeed, shall all who sleep in the earth bow down; before him shall bow all who go down to the dust, and I shall live for him. **30** Posterity will serve him; future generations will be told about the Lord, **31** and proclaim his deliverance to a people yet unborn, saying that he has done it.

Hebrews 5:7

In the days of his flesh, Jesus offered up prayers and supplications, with loud cries and tears, to the one who was able to save him from death, and he was heard because of his reverent submission.

One: This is the Word of the Lord.

Many: Thanks be to God.

The day dawns crisp and clear. It is cool outside; windbreaker weather. When she walks down the driveway to retrieve the morning paper, she waves to the neighbor. It's his day off and yet he's already out the door for a day full of errands, serving lunch at the Soup Kitchen, coaching the kids at the Y, and probably dying eggs for Easter. She marvels at the metabolism that allows him to move so fast, sleep so little, and wear shorts in the middle of December. Winter, summer, fall, and spring, he is on the go.

Picking up the paper, she feels the sting of her back announcing to her brain that yesterday's run was a bit too ambitious. Yet, the pain is assuaged by the pride of having run 20 miles. She's right on schedule for the Boston Marathon in a few weeks. She breathes in the invigorating spring breeze and gives thanks for the beauty of another sunrise before commencing the morning routine, the efficiency of which even the engineers over at M.I.T. could not duplicate. With one hand she's packing lunchboxes and reaching for the cereal bowls with the other, all while barking orders to the kids that cover everything from whether the beds have been made and the teeth have been brushed to the sufficiency of the wardrobe and the submission of every document that requires her signature.

By the time the school bus arrives, every child has been packaged, zipped up, and outfitted with backpacks, lunchboxes, and notes to the teacher. She waves goodbye at the bus stop, and jogs back to the warmth of a coffee mug and the regimen of reading her daily devotional, stretching the lactic acid out of her hamstrings, completing her core exercises, and heading out for today's run. It's Tuesday, so she'll have to be back in time to shower, dress, eat, and get to the school to volunteer in the first grade class at noon. After that, it's a late lunch with her husband at the club. Her life is a monument to her father's two cardinal rules: A place for everything and everything in its place; and Proper Preparation and Planning Prevent Poor Performance.

A place for everything and everything in its place. Proper preparation and planning prevent poor performance. That is her life and she is good with that. The disciplined routine makes her feel secure, comfortable, confident. She is equipped for each morning with a plan *so that she knows what to expect*; except . . . nothing prepared her to expect this.

The iPhone is ringing when she returns from her run. The voice on the other end is frantic, borderline hysterical. "Where are you? I've tried to call you at least eight times!!" A dear friend down the street breathlessly utters the words that will turn her life inside out and take her into a desert valley so dry and so dark she will despair of ever finding her way out.

"There's been a shooting at McArthur." Good Friday arrived early for Lauren Deland and for many in our church and community this week. Lauren permitted me to share the heart of one who wasn't planning on choosing hymns for her husband's funeral last week.

Along with Lauren, we are a people undone, broken, dazed and confused. I cannot fathom the pain of loss you may well be experiencing right now. This is one of those times when among the worst things you could possibly hear are the well-intentioned, but seriously off-the-mark condolences you will most likely try to deflect with grace: "I know how you must feel;" and "Everything will be all right." Both statements are lies. No one can know how or what you are feeling in the aftermath of this senseless evil, and we can't say everything will be all right, because we don't know. All right seems like a fictional zip code right now.

It would be folly for me to stand up here and seek to offer an adequate theological explanation for the evil that befell our community on Tuesday. I don't know that there is one. Newsweek this week sought to offer the perspectives of the Hindu, the Buddhist, the Muslim, the Jew, and the Christian without much success. In the end what we can only say is that there is an evil in the world. Paul said, "For now we see in a mirror dimly," the Greek here actually suggesting that life, as we know it, is a riddle. And at times like this that mirror seems mighty cloudy and our minds feel mainly muddled.

In the wake of this week's trauma, there are some things we know from past experience. The false promise that this will never happen again will be made; Pat Robertson will say something stupid; restrictions will be debated; blame will be cast about like candy at a parade; claims will be made that society is no longer fraying at the edges but cracking at its core; and news reporters will be tripping over one another trying to beat the other guys to a scoop about anything from the important to the farcical. Yes, in the wake of tragedy our attention will usually be drawn to this theater of the absurd.

One way to deal with this is to do what our society tends to do so well and that is to suppress and evade it with our stoic resolve. There are Spring

Break trips scheduled, there are Easter meals to be planned, school projects to complete, committee meetings to organize, minor inconveniences about which to complain, baseball games to watch. Yes, one way to deal with our doubts, questions, and fears is to suppress them. Go on living as though they are not there. Besides, we just don't have the time. And yet, I would suggest to you that there is another way, and that is to face the questions, give them voice. Faith, after all, is not about having all the answers. No, it is more about wrestling with and living with the questions.

Confront the question. Follow the example of the psalmists who were never shy about asking the question that if not on our minds and hearts right now, will be at some point in our lives. Where in the world is God in all of this?

When that which threatens life comes near and cynicism or despair knocks at the door, there are some who try to pull away from God, or at least try to hide their honest feelings and fears from God, when what they most need is to pour out their true emotions to God. For if God is God then God can take that. In fact, God wills to take that. For God has not despised the affliction of the afflicted. The One who heard the cries of Israel in Egypt will not hide his face from our explosion of emotions. God will not close his ears when we approach him with our honest fears. Faith includes holding the worst of life up to God.

Our model for this, as in all things, is Christ, in whose name we pray. We read in Hebrews that, "In the days of his flesh, Jesus offered up prayers and supplications, with loud cries and tears, to him who was able to save him from death, and he was heard for his godly fear." Indeed, on Good Friday we will read the haunting prayer that Jesus offered up from the cross: "Eloi, Eloi, lama sabachthani (My God, my God, why hast thou forsaken me)." This raw lament is taken from the first line of our Psalm text this morning. Psalm 22 is a combination of two prayers: a psalm of lament and a psalm of thanksgiving, and it is important to note that in the tradition of the time, citing the first words of a text was a way of identifying the entire passage.

So in weaving this text into the Passion narrative we are to understand that the God to whom we lift our laments is also the God who delivers us from the evil that encroaches. "He has not abhorred the affliction of the afflicted; and he has not hid his face from him, but has heard, when he cried to him."

This psalm was written for liturgical use, which is to say that this was not just the prayer of one individual but was offered for use as a prayer for all who suffer or feel threatened. And, immediately we see that the petitioner holds nothing back from God. "My God . . . why hast thou forsaken me? Why art thou so far from helping me, from the words of my groaning?" Crying day and night, the petitioner finds no solace or rest. Remember the

New Testament challenge to prayer where the person in need knocks on his neighbor's door at midnight, and finally the neighbor answers his need? It is a challenge to keep on, keeping on in our prayer life in spite of our impatience with God's timetable. Yet, we have all known those times in life when we've knocked and knocked until our inflamed knuckles scream for mercy. When do you begin to feel ridiculous and give up? "Why art thou so far from helping me?"

But then the psalmist remembers, and memory is so important for faith. "Yet thou art holy," he prays, "enthroned on the praises of Israel. In thee our fathers trusted, and thou didst deliver them. To thee they cried, and were saved; in thee they trusted, and were not disappointed."

Memory for the psalmist, for us, offers the verification that ours is a God who acts, and sometimes, memory is all you've got: The memory of a baby being born; the memory of a deliverance from a threatening situation; the memory of a time of worship when you felt so full of the presence of God. It may be all you've got, but it is enough to spark the energy for prayer.

When you feel you're not getting an answer; when you feel your prayers are reaching no higher than the ceiling of the darkened room in which you hide and cry; when your knuckles are bleeding from knocking on the unanswered door; there is only one thing to do. Pray again.

And so, remembering that ours is a God who acts, the psalmist prays some more, holding nothing back.

"I am a worm," he laments, "and no man; scorned by men, and despised by the people." He describes the mockery of those who scorn his faith. The imagery of the lions and the bulls evoke the power of that which threatens him. He feels like hunted prey. Everyone dreads feeling threatened. The threat of violence. The threat of death. The threat of a layoff. The threat of illness. The threat of enemies both real and imagined. Sometimes you feel like you are cornered by a ravenous dog.

But again he remembers. "Upon thee was I cast from my birth, and since my mother bore me thou hast been my God." And so he keeps praying. "O thou my help, hasten to my aid!"

That Jesus, the Son of God, uses this prayer; that Jesus, the Son of God, experiences the threats, the wounds, the sense of abandonment contained in this prayer means something, doesn't it? If God felt the crown of thorns piercing his head and felt the nails impale his hands then you cannot say he doesn't know how you feel. "He has not despised or abhorred the affliction of the afflicted." In Jesus, God took our pain on as his pain. This psalm of lament therefore concludes as a psalm of praise and thanksgiving lifted up by the whole congregation. "The afflicted shall eat and be satisfied; those who seek him shall praise the Lord! May your hearts live forever . . . All the ends of the earth shall praise the Lord . . . Posterity shall serve him; men shall tell of the Lord to the coming generation, and proclaim his deliverance to a people yet unborn."

Our hope is that the One who delivers is also the One who suffered. Jesus rose from the dead in victory over all that would threaten or destroy human life. As Peter proclaims, "By his wounds we are healed."

And so, along with the psalmist's prayer, a psalm that Jesus claimed for us, our laments can become songs of thanksgiving. "For he has not despised or abhorred the affliction of the afflicted; and he has not hid his face from him, but has heard, when he cried to him."

God has not despised or abhorred the affliction of the afflicted.

Because Jesus Christ, who was nailed to a cross, claimed the fullness of Psalm 22 for us; because Jesus Christ, who was released from death's tomb on the third day, claimed the fullness of Psalm 22 for us, we can pray in all circumstances, we can lift our cries to God when this world's threats overwhelm us, we can trust that our God is a God who hears and our God is a God who delivers. "The afflicted shall eat and be satisfied; those who seek him shall praise the Lord!"

Isn't it curious that those who have suffered the most are often the ones who understand this the most? A colleague of mine in Florida has taken several mission trips with his church to Haiti, the most impoverished country in the western hemisphere. He once traveled to a hospital there, but to call it a hospital is a bit of a stretch. No sterile environment here. Ill-equipped, rusty, rudimentary tools, an abundance of insects. John was ushered into a so-called recovery room where a man was brought in who had just had his gangrenous legs amputated.

He was muttering something in French and it was hard to hear, so John leaned over and after a moment finally understood what the man was saying, "Merci Mon Dieu. Merci Mon Dieu." Thank you, my God.

This is a most unsettling, uncertain time. We are heartbroken. We are confused. But God shall not abhor the affliction of the afflicted. For in Jesus Christ, who took on our pain, who conquered the grave, who claimed this prayer for us, we shall be delivered. "Posterity shall serve him; [people] shall proclaim his deliverance to a people yet unborn."

Friday, as the Cannon family gathered for Marge's funeral, there was sorrow and a somber sense of loss, but there was also joy as cooing adults took turns holding a beautiful little red-haired infant and there was delight as we were beguiled by the coy grin of a one-year-old. Death was tempered by the budding of life. Our hearts were pierced this week by murderous rage, but our hearts shall not cease to swell at the news of a longed for pregnancy or the sight of a giggling infant. Joy is possible even in the dark passages of life and the uncertainty and fears that tomorrow may bring. Amen.

7

On the Third Day

"I will die but that is all I will do for death."

—EDNA ST. VINCENT MILLAY

I WOULD SECOND EDNA'S motion as I observe a world where death is dreaded more than life is celebrated. Why do we give death so much power? Rather than death casting a pall over life, shouldn't life cast its glow over death?

In the Gospel of Mark, when Mary, Mary, and Salome approached the tomb on the third day, they were not holding out hope for life; they were expecting death. We know this because if they had expected life they would have brought food for the savior instead of spices and oils for a dead friend. The sunlight may have illumined the stony, dusty path before them, but, because of the gloom of death, the women were certainly fumbling through the dark.

At the tomb, they were surprised and terrorized. A young unnamed man dressed in white offers the first, and honestly the only necessary, Easter sermon. Mark writes, "Do not be alarmed; you are looking for Jesus of Nazareth, who was crucified. He has been raised; he is not here. Look, there is the place they laid him. But go, tell his disciples and Peter that he is going ahead of you to Galilee; there you will see him, just as he told you."

Here, the whole of scripture, the entire history of God with his people is wrapped into these few short words. But, honestly, I doubt that the women heard any word but *go*. Long ago, physiologist Walter Cannon came up with the idea that our sympathetic nervous system initiates what he called the *fight or flight response*. In response to threats or stress we are wired to either fight or flee, and most folks would be right there with the women. Coming upon that scene, seeing what they saw, the majority of people are not kneeling in prayer; they are lacing up their Nikes and getting out of there.

That this is the way scholars say Mark's gospel originally ended dismays believers and skeptics. In fact, the literal translation reads, "To no one anything they said; afraid they were for..." Tom Long says, "It is almost as if the author of Mark had suddenly been dragged from his writing desk in midsentence."[11] The great preacher Fred Craddock had the courage to ask the question that troubles all of us, "Is this any way to run a resurrection?" Come on, Mark, where are the breakfasts by the seashore? The miraculous catch of fish? The holy conversation and burning hearts on the road to Emmaus?

We like simple happy endings, like *You've Got Mail* and *Hoosiers*. Only the movie critics like gritty unresolved stories and relationships. We yearn for a clear, distinct, happily ever after resolution. Mark, in contrast to the others, leaves us with a dangling preposition, and everybody knows you are not supposed to end a sentence, much less a gospel, with a preposition.

How many Passion plays have you seen that end with a confused, frightened cast and a preposition? No, every one of them seems to have Jesus walking out of a chicken wired, paper mache tomb wearing a silver-sequined, James Brown-lookin' robe, gleaming like a big ol' disco ball, his hands raised as if somebody's scored a touchdown.

My dad is from Missouri where they'd say, "Show me a risen Jesus!" People want a clear, irrefutable resolution. And if it's not there, they may just add one of their own. That's what happened with Mark's gospel. Later editors, or what seminarians call redactors, would not abide Mark's unresolved tension and so they added a couple of extra endings.

"To no one anything they said; afraid they were for . . ." What was Mark doing here? Maybe, just maybe, Mark knew exactly what he was doing. He leaves you there with Mary, Mary, and Salome, frightened and confused, running out of the tomb into the Sunday morning sun, blinded by the darkness—the darkness of death, the darkness of doubt, the darkness of anxiety and fear. They had heard the good news, or at least the good news had been spoken to them, but they had not physically, with their own eyes, seen the risen Christ.

There is a question that tugs at worshippers, preachers, and prophets on Easter. Is it true? Faith is a matter of trusting that what the young man

11. Long, William, *The Christian Century*, April 4, 2006.

said is true without having seen it. "Do not be alarmed; you are looking for Jesus of Nazareth, who was crucified. He has been raised; he is not here."

It is interesting that Christians tend to focus on an empty tomb each Easter, when the Bible says Jesus wasn't there. If you want to see him, you have to go to Galilee. Maybe our Easter hymns should be pilgrim psalms inviting us to pick up our Easter lilies, put on our hiking shoes, and get on the road to Galilee. You see, death does not mark the end of the story. Maybe that's why Mark ended his gospel with a preposition. The story is still being written wherever the risen Christ appears in the Galilees of our lives.

Mark gives us a clue to this in the spare first words of his gospel. Matthew begins with an elaborate genealogy that walks us through the history of God with God's people. Luke gives us a beautifully rich account of Christ's birth. John gives us a profound and deep theology lesson, but all Mark gives us as an introduction is this: "The beginning of the good news of Jesus Christ, the Son of God."

It's hard to get much of a Christmas pageant out of that. But Mark offers something believers need to know as they fumble through the dark. "The beginning of the good news of Jesus Christ, the Son of God." The beginning. You see, the story of faith is still being written, and, like the women at the tomb, you will find the risen Christ in the Galilees of your lives.

Fumbling through the dark. That's the way a school nurse once described my life with autism to my mother. Not a good idea. She must have put a hurtin' on that nurse's ears for half an hour. At the end of the whuppin' she concluded. "Zachary is not fumbling in the dark, he's searching for the light. He may get a few bruises as he bumps his way along, but who the hell doesn't? He'll get there all the same."

Well, I did get here and the warmth of the light envelops me with peace as I observe the seasons of life in Edinburgh and at St. Martin. Summer, Fall, Winter, and Spring. The cynic would say they are fumbling through the dark, but I know they are searching for the light, and they'll get there all the same.

44917942R00127

Made in the USA
Lexington, KY
17 September 2015